IMAGES of America
SULLIVAN COUNTY BORSCHT BELT

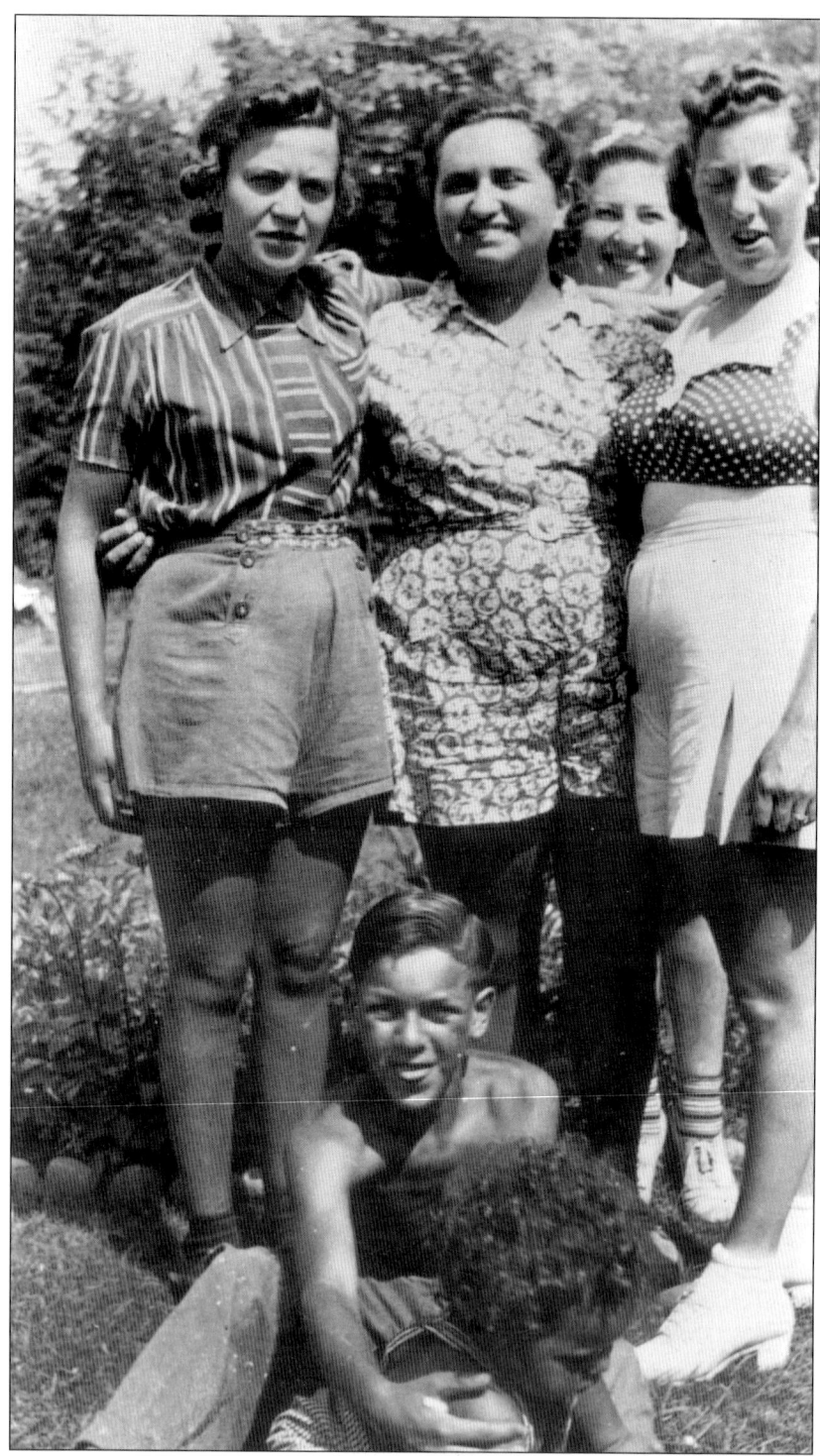
Bungalow colony women pose with two kids on the lawn of their summer resort in Woodbourne c. 1942. During the week, bungalow colonies were ruled by women. The balance shifted on the weekend, when the men came up. That was party time.

IMAGES
of America
SULLIVAN COUNTY BORSCHT BELT

Irwin Richman

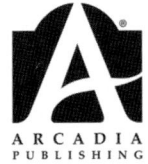

Copyright © 2001 by Irwin Richman
ISBN 978-0-7385-0541-1

Published by Arcadia Publishing
Charleston SC, Chicago IL, Portsmouth NH, San Francisco CA

Printed in the United States of America

Library of Congress Catalog Card Number: 2001088816

For all general information contact Arcadia Publishing at:
Telephone 843-853-2070
Fax 843-853-0044
E-mail sales@arcadiapublishing.com
For customer service and orders:
Toll-Free 1-888-313-2665

Visit us on the Internet at www.arcadiapublishing.com

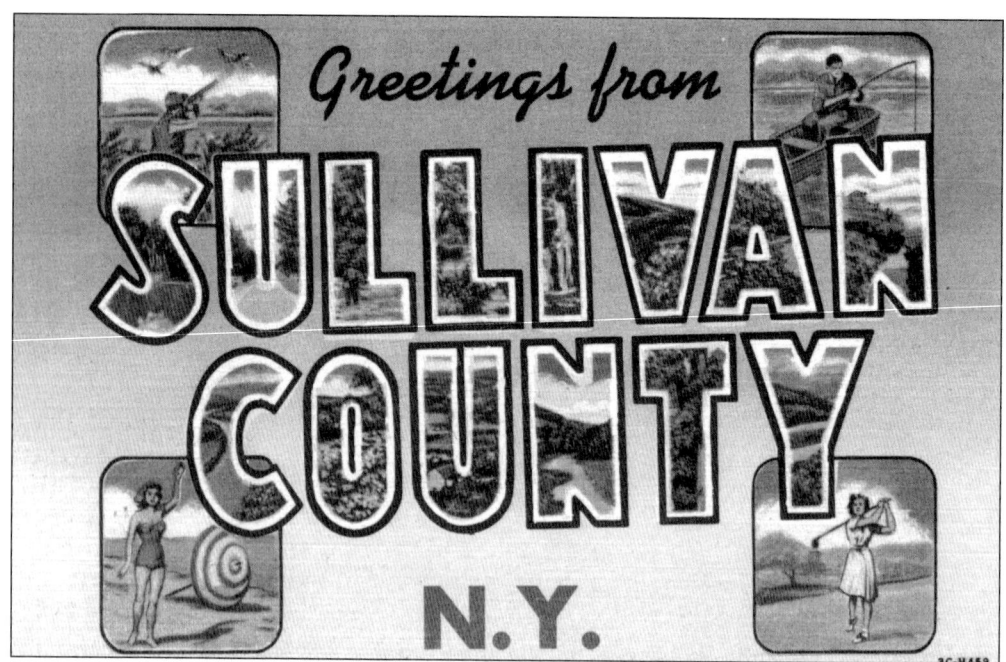

This 1940s Sullivan County montage postcard was printed in Chicago but distributed by New Hillig Studios of Liberty. The images are generic. You could certainly golf, hunt, and fish in Sullivan County. But where could you find an ocean to play near? Fantasy and resorts go together.

Contents

Introduction: Entertaining a Million Jews		7
Acknowledgments		10
1.	Before the Borscht Belt	11
2.	Resort Towns and *Shtetlach*	33
3.	*Kuchaleins* and Bungalow Colonies	69
4.	The Hotel Age	97

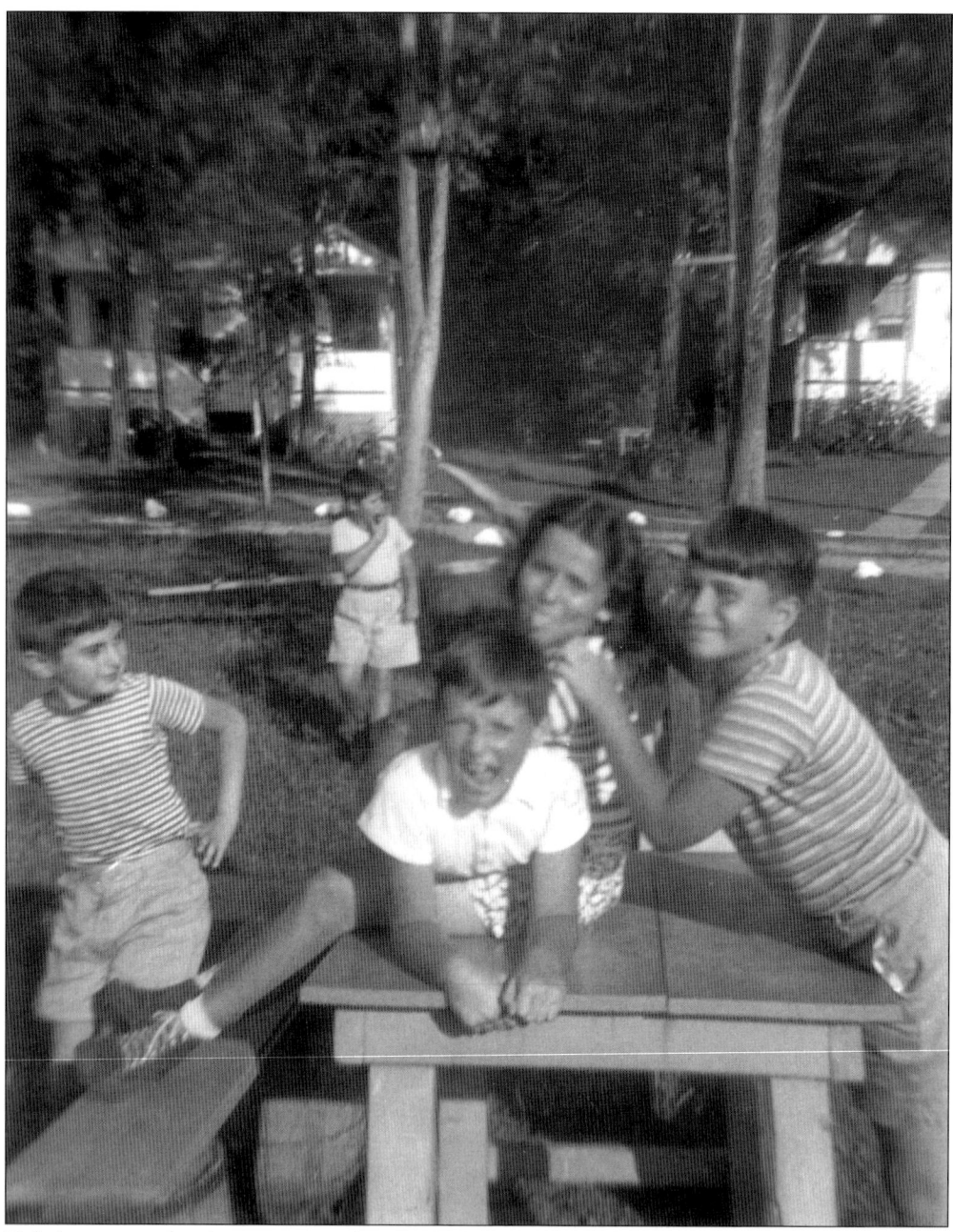

Kids ham it up for the camera in this c. 1946 image. Bungalow colonies, such as this one in Woodbourne, were about safety and community. In the summer, kids had time to be children and just "noodle around" at impromptu play.

INTRODUCTION: ENTERTAINING A MILLION JEWS

It was a world we never realized was unique. Sullivan County was the playground of millions of Americanizing and American Jews. Most of them came from New York City, seeking relief from the heat of the Lower East Side, the South Bronx, or Brownsville. Later they also came from Flatbush, the Grand Concourse, and Queens. They were going to a *haimish* (homey) enclave, set apart from a restrictive and often unfriendly gentile environment. In 1879, for example, the president of an exclusive Coney Island resort had announced that he would not allow Jews into his hotel. "We do not like Jews as a class," he proclaimed.

Jews had to create a resort world of their own, and the Catskill Mountains of New York State beckoned. In 1883, the Fleischmann family, Jews of Hungarian origin, bought 60 acres near the town of Griffin's Corners. This village was later renamed Fleischmanns after the yeast and distilling magnate Charles F. Fleischmann, whose family and friends built homes of unheard-of luxury in northern Ulster County. The door was open. Less affluent Jews bought neighboring boardinghouses. Soon the nearby towns of Hunter and Tannersville were also Jewish resorts. This area, however, was not to be the Borscht Belt of legend. Here the story moves a bit to the south into the Showangunk, or southern Catskill region.

About 2.3 million Jews, mostly from eastern Europe, immigrated into the United States between 1880 and 1924, when restrictive legislation halted the flow. More than half of them chose to settle in New York City. Some came from big cities like Lodz, Vilnius, Warsaw, or Odessa, but most came from small towns, *shtetlen* or *shetlach*. Many of the Jews who had been farmers in the old country wanted to reestablish their bucolic lives in America. The Jewish Agricultural Society was ready to help them. Because of the proximity to New York City and the cheap land, the lower Catskills—and especially the Neversink Valley of Sullivan County—were very attractive.

The railroad had arrived in the region in the early 1870s. By 1878, the New York, Ontario, and Western Railroad was producing an annual publication, *Summer Homes*, to promote the area. Thanks to the railroad, thousands of New Yorkers flocked to Sullivan County. Gentile farmers took in gentile boarders, and boardinghouses and hotels grew in importance. Many catered to working-class German and Irish immigrants. A few hotels were semi-elite. Jews first entered this Christian world of farms and summer resorts as early as 1892, when Yana "John" Gerson bought an abandoned farm in Glen Wild, near Woodridge. He soon built a successful dairying operation and a boardinghouse. Others followed. Jews were not welcomed, but they persisted. By the 1920s, the Borscht Belt of Sullivan County was firmly established as a Jewish resort, a place where Jews could feel at home.

The terms "Sullivan County," "the Catskills," "the Country," "the Mountains," and "the Borscht Belt" became synonyms for the famed resort area. Geographical names, however, are arbitrary—settlement patterns seldom follow the dictates of the map makers. Classic Borscht Belt Sullivan County is really only the eastern part of the county, with a bit of southern Ulster County included. The western part of the county, which borders on the Delaware River, never developed an extensive resort industry, although it is now becoming an increasingly expensive center of second homes, often for expatriates from the Borscht Belt. The Rockefeller family has even developed a very private enclave of second homes along the banks of the Willowemoc Creek, near the town of Lew Beach, a haven designed to preserve this world-famous fly fishing stream.

Most of the soil in the lower Catskills is poor, and few Jewish farmers (like their Christian predecessors) could scratch more than subsistence living from the unyielding ground. Many followed the lead of Yana Gerson and started taking in boarders. You could not only rent out parts of your farmhouse but also feed the boarders the food you raised and had trouble marketing. As inexpensive as boardinghouses were, some New Yorkers could afford only cheaper accommodations, and the *kuchalein,* "cook for yourself," was born. Now the farmers only had to rent out rooms. The summer people all shared a common kitchen, outhouses, and bathtub, which was often set out behind the barn, with separate hours for men and women. Many *kuchaleiners* never used these often filthy tubs and preferred to wash in the Neversink River or a nearby lake. They could also buy the farmer's produce. Sometimes they had to buy food from their landlord. Because so many early resorts developed from farms, many renters referred to the landlords as farmers, whether they farmed or not.

There were hundreds of *kuchaleins* but, by the 1920s, there was a demand for more privacy. Some "farmers" started to build shacks on their grounds. These structures usually had no cooking or plumbing, and tenants shared the common facilities with the rest of the *kuchalein*. By the mid-1930s, a few of these shacks added a kitchen and a bathroom, and the rental bungalow was created. Soon the very distinctive Borscht Belt resort-type bungalow colony came into being. "What is a bungalow colony and who goes there?" asked Michael Straus in the *New York Times* in 1956. "A bungalow colony is usually an oval cluster of cottages bordering on a greens sward at the opposite ends of which are a day camp for children and a social hall for transient fathers." While this description is perhaps overly elegant, by 1956 there were well over 2,000 bungalow colonies in the region of eastern Sullivan County and southern Ulster County. The typical bungalow had two rooms: a kitchen and a bedroom. A more luxurious unit might have two bedrooms. No bungalow had a separate living room, but there might be a screened porch. During the week, the resort was a matriarchy. The mothers stayed up with the kids, and the fathers came up on the weekends. If they had a vacation, fathers might spend a week or two.

By the 1950s, Bungalow colonies had evolved from crude clusters of shacks with few amenities into comfortable resorts. Although the average resort might have about 20 units (often a combination of apartments and bungalows), there were large places, such as Cutler's Cottages in South Fallsburg or the Ideal near Monticello, which counted accommodations in the hundreds. The small resort owned by the author's family only accommodated 13 families. Soon, the larger resorts started mimicking the area's famed hotels, offering professional entertainment and even an occasional indoor swimming pool. The question of who went to a bungalow colony and who went to a hotel was based on preference rather than economics. If you wanted three big meals a day and the opportunity to change clothes all day, you went to a hotel. If you wanted a more casual experience, you went to a colony. The 1999 film *To Walk on the Moon* beautifully depicts the vanished world of the Borscht Belt bungalow colony. It also answers the question, "Did bored wives ever have affairs?" Yes, but more probably had affairs at the hotels than at the bungalow colonies.

Catskill hotels were the most famous resorts of the Borscht Belt. Some, like the Sha-wan-ga Lodge were started as Christian hotels, but most others evolved out of Jewish farms and boardinghouses. A list maintained by the Catskill Institute records more than 1,000 hotels that once existed in the region. At the industry's height, from 1950 to 1970, it seemed as if there was a hotel on every hill or around every bend. The hotels ranged from the lowly "*schlock* houses," or dumps that were little better than run-down boardinghouses, up to grand palatial hotels. The hotel names Flagler, Concord, Grossinger's, and Nevele resonate with upper-middle-class Jewish glamour. Brown's Hotel, the Aladdin, Shenk's Paramount, the Esther Manor, the Nemerson, and hundreds more served a rapidly Americanizing middle class. From the early years, Catskill hotels were famed for food. Hotels were expected to serve huge, order-whatever-you-want meals three times a day. The meals usually offered Jewish favorites, never giving up on lox, herring, and brisket. To the extent that a kosher kitchen would allow, hotels also served variations of Chinese and Italian food. Most hotels were kosher until a few broke with the pack and began serving "Jewish American cuisine," which meant that you could have lox and eggs for breakfast and grilled lobster for dinner.

Entertainment was famous in the Catskills, and hotels vied with one another to best amuse their guests—first in makeshift rooms and then in casinos, full-fledged theaters, and finally in lavish nightclubs. Entertainers whose careers developed in the Borscht Belt are legendary. They include Sid Caesar, Danny Kay, Jerry Lewis, Eddie Fisher, Henny Youngman, Buddy Hackett, and hundreds more. At the height of the Borscht Belt era, more than 600 resorts offered one or more shows on any given Saturday night.

The Borscht Belt and its heart, Sullivan County, became synonymous with glitz. "More is better" was the Catskill slogan. Every year brought improvements: new swimming pools, tennis courts, fabulous nightclubs, and special teen lounges. It is no accident that many of the developers of Miami Beach and Las Vegas spent their childhoods in Sullivan County. While several movies were set in Catskill hotels, *Sweet Lorraine* was actually made there and tells the most authentic story.

Today the *kuchaleins* are gone, killed off by changing lifestyles and prosperity. Only a handful of traditional hotels remains in Sullivan County. The bungalow colonies are mostly gone as well. Today's Jews, who continue to go to the Catskill resorts and especially the bungalow colonies, are the ultra-Orthodox and the Hasidim. Why do they come? Because their religion demands a community that provides them with kosher food and Orthodox services. Why did normative Jews abandon Sullivan County? The answer is complex. The rise of suburbia, the women's movement, and air conditioning all changed society, as did Civil Rights legislation of the 1960s that outlawed discrimination at places of public accommodation. Cheap airfares opened the world to the Americanized, worldly Jews. As one hotel owner lamented, "I used to compete with the hotel down the road; now I compete with the world." It was an uneven battle, and the world won. The Borscht Belt of legend is no more. Read on and share the dream of what once was.

"The Cottage"
Bainbridge, Pennsylvania
January 2001

Acknowledgments

Every book is a collaborative enterprise. For me, this book on Sullivan County's Borscht Belt is a blend of scholarship, collegial cooperation, and memories. Many people in my past form what is essentially a Jewish "McNamara's Band." First and foremost, there were my grandparents Abraham and Bayle Richman, who created the small bungalow colony in Woodbourne that later served as my introduction to the history and culture of the Catskills. My mother, Bertha, ran the colony for many years after my grandmother's death. My father, Alexander, demonstrated to me how much time could be spent playing pinochle in a summer. My brother, Seymour, taught me how to hold my breath the many times he held me under in the Neversink River.

We had many tenants over the years. Some were unforgettable. Schmuel and Raizel Dubofsky were at Richman's almost every summer since it opened in 1937. Mary and Morris Ossip were there almost as long. Morris was our resident poet laureate. His Yinglish poems always summed up our summers. Mary Cohen, a seller of legal drugs by profession, was a delightful raconteur and singer. Her daughter, Jeanne Reynolds, was a popular Borscht Belt entertainer who, over her long career, transformed herself from a blond bombshell into a lusty Sophie Tucker–like entertainer.

There were owners of other bungalow colonies: Leo and Sophie Kassack and Meyer and Stella Furman, whose colonies I worked at, and our resort-owning neighbors, the Franks and the Abe Furmans, who are part of the memory.

Then there were the townspeople. Meyer Lebed, who ran a local drugstore, was the village jokester. Much less colorful was his competitor across the street, Abe Godlin, who was the son of a Jewish pioneer of Woodbourne and owned half the town. Hymie Kanowitz, our milkman, delivered dairy products to us for years. As special favors for his old customers, he might pick up a rye bread and newspapers, especially the Yiddish-language *Forward*. Pamela Gugig had the first antiques shop in Woodbourne and later became known as "the Lady Auctioneer." Two marriages later, she is Pamela Moore Epstein.

Two of my former professors, Wood Gray and Wallace E. Davies, instilled in me a love of social history, which has led to my work on the Catskills. My current colleagues at the Harrisburg campus of the Pennsylvania State University have always been supportive. I especially want to thank Bill Mahar, my school director, who has always done his best to help me in my projects, as has Howard Sachs, our dean for research and graduate studies. Linda Seaman typed the manuscript, and our efficient reference librarians helped me check facts. Phil Brown, president of the Catskill Institute, leads my professional cheering section.

My very remarkable wife, Susan—a mathematician and talented administrator, who had never been to the Catskills until we met—urged me on. Lastly, I do my books so that people can enjoy them today, but also so that tomorrow's generations can learn about a past age. My *nachas* are our sons, Dr. Alexander E. Richman and (future physician) Joshua S. Richman, and our daughter-in-law, Kristin Graham Richman. In a class by himself is our grandson, Benjamin David, who was almost born on the Fourth of July, right at the start of the summer season.

One

BEFORE THE BORSCHT BELT

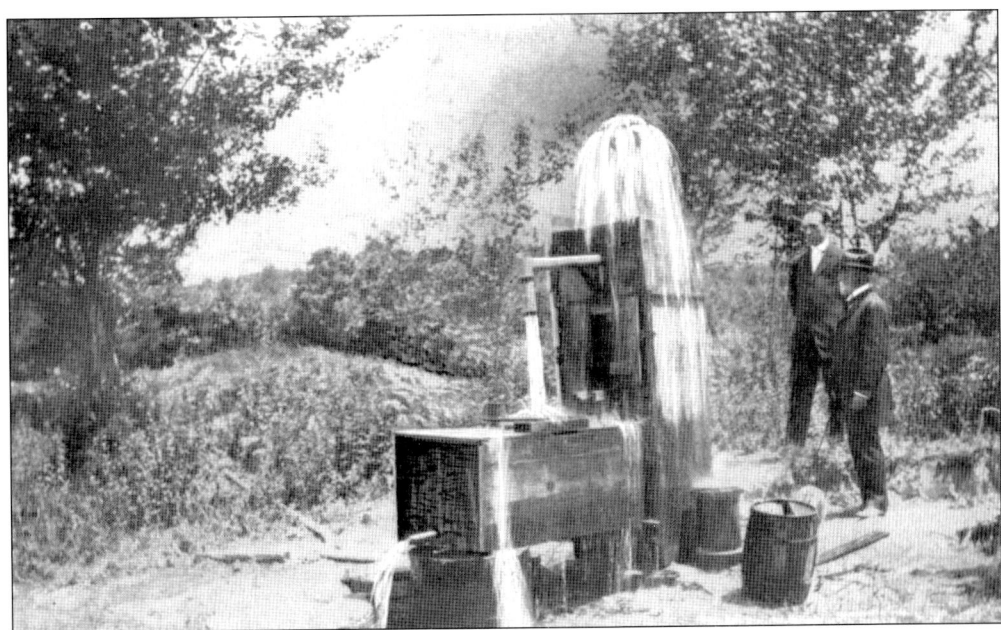

Water is important to the Sullivan County story. Samuel Colcord's well, shown c. 1910, was a major attraction. A message on the back of this postcard informs us that "90,000 gallons per day . . . rises 26 feet above the ground [and] hundreds of people came to drink it daily." Today the water is commercially bottled.

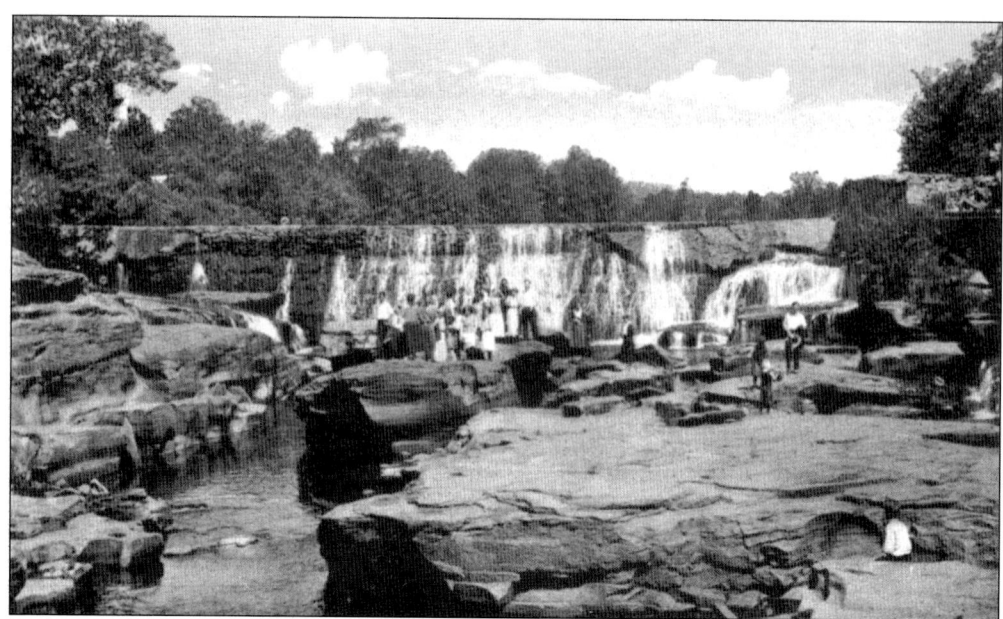

The wonderful falls at Fallsburg—or "Old Falls," as locals called it—fell over a dam built to create a millpond for a gristmill and the nearby Palen leather tanneries. The tannery consumed 4,000 cords of tanbark and 400 cords of wood each year. Its vats could treat 25,000 hides at a time. When the industries died, the dam stood for many years, creating a popular spot to visit. Although the dam is long gone, the picturesque rock formations remain. In 2000, a new pavilion was built to provide a scenic vantage point for the beautiful site. Unfortunately, the stone arch bridge near the falls has long been replaced by a prosaic concrete and steel highway bridge.

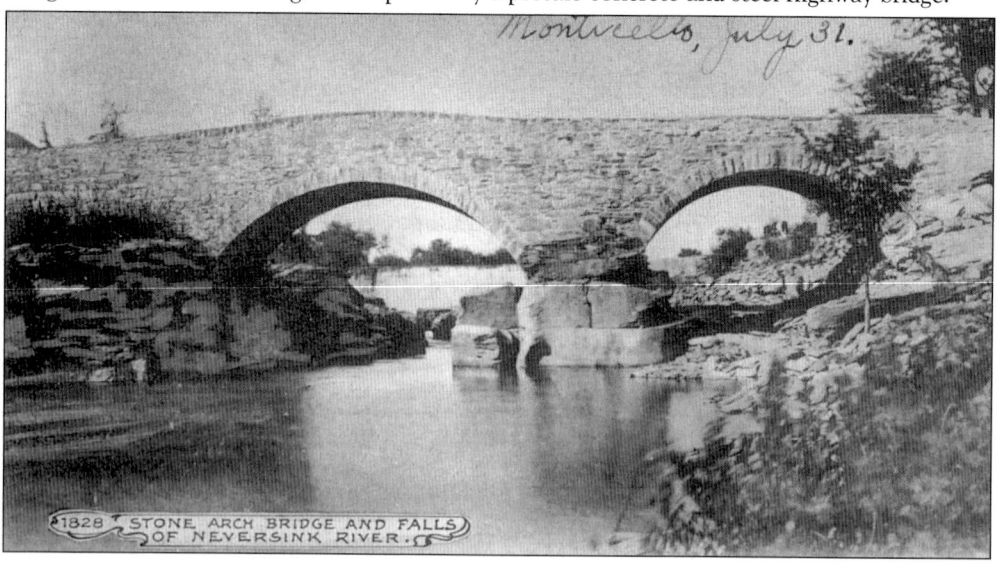

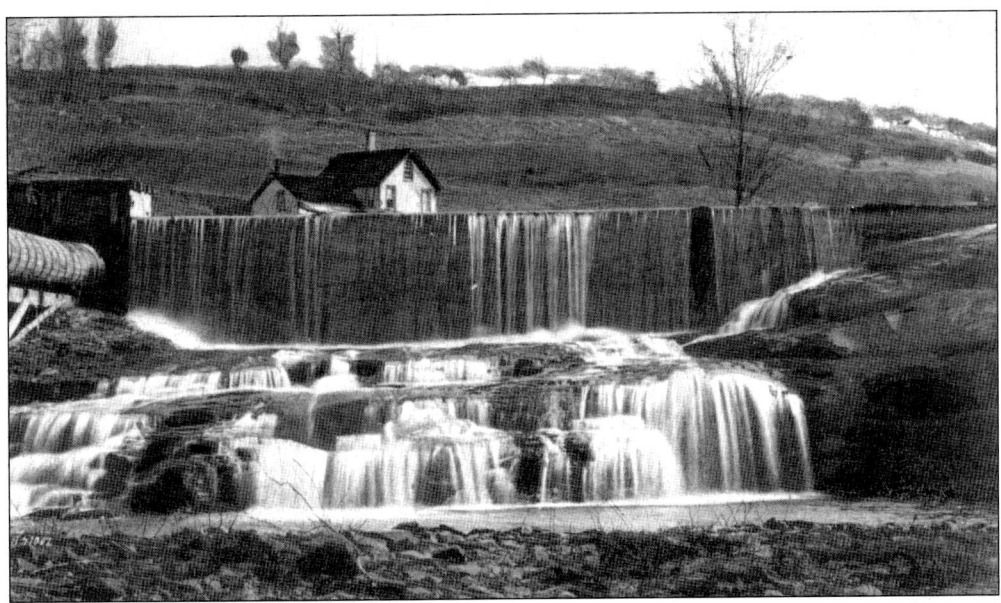

Every agricultural community needed to have a gristmill to process grain into flour. Mills need millponds, or reservoirs, to impound water for use during dry spells. Excess water falling over the dam in wet weather was often dramatic. Above, in a 1907 view of Ferndale, the mill is to the left, mostly out of view. The miller's house is visible to the back. Below, at Liberty, the miller's house stands on a hill overlooking "the Old Grist Mill."

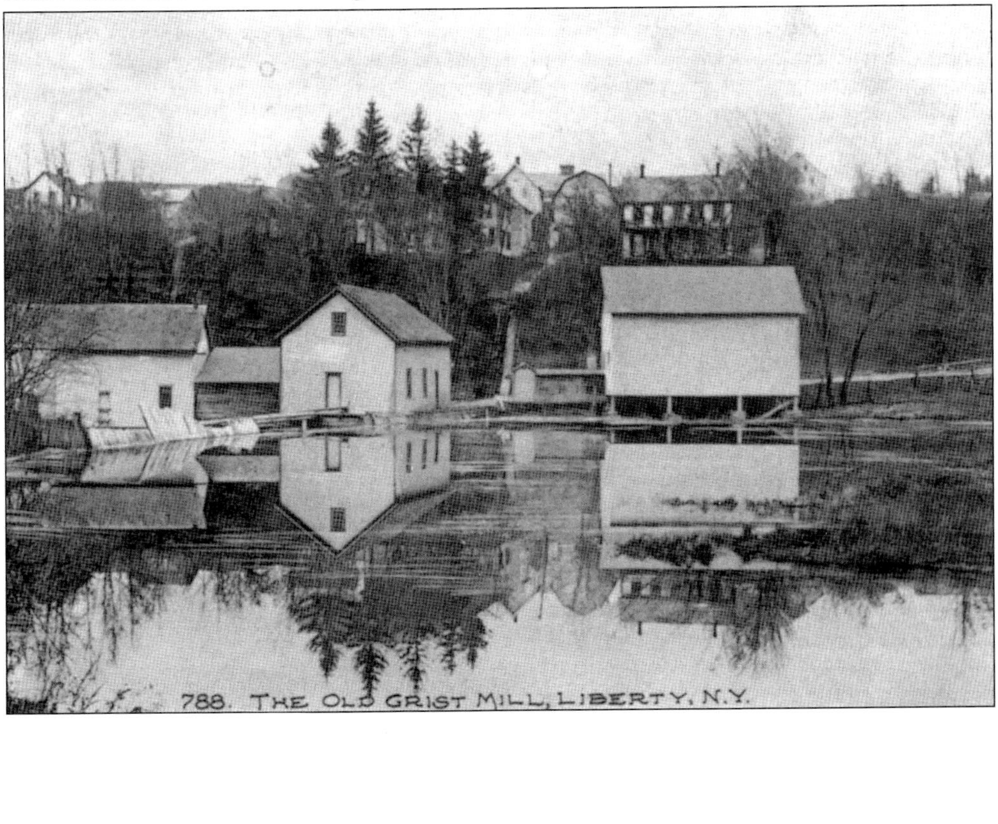

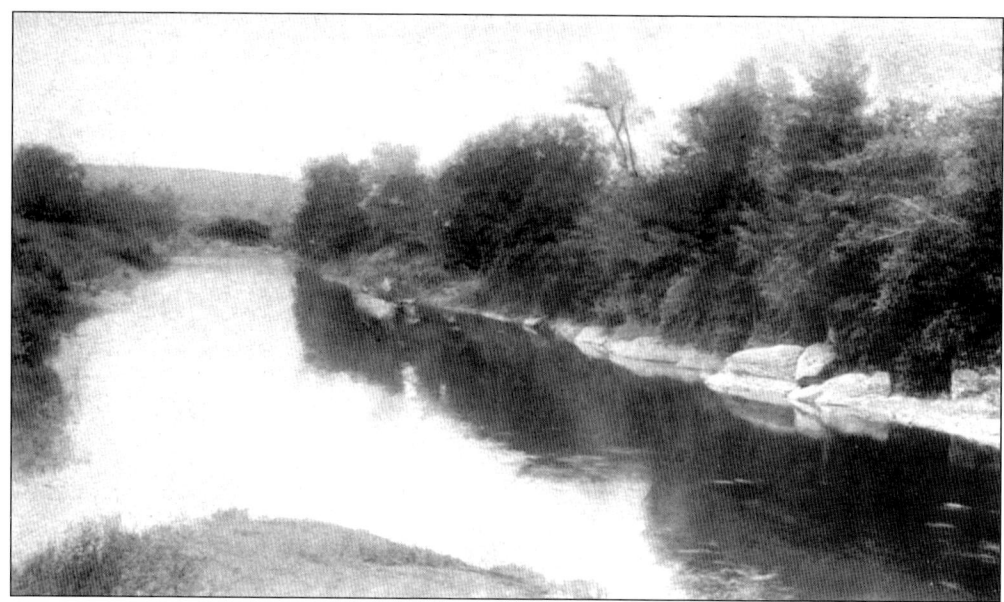

The Neversink River, a tributary of the Delaware River, is Sullivan County's major waterway. It is especially picturesque near Hasbrouck, a town named for a member of a French Hugenout (Protestant) family, living in New York State since the late 17th century. The nature of the river changed dramatically in the 1960s after the City of New York dammed it as part of its Neversink Watershed project, which now supplies the city with drinking water.

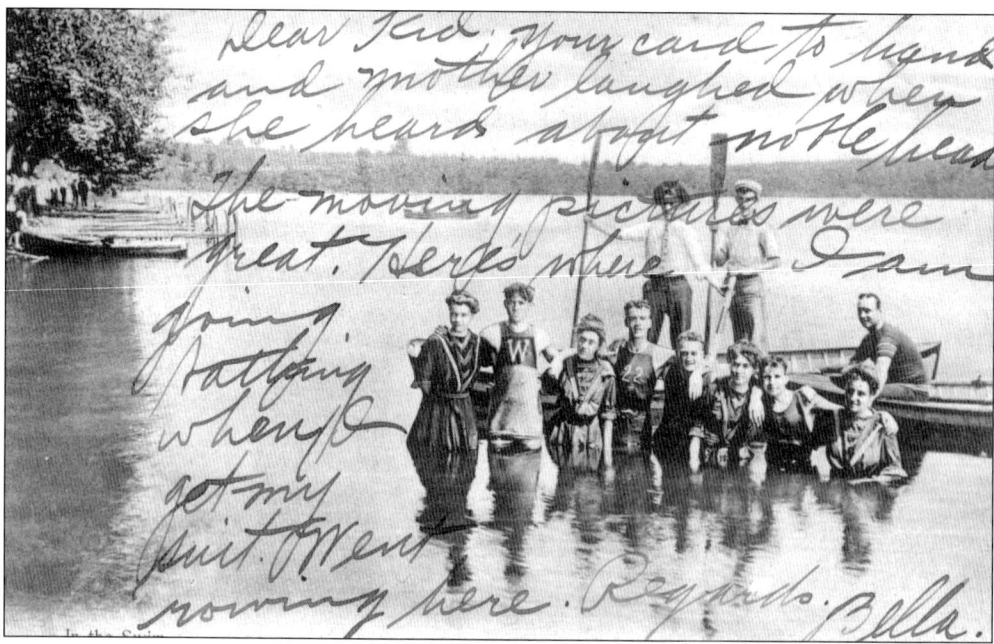

Sullivan County's many lakes helped make the area an attractive vacation spot. Mailed in 1910, this postcard clearly shows that Bella was having the time of her life in Loch Sheldrake. The girls shown had the most fashionable swimwear, but Bella was waiting to get her swimsuit.

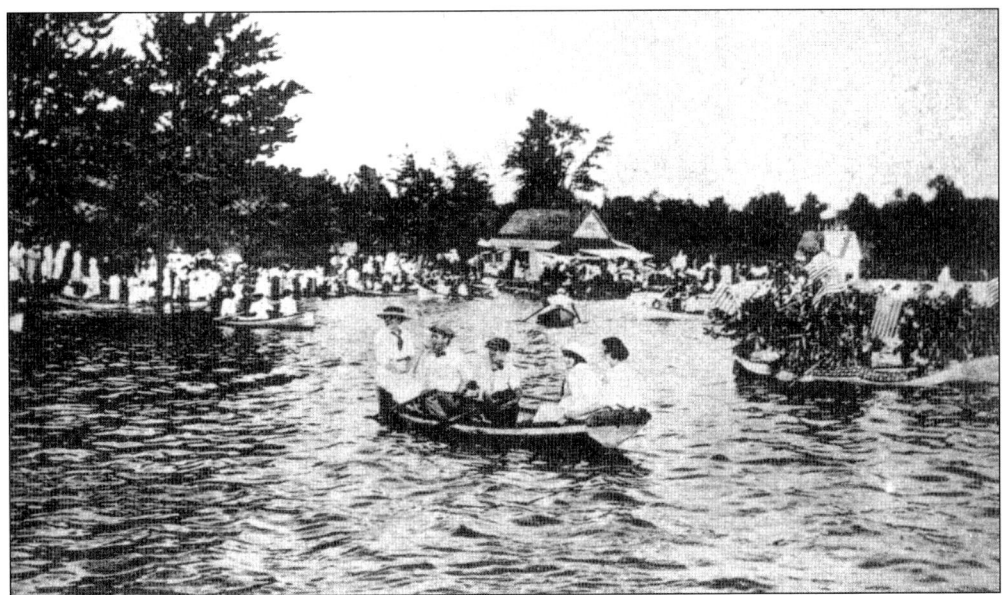

Regatta Day was an important event during the summer. Often held on the Fourth of July, summer people and locals enjoyed the festivities. Before it was renamed by the New York, Ontario, and Western Railroad (O & W), Kiamesha Lake was called Pleasant Lake.

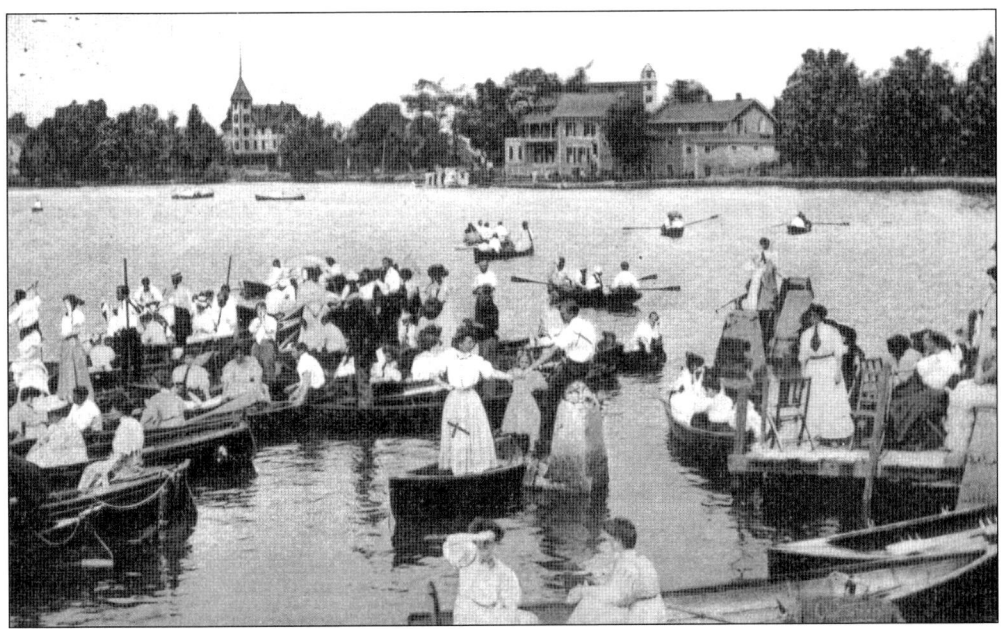

This postcard was mailed by Velma Turner in August 1909. Vacationing Velma marked an X on her image. She is holding hands with her husband, Percy, marked with a less noticeable X. Saturdays were festive days of fun for guests of local Christian hotels and boardinghouses.

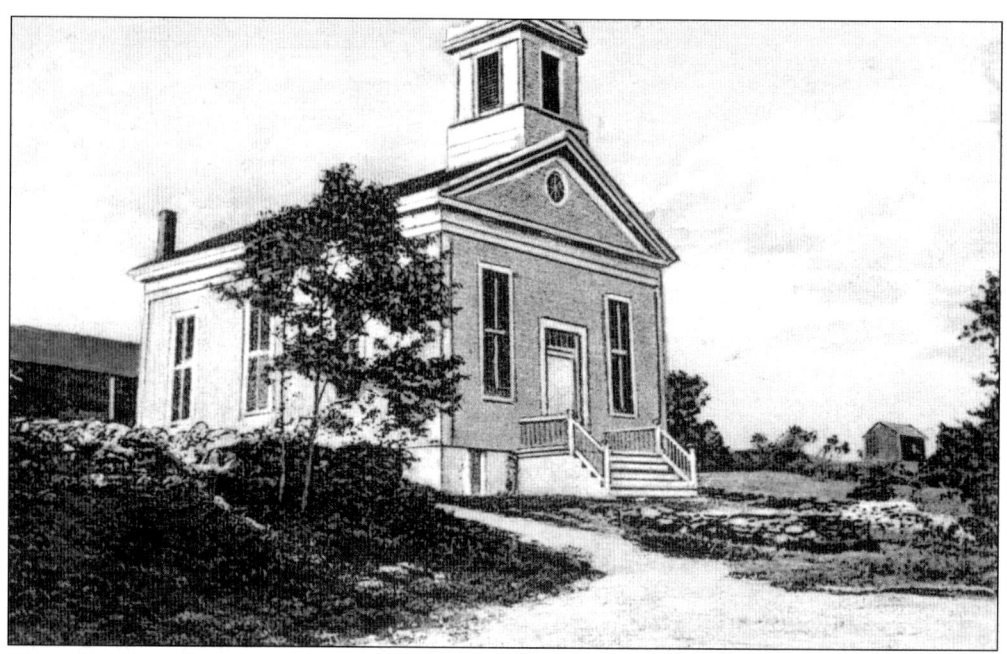

Ulster Heights, a hamlet in Ulster County near Ellenville, was proud of its Greek Revival–style church. Locals such as Otto Johnson built boardinghouses on their farms to accommodate summer visitors attracted to the hamlet by its small lake. The vista is serene and relaxed.

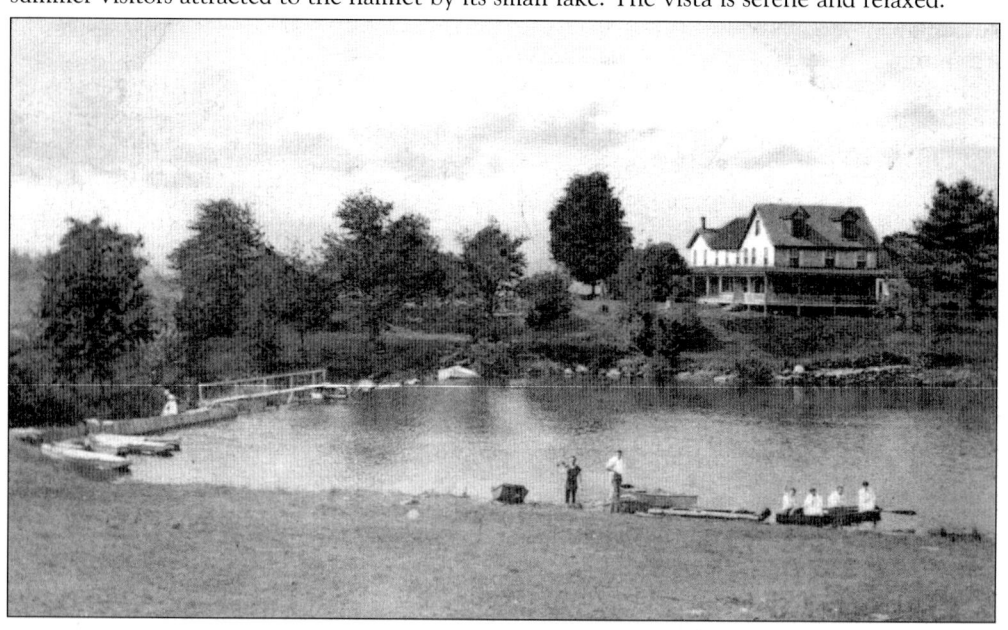

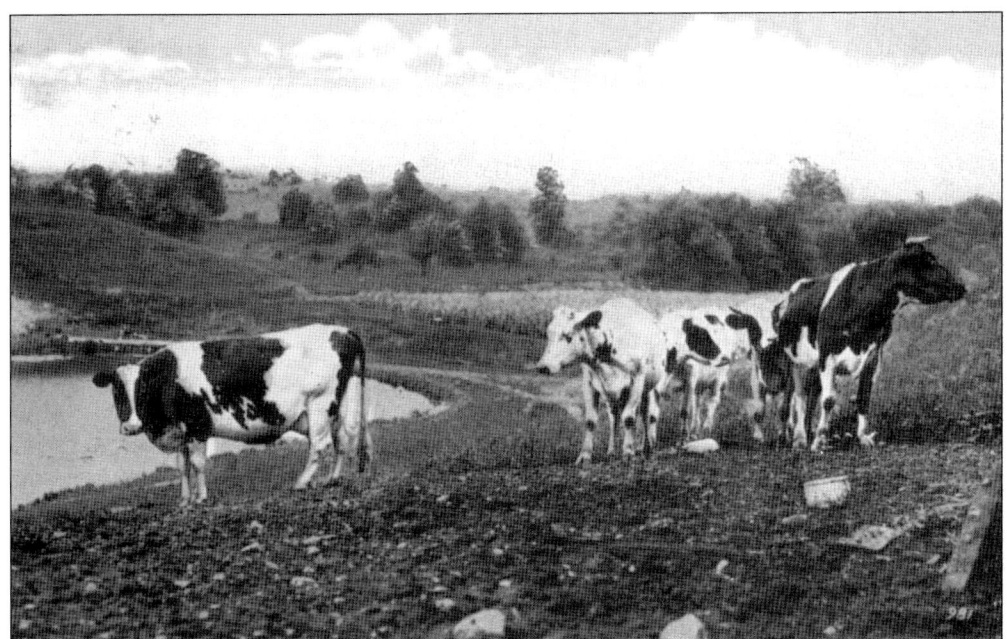

In the 1920s, when these postcards were mailed, agriculture was still very important to Sullivan County. It would remain so until after World War II. Scenes of domestic animals in pastures could be seen along both paved and dirt roads. In the 1950s and 1960s, the chicken and egg industry also boomed in the Catskills. Resorts and animal smells never really went together and, in governmental actions, the farms usually lost.

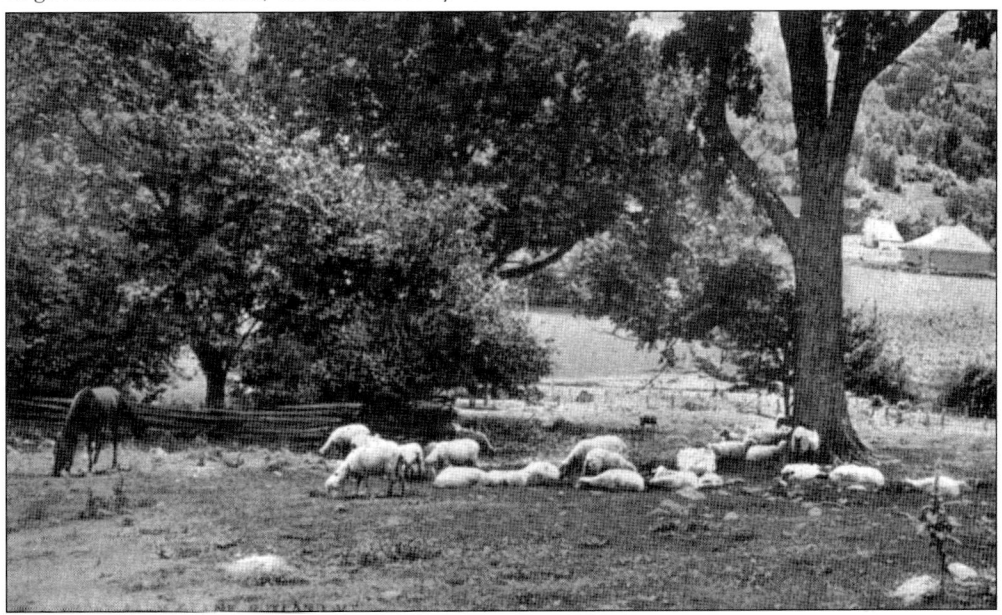

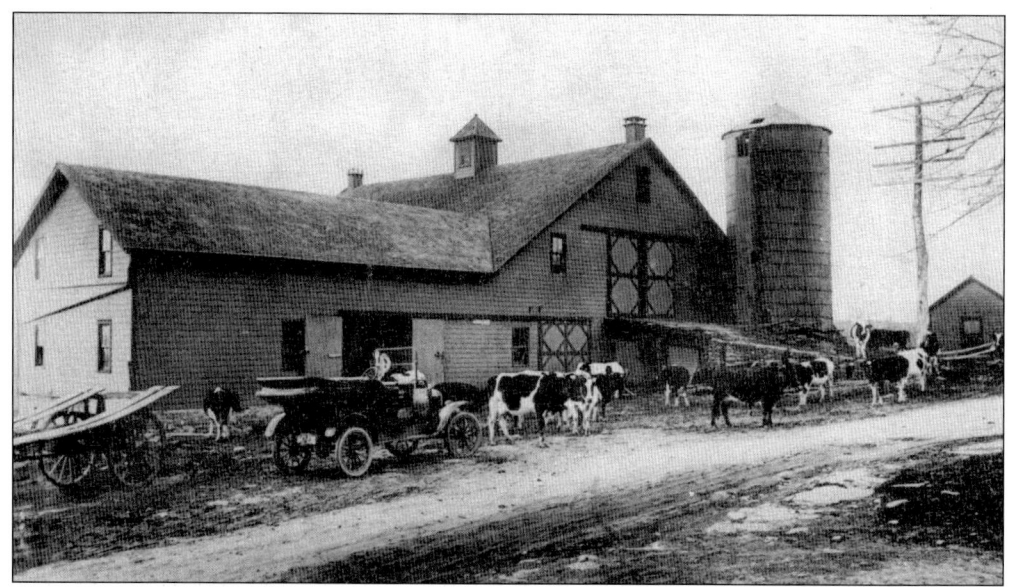

Dairy farms were popular tourist stops for city visitors. Many farmers would sell raw milk to travelers. The Hurleyville dairy, above, eventually gave birth to its own resort, the Wayside Inn. This was a familiar pattern in the region, one that accelerated in the 1920s.

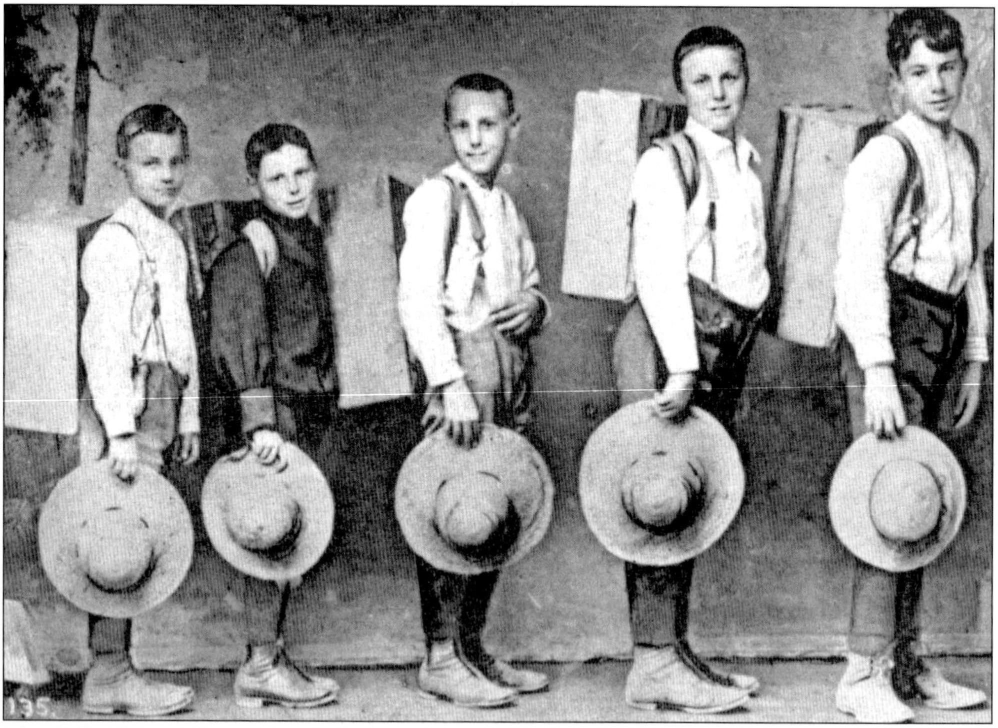

The hills above Ellenville were covered with blueberries, which were picked in commercial quantities by whole families and sometimes by packs of boys whose agility allowed them to get to difficult spots. Their story has been told in *The Huckleberry Pickers: A Raucous History of the Shawangunk Mountains*.

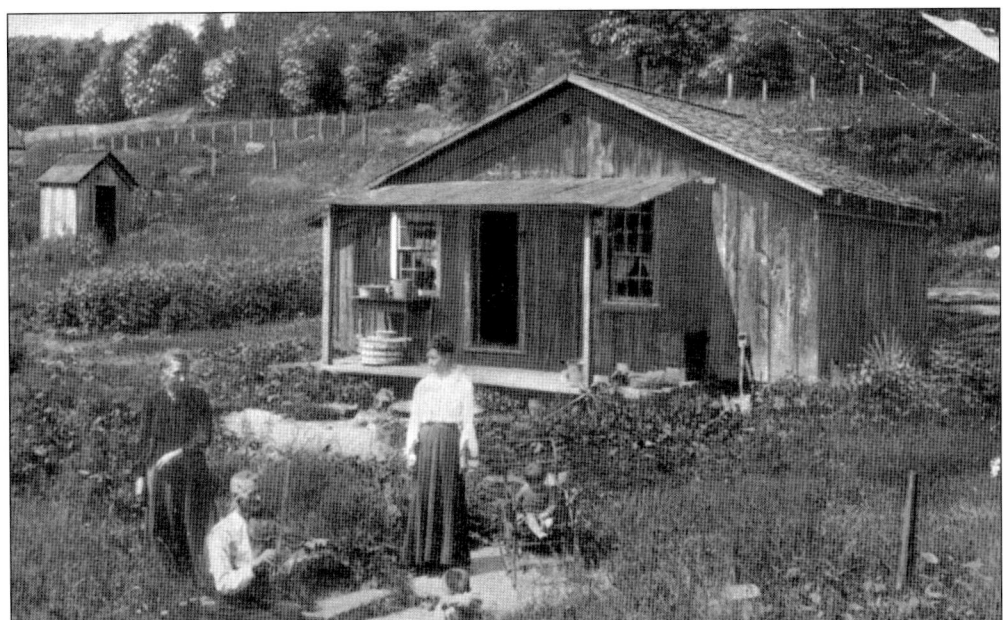

Photographed c. 1910 by Otto Hillig (1877–1956), this Sullivan County scene is reminiscent of Appalachia. It represents, however, the lifestyle of many of the subsistence farmers who lived in Sullivan County until well after World War II.

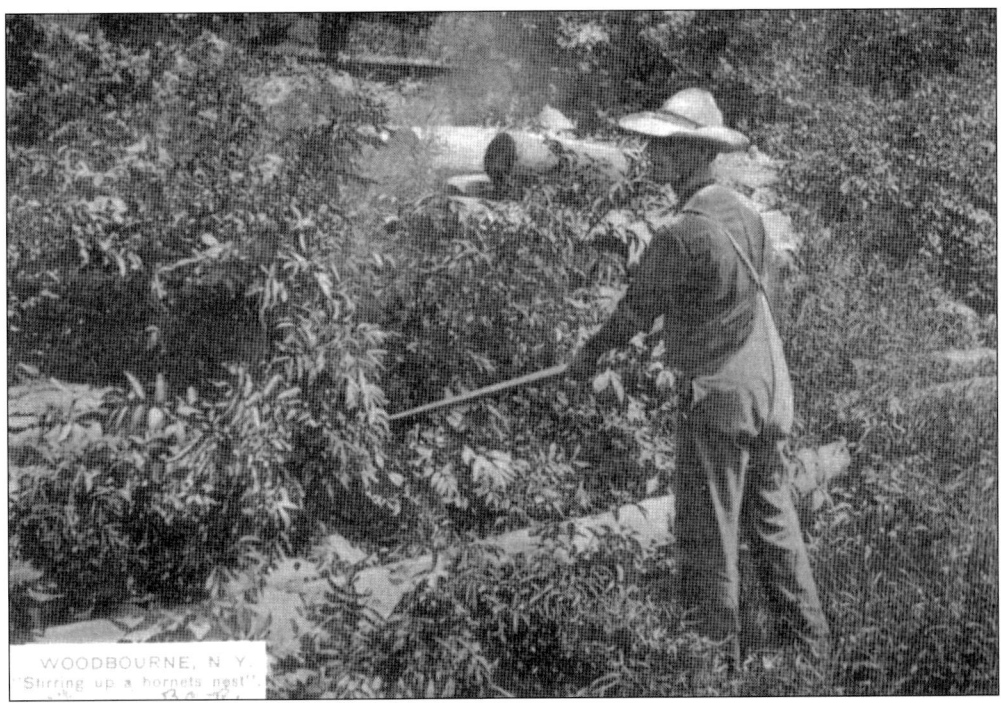

What precisely is this rustic man doing? He is properly static for someone stirring up a hornet's nest. The message on the back of this c. 1910 postcard is enigmatic: "Well, here is your card Agnes. Am staying here for one week. You don't need to tell me what it said in *that* letter." It sounds as if more than one hornet's nest was being stirred.

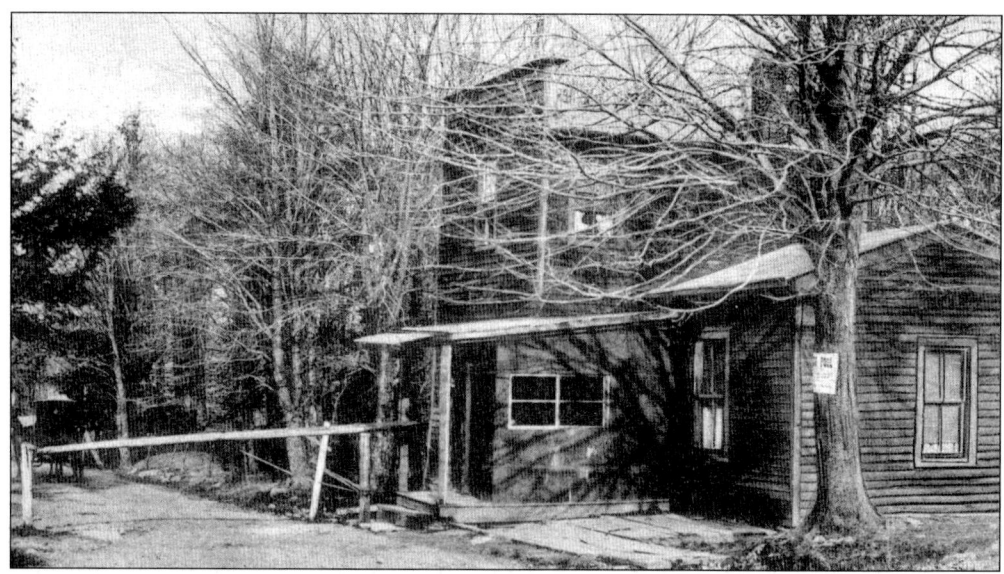

Many of the first roads in Sullivan County were toll roads, as was this one near Monticello. Very early in the 20th century, tollhouses were considered quaint relics of a passing society. Road improvements forced by the automobile made them obsolete. The first modern toll road in America was the Pennsylvania Turnpike, which opened in 1940.

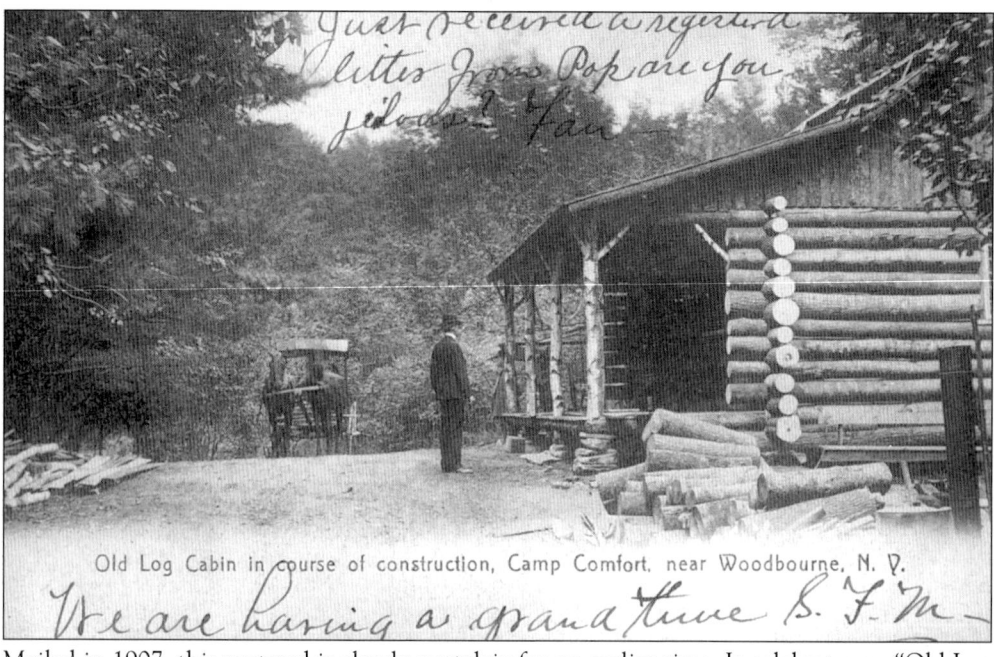

Mailed in 1907, this postcard is clearly nostalgic for an earlier time. It celebrates an "Old Log Cabin" being built. "Camp Comfort" was a popular picnic spot for both summer and year-round people in eastern Sullivan County.

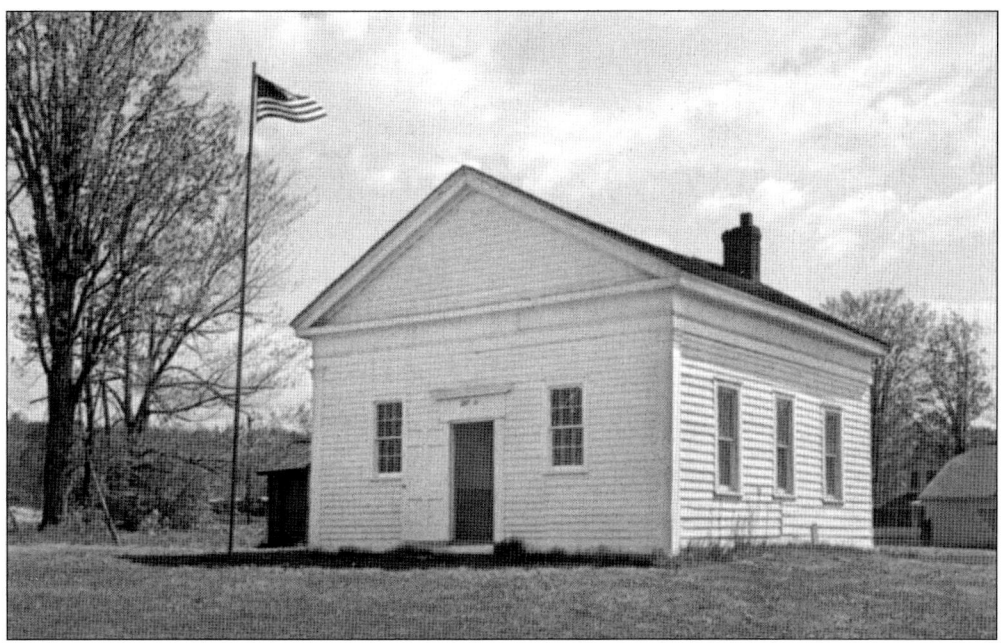

One-room schoolhouses dotted the Sullivan County landscape. The Greenfield Park Schoolhouse, just over the county line in Ulster, was built before 1836 and was used for a century. The school housed the eight elementary grades, including both Christian and Jewish students. Dave Levinson, who later developed the nearby Tamarack Lodge into a major Borscht Belt resort, went here as the son of a nearby Jewish farmer. The school is now maintained as a museum by the Greenfield Park Historical Association.

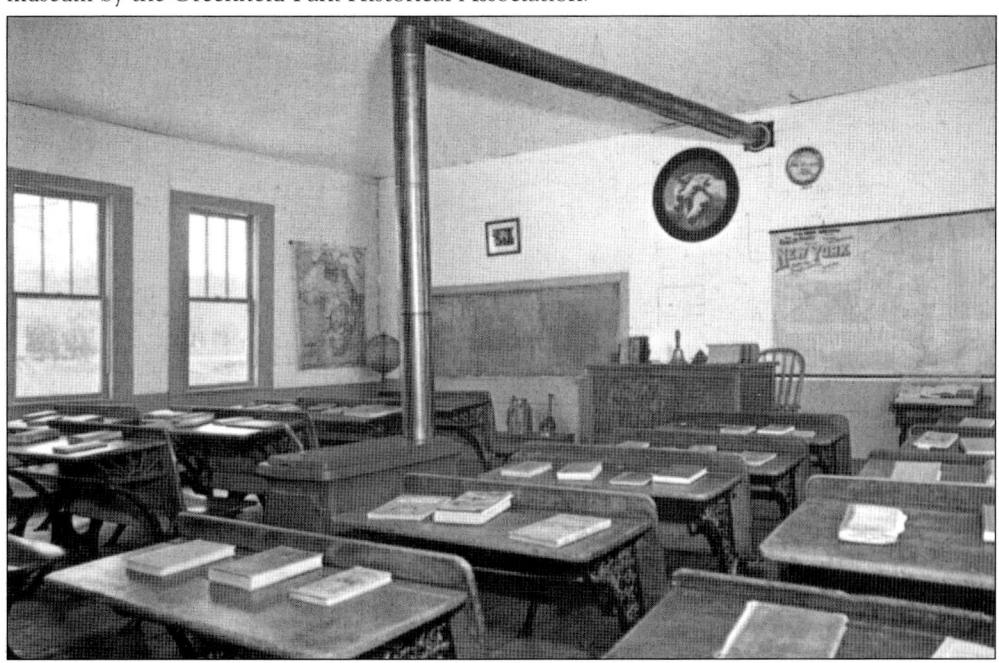

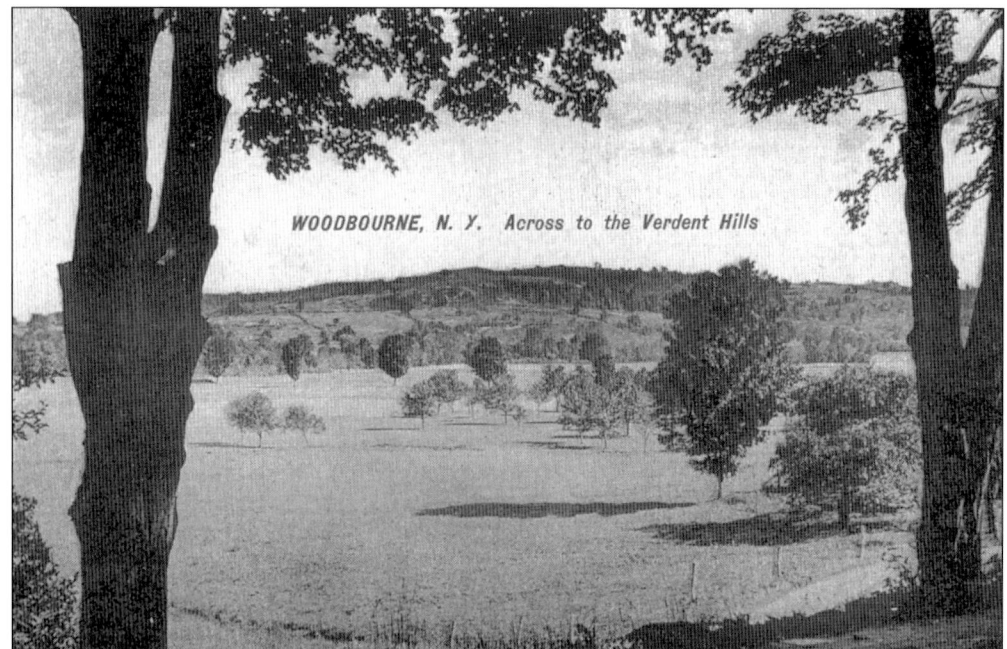

Mailed in 1909 from South Fallsburg to an aunt in Hasbrouck, this postcard shows a beautiful sweep of meadow with low hills beyond. In the 1930s, New York State built a prison on the closest of the "Verdant Hills."

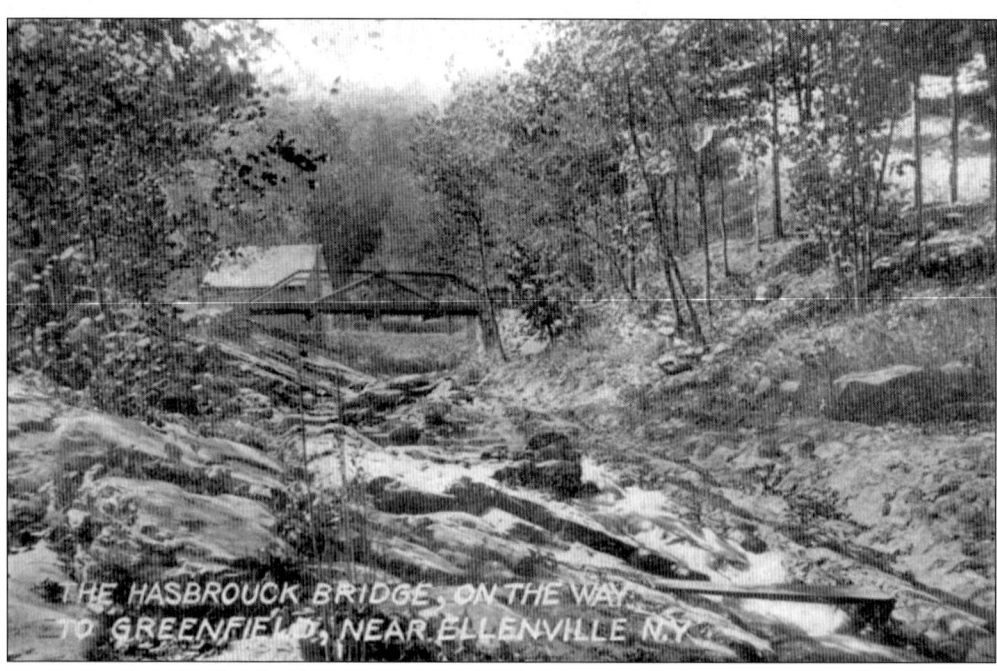

Demonstrating that locals often sent postcards of picturesque scenery to one another, this card of the Hasbrouck Bridge was sent by one Hurleyville resident to another. Hurleyville is about 6 miles from Hasbrouck.

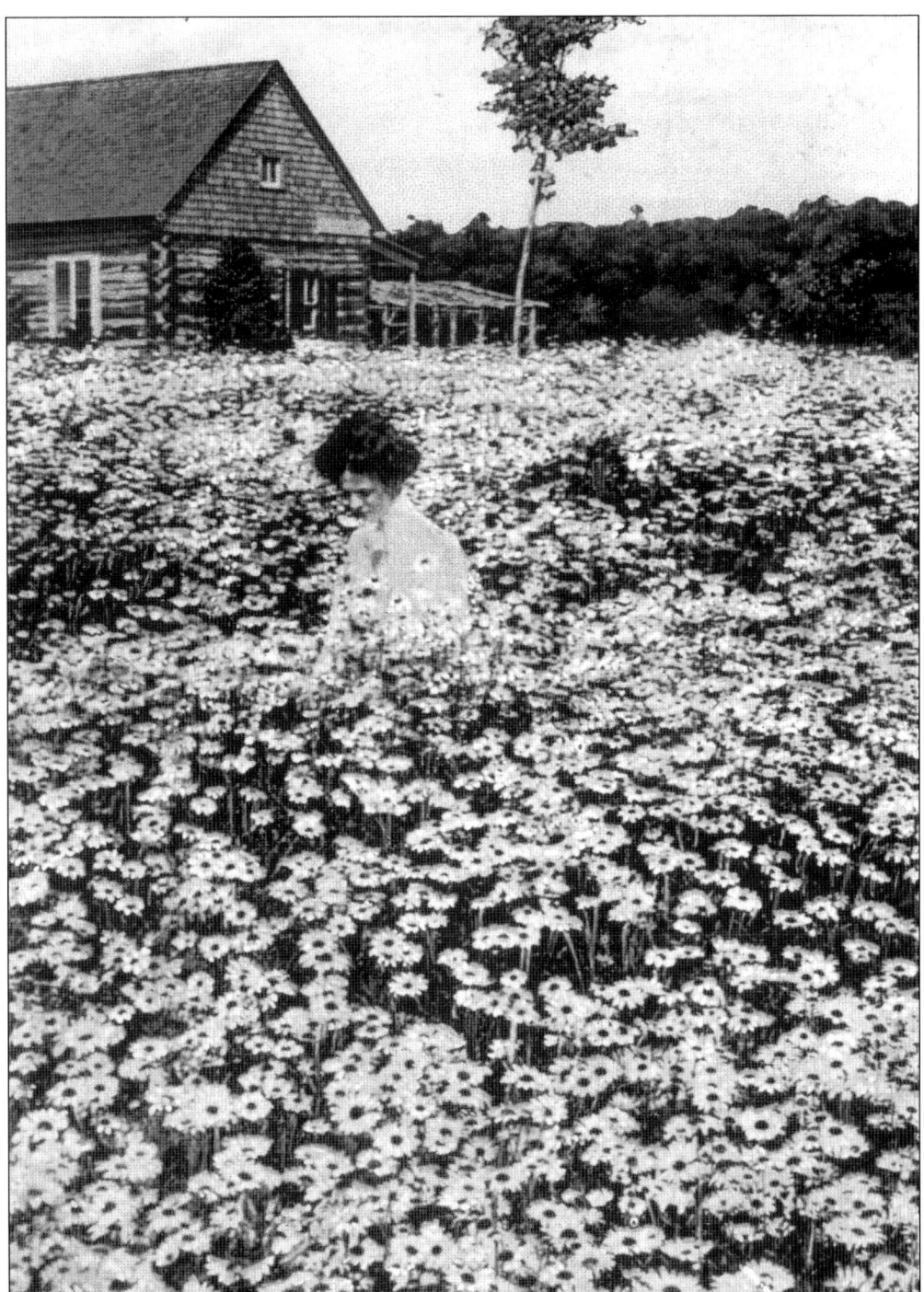

It is hard to remember that the oxeye daisy is not a native plant. Imported from England, it now grows wild throughout Sullivan County. This field was photographed by Otto Hillig (1877–1956), one of the region's most important postcard makers. He sold this image with many different town legends. This one is marked "Monticello." Note the quaint log building in the background.

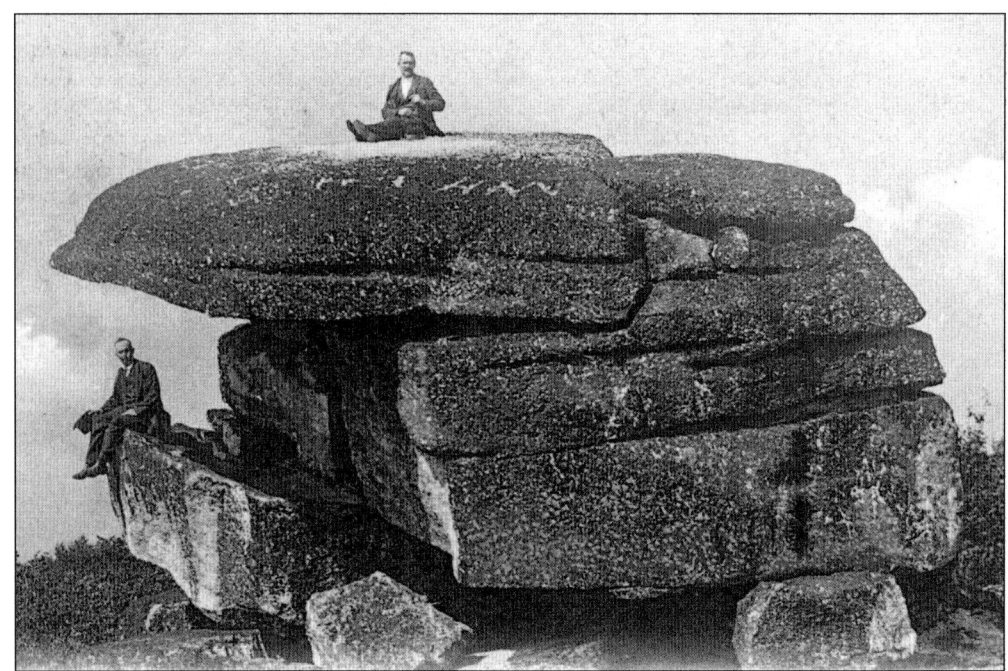

Visiting impressive rocks was an important tourist pastime. Daredevils would pose in precarious positions. High on a hilltop near Ellenville, Big Indian Rock was a popular destination for picnickers. This 1907 postcard was sent to Mae Grady of Halsay Street in Brooklyn.

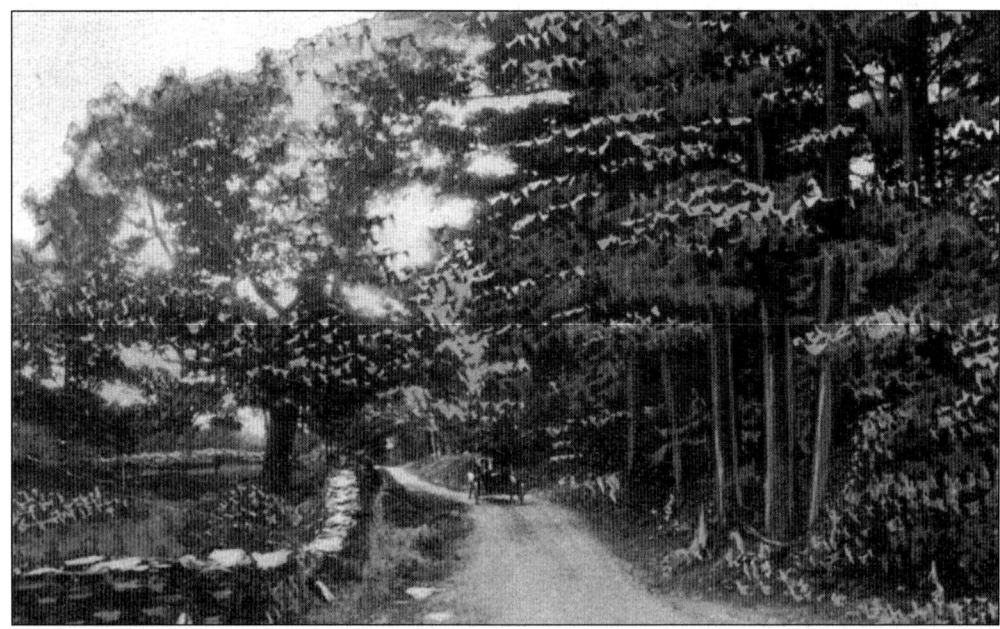

Merriewold Park was an intellectual community founded by social theorist Henry George (1839–1897). Once only a summer community, it is now home to many residents year-round. On this 1924 postcard, showing the road near Merriewold, a woman named Martha writes, "It is just grand here have not been to Monticello but we took a ride to Mongaup Hills yesterday."

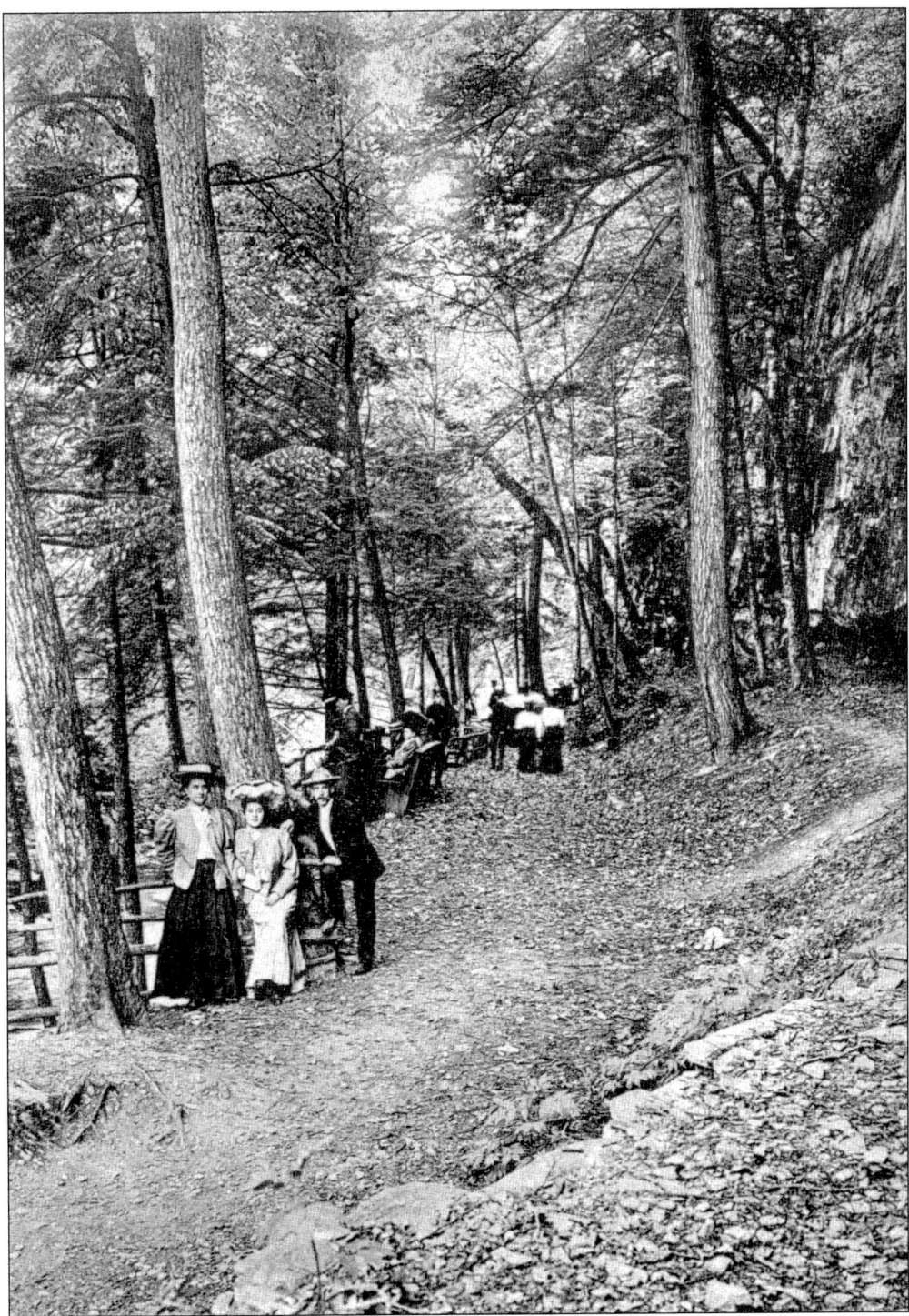

Lovers Lane, located on Lake Ophelia (now under Route 17), was a popular strolling place in 1912 when Grace Tracy sent this postcard to her friend K. Boyer in Reading, New York. The grouping in the foreground is unusual for a Lovers Lane scene.

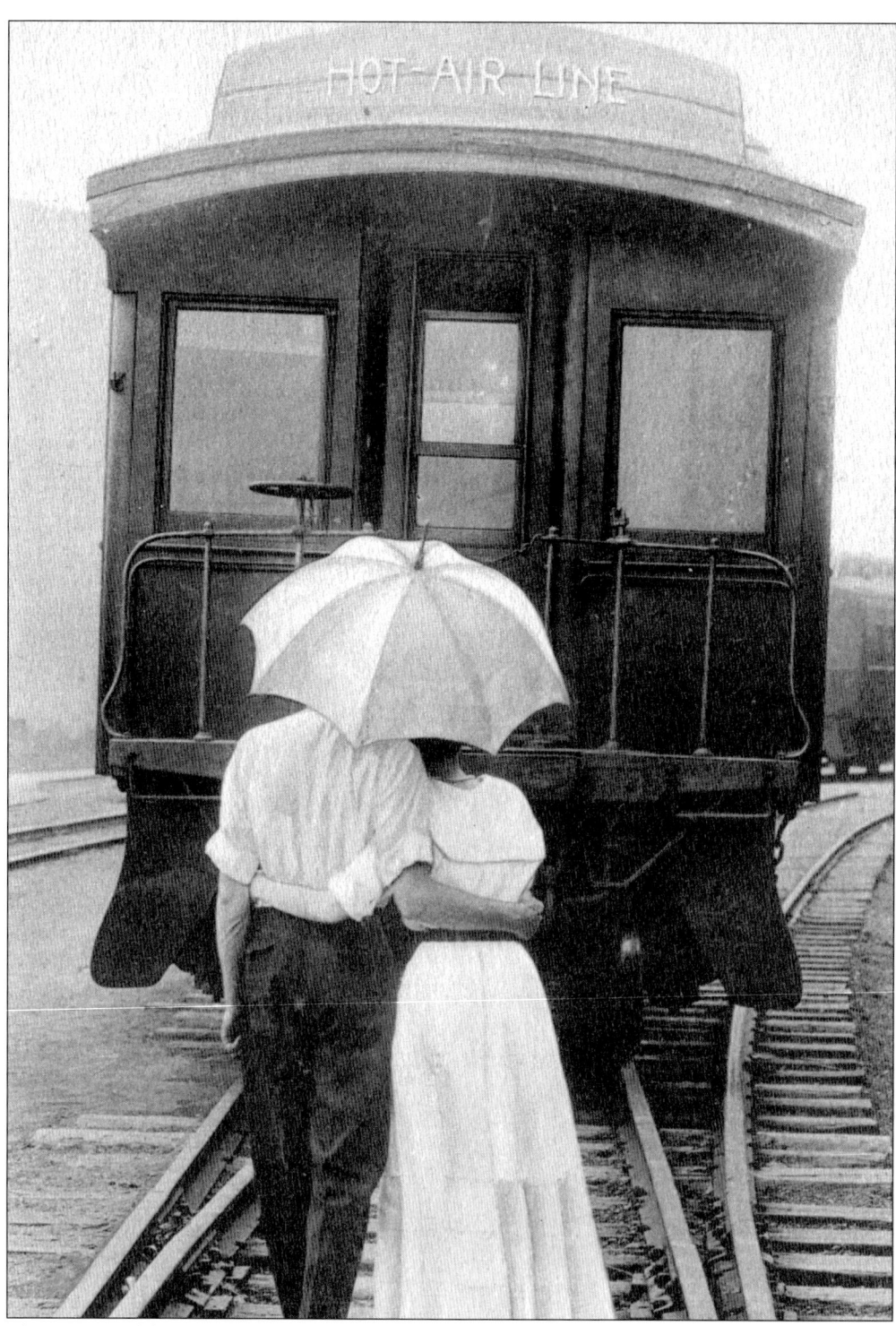
The coming of the railroad opened Sullivan County to tourism. The train had made honeymoon trips to Niagara Falls almost mandatory. This postcard is labeled Loch Sheldrake, but the same image has been impressed with the names of other towns as well.

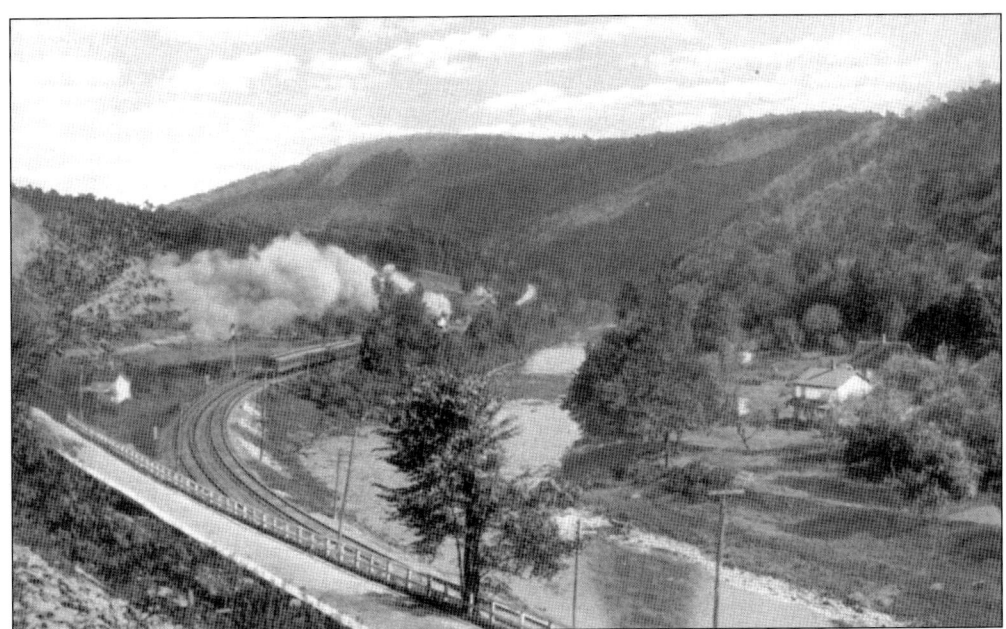

This "machine in the garden," as the railroad has been called, was photographed c. 1920 by Otto Hillig between Parksburg and Livingston Manor, where the New York, Ontario, and Western Railroad ran along the Neversink River. New York Route 17 is in the foreground.

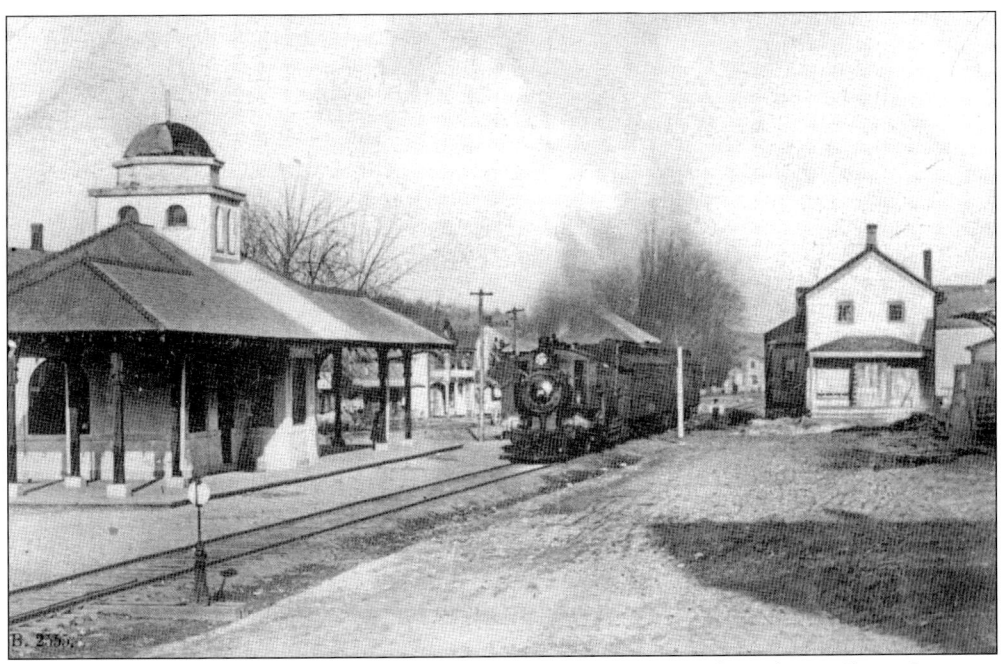

The more prosperous and successful towns in eastern Sullivan and southern Ulster Counties had railroad stations that quickly became the center of town activity, as was this station in Kerhonkson. In summer, the railroads brought tourists. All year, the railroad allowed locals easy access to nearby communities and a relatively direct route to New York City.

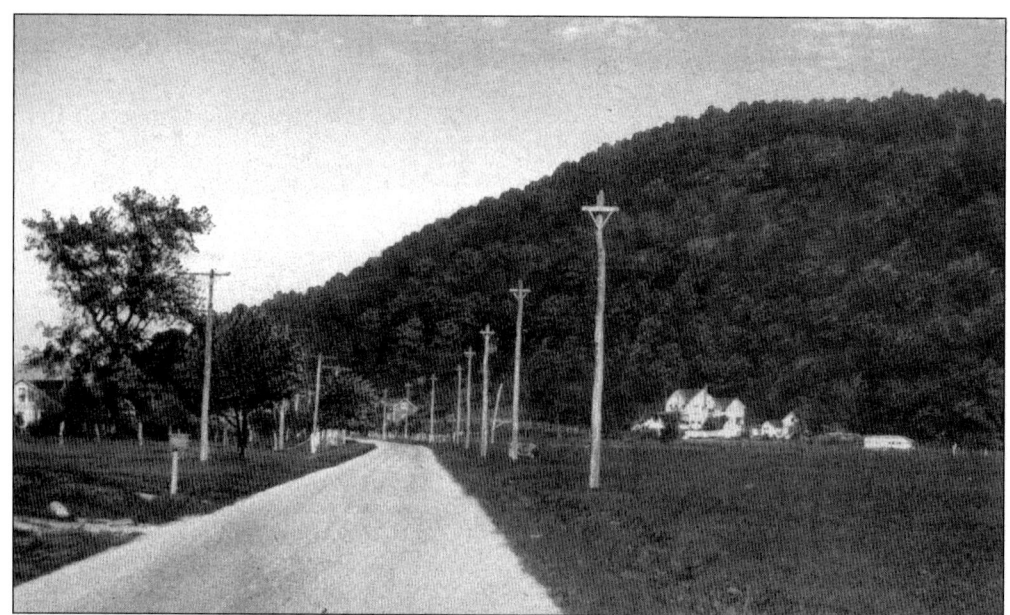

The automobile and highways had an even greater impact on Sullivan County than the railroad did. Buses and cars quickly replaced the railroads as the premier people movers. This highway, probably New York Route 17, was photographed by Otto Hillig c. 1920.

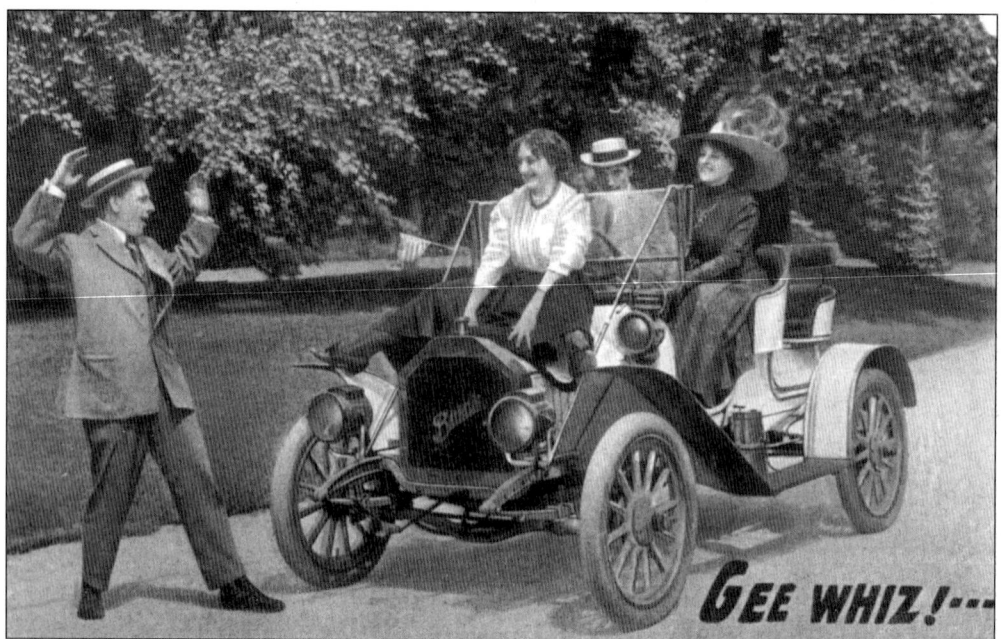

This postcard was sent to Maude Hindley of Monticello in 1911 by her friend Edna, who was visiting in New York City. The message was simple: "We are having a swell time doing stunts like this." Moralists were alarmed, but Sullivan County was changed forever by the automobile.

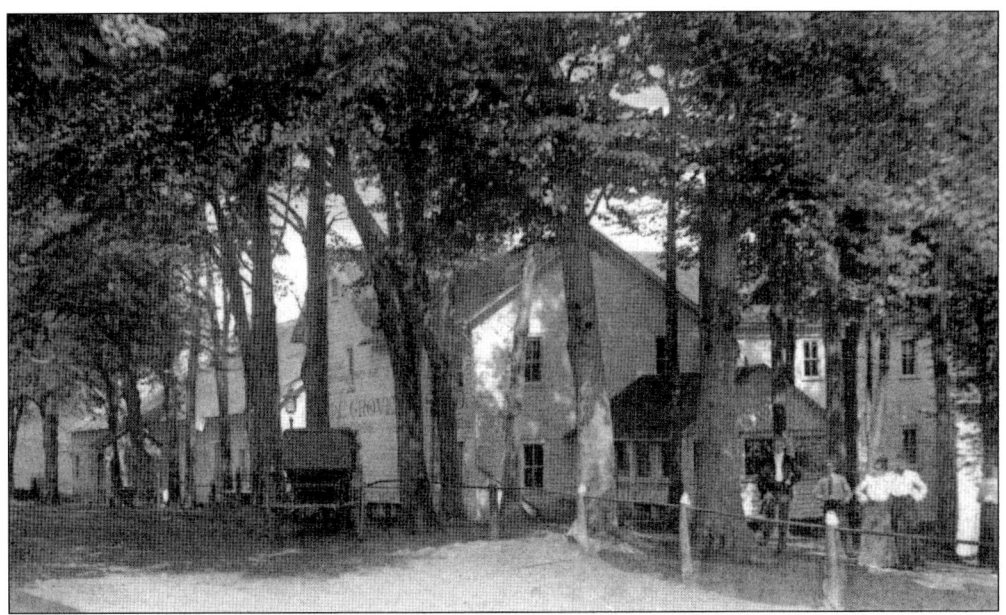

The above postcard, showing the Maple Grove Casino in Loch Sheldrake, was mailed to Alma Foster in Westport, Connecticut, in 1906. That year, Sheldrake (the "Loch" was later added by the New York, Ontario, and Western Railroad) had 23 boardinghouses and guesthouses. To extract money from summer people, H.M. LeRoy opened the Maple Grove Casino, which boasted Sullivan County's first bowling alley, below. LeRoy offered "free dancing in the casino every afternoon and evening except Sunday." His casino also featured a "temperance bar," which presumably served only nonalcoholic beverages.

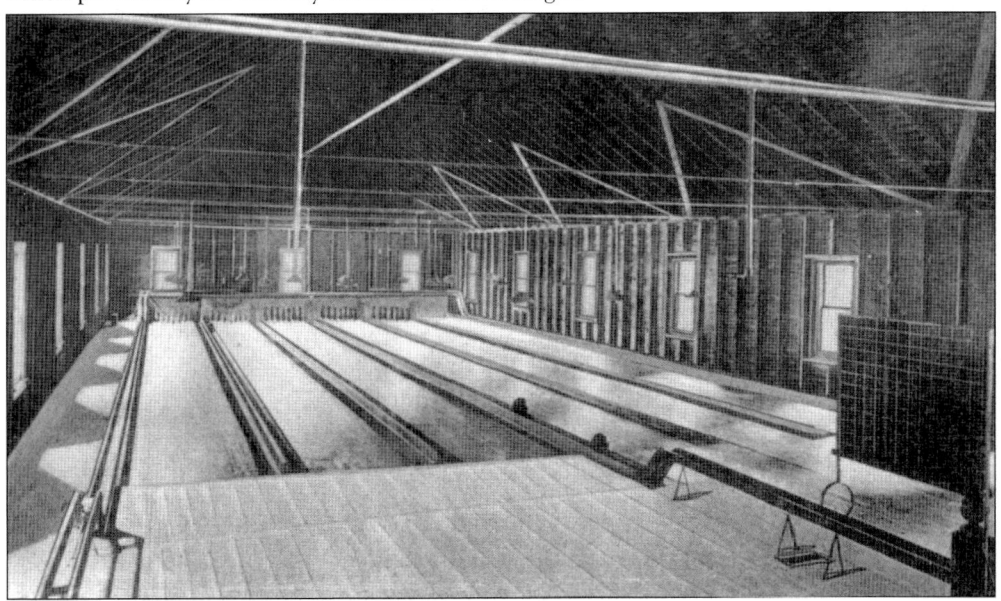

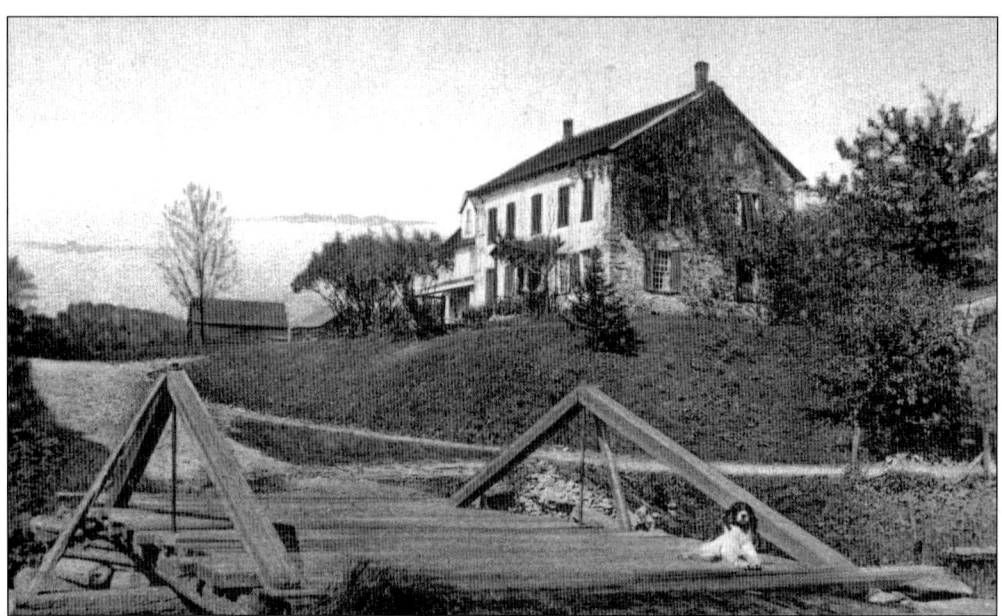

The Old Stone House in Hasbrouck, above, was built early in the 19th century by a descendent of a French Huguenot family who had settled in the nearby Hudson Valley in the 17th century. The building later became a boardinghouse and, covered with jerry-built additions, was a *kuchalein*. It is now restored and maintained as a historic house. Mrs. H.J. Duffy's Woodland Cottage is typical of the region's late-19th-century farmhouses that took in boarders.

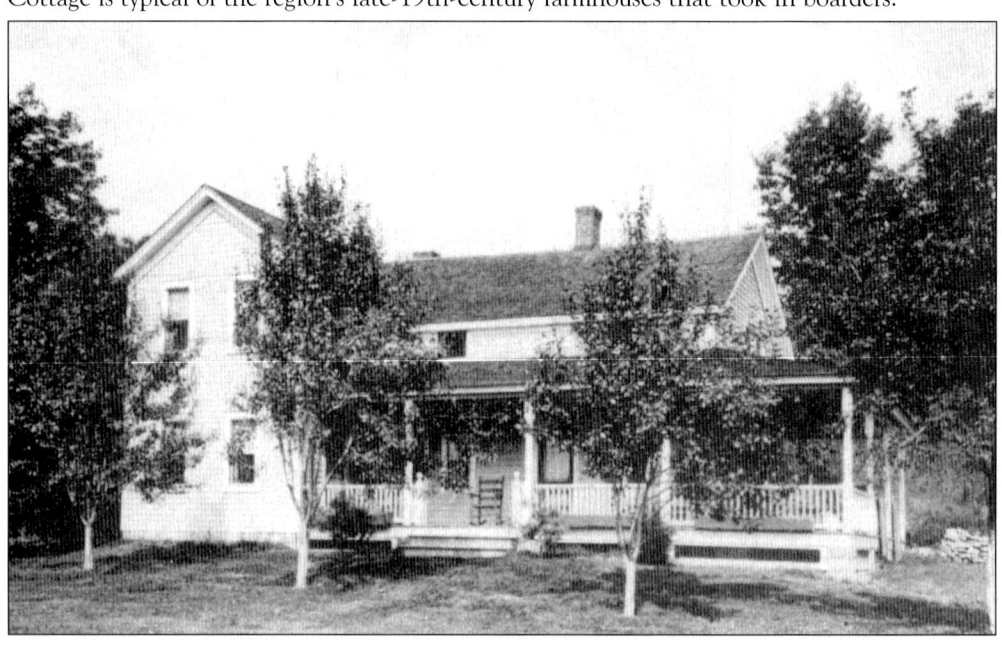

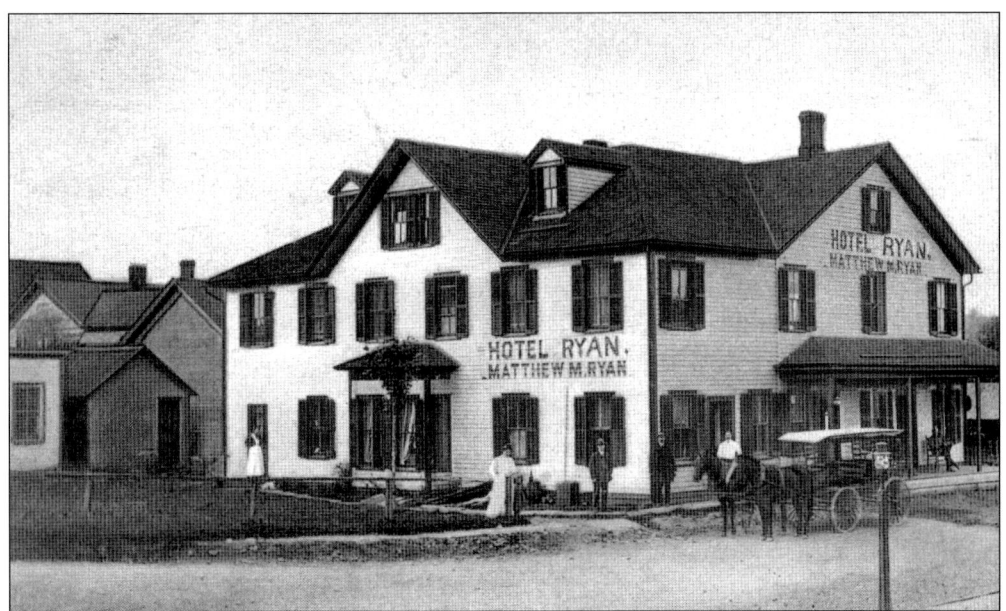

The Hotel Ryan in South Fallsburg was run by Matthew M. Ryan. Many of the earliest hotels in the county catered to an Irish or a German clientele. On this postcard mailed in 1904, a traveler reports having had dinner here on his way to nearby Woodbourne. Unfortunately for history, he did not critique the meal.

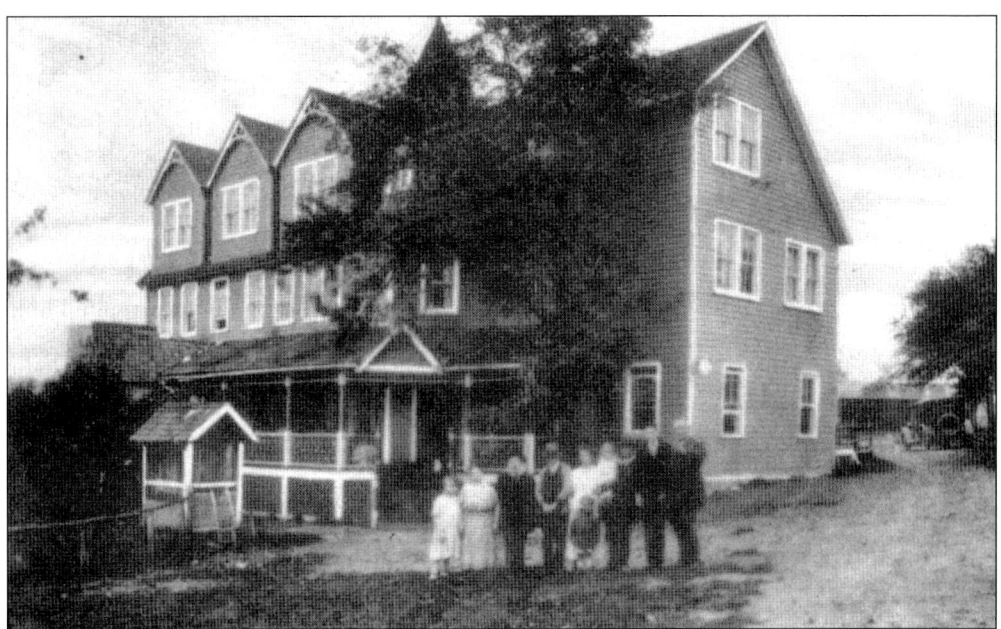

This c. 1910 image shows the Birkil Farm House, which had just been built for summer boarders. The rough grounds are a reminder of the bucolic origins of many resorts.

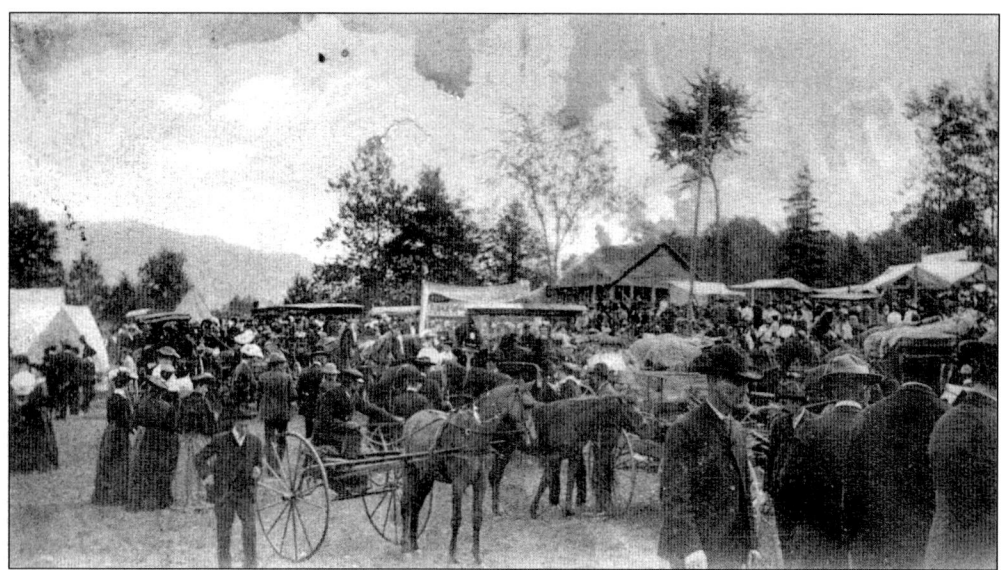

The Little World's Fair, held in Grahamsville at the end of August, is one of New York State's oldest continuing agricultural fairs. It remains popular with both local folks and visitors. This c. 1905 postcard was printed in Germany, where most early postcards were produced.

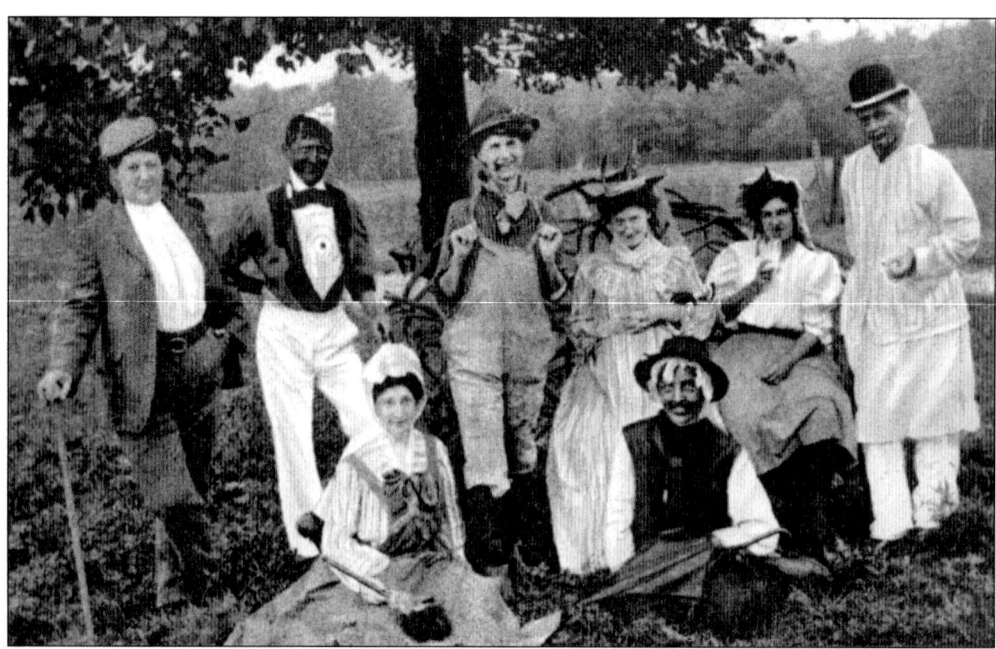

Entertainment was homemade during the summer. Dressing up in costume was a popular pastime, and outfits were usually impromptu. Two of these men are in blackface. Printed in Germany, this postcard is marked Ferndale, New York.

Two
Resort Towns and Shtetlach

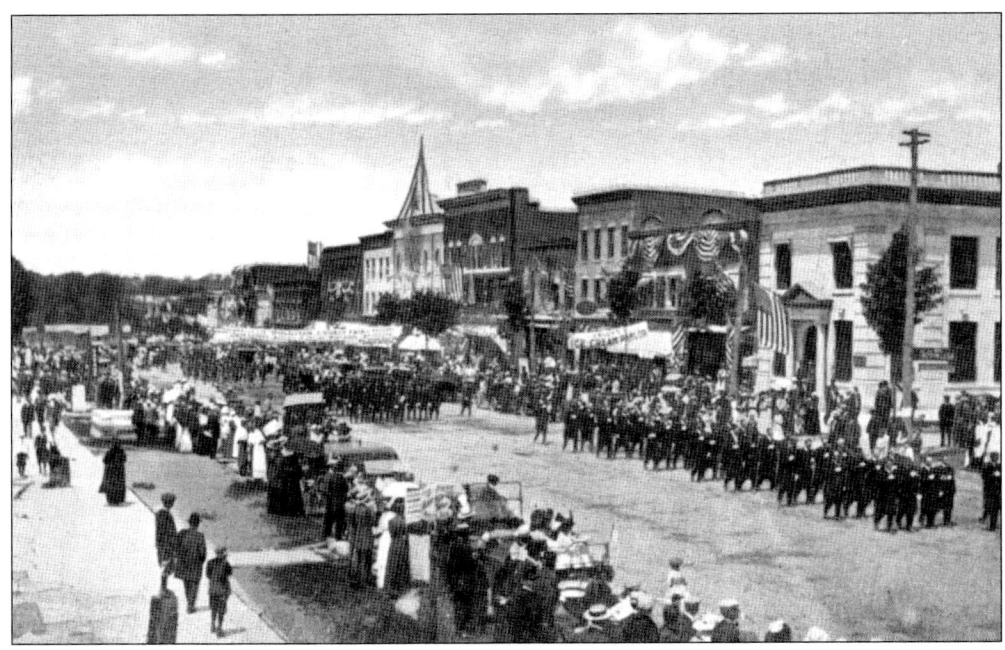

Broadway, Monticello's wide main street, has long been a popular place for parades. Published c. 1910 in nearby Middletown in Orange County, this postcard shows a parade in late summer. The banner being carried by the group in the middle ground advertises the now defunct Sullivan County Fair.

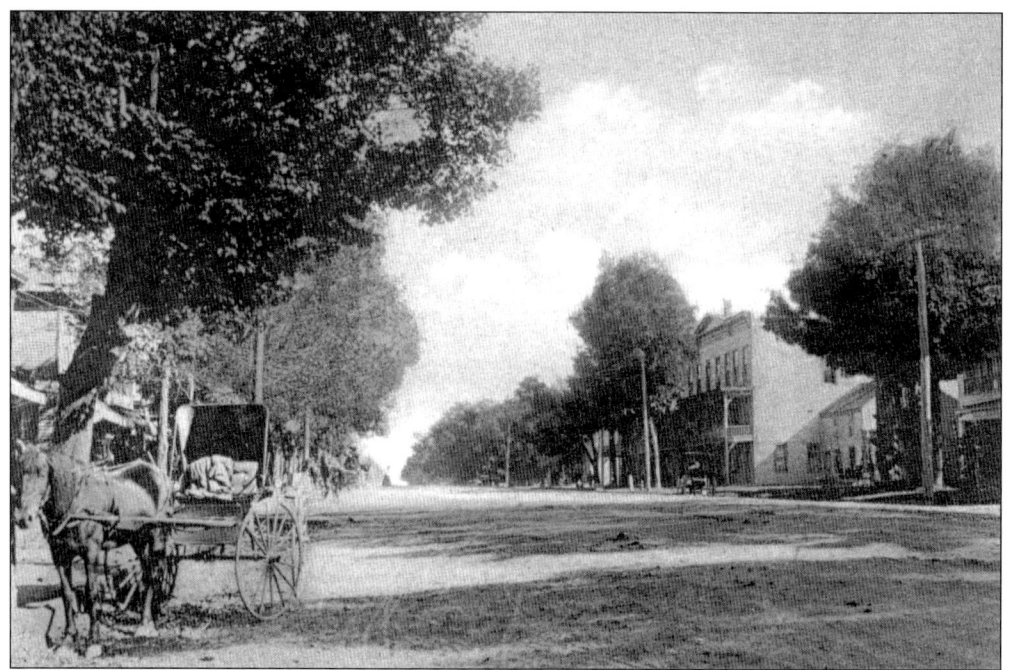

Monticello is the seat of Sullivan County and its largest town. Nevertheless, it took a long time for even its principal street, Broadway, to be paved. These c. 1910 views show what is essentially a sleepy town, before the boom years of the Borscht Belt era. The monument seen below, which now stands on the courthouse lawn, honors the Sullivan County soldiers and sailors who served in the Civil War.

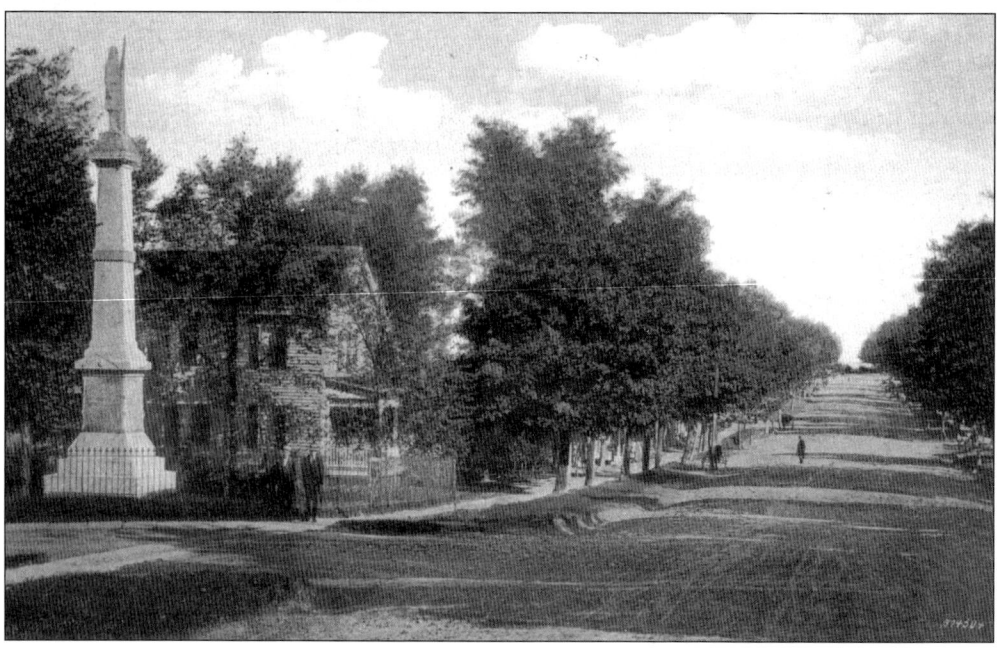

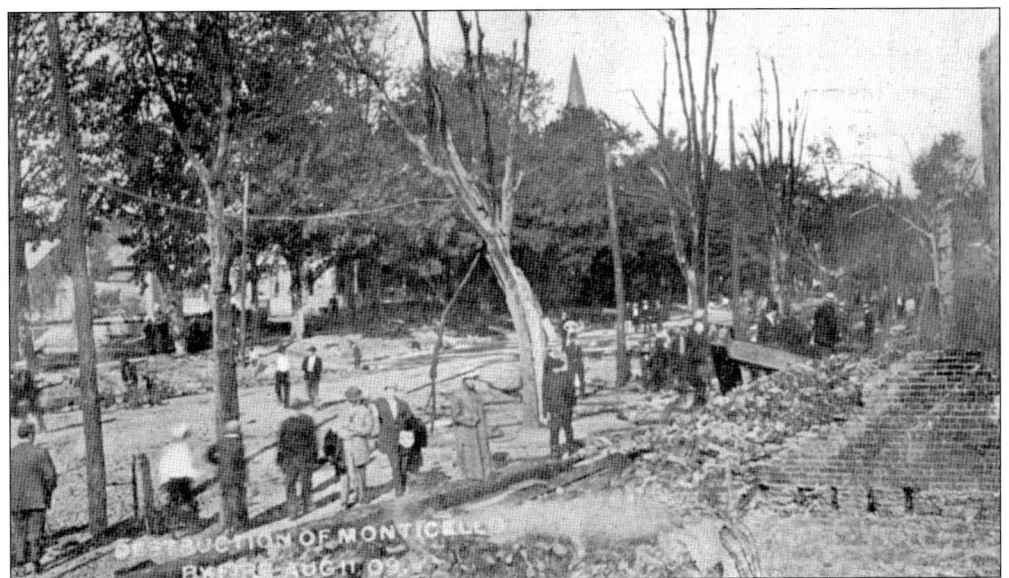

A devastating fire on August 10, 1909, destroyed much of downtown Monticello. Prosperous, if still quiet, the town was quickly rebuilt. In the 20th century, a number of fires have devastated local communities and resorts. In 1913, Liberty, Sullivan County's second largest town, suffered from a major fire as well.

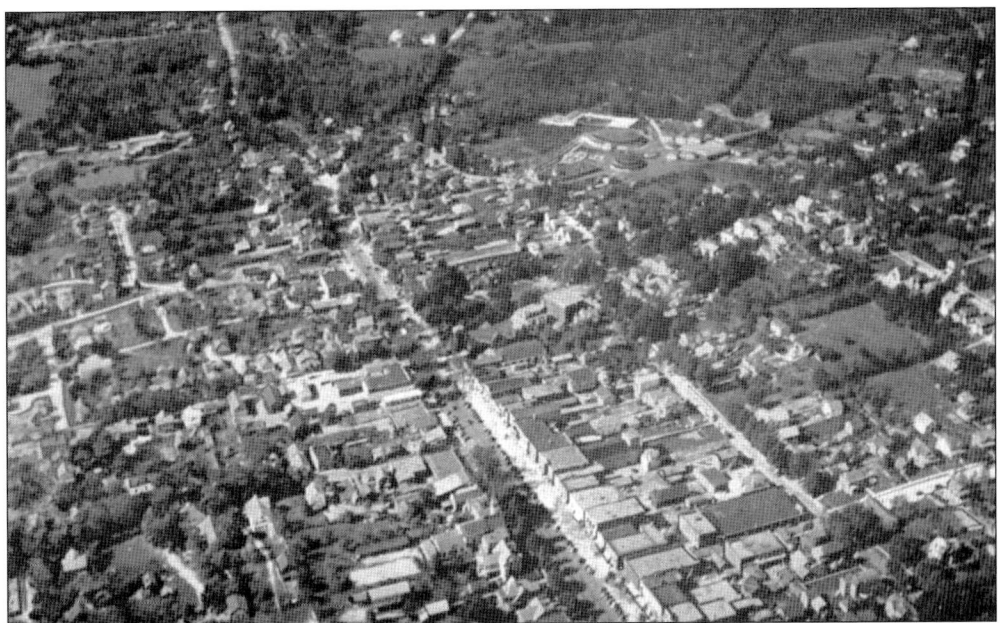

Monticello was photographed in 1931 by Otto Hillig (1877–1956), Sullivan County's premier photographer and aviation pioneer. Hillig was one of the first Americans to fly across the Atlantic. Wealthy and flamboyant, he built a castellated house that overlooked Liberty until it fell into ruin in the 1980s.

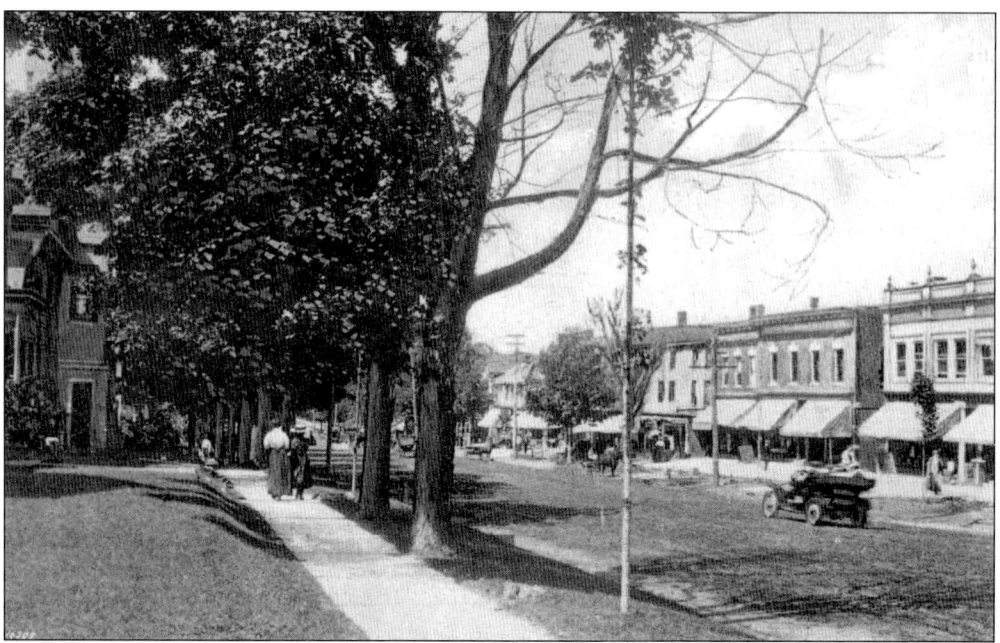

Monticello, founded when Thomas Jefferson was president, was named for his Virginia plantation. As shown above in 1912, Monticello was a prosperous county seat with a large downtown that had been rebuilt after the disastrous 1909 fire. Some 40 years later, the town reached its economic zenith, as shown below. Every store is rented, and most have new post–World War II facades. *Carpetbaggers* is showing at the Rialto. The back of the lower postcard proclaims, "View shows part of the Broadway business district. Monticello is the heart of the famous Sullivan County vacationland—a land of beauty, mountains, lakes, rivers, trout streams, the finest hunting in New York State. Lavish hotels, motels, bungalow colonies cater to hundreds of thousands of vacationers every year."

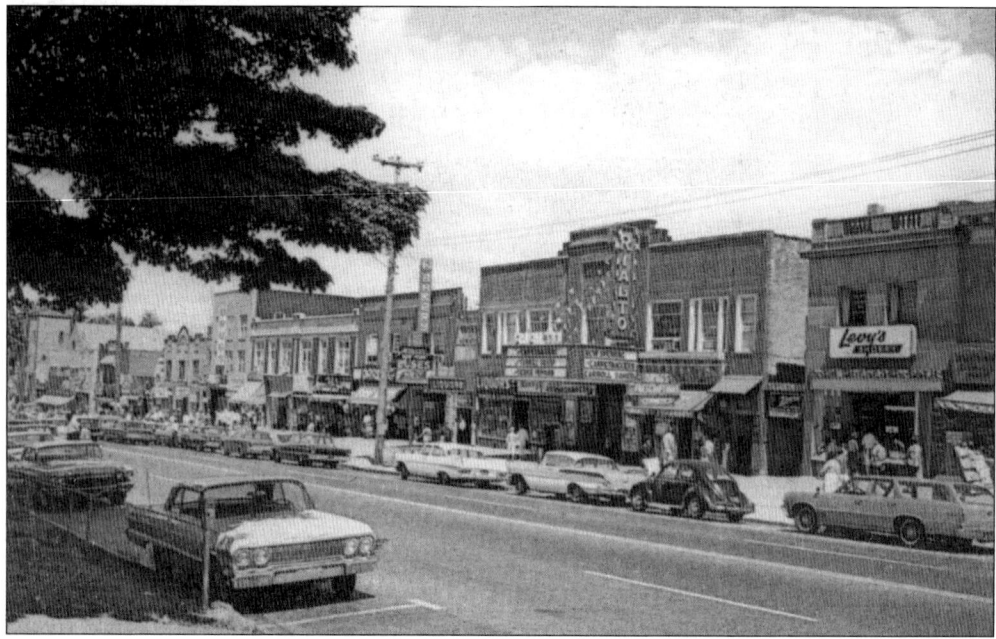

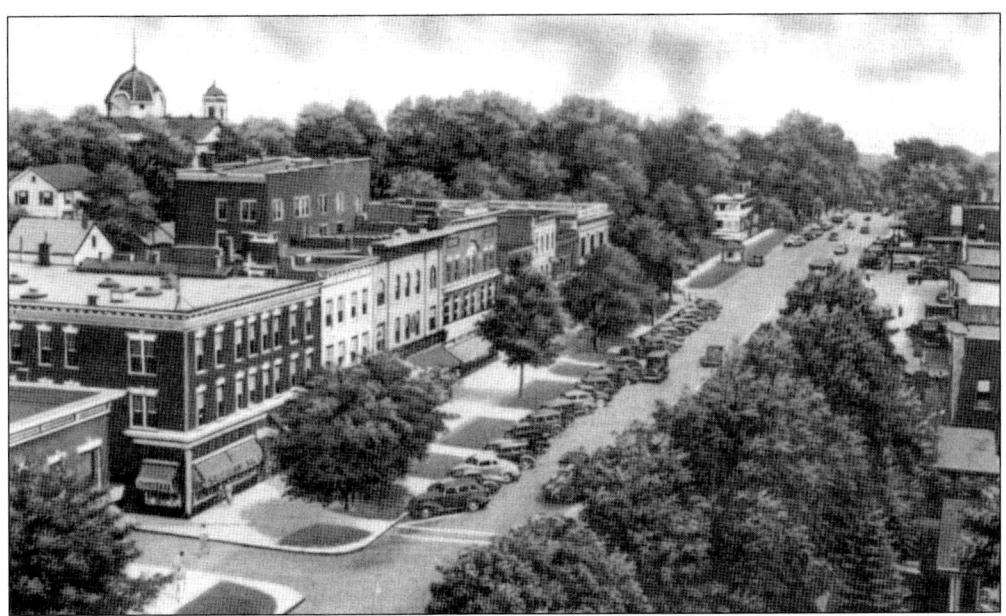

Monticello began to boom in the 1920s. By the 1930s, it was the unchallenged capital of the Borscht Belt. The dome in the background of the above image is the Sullivan County Courthouse. Below, people mill about on Monticello streets. Next to the F.W. Woolworth store is the Hammond and Cooke department store, Sullivan County's largest. There is a wonderful description of Monticello during this era in the novel *Summer on a Mountain of Spice*, by Harvey Jacobs.

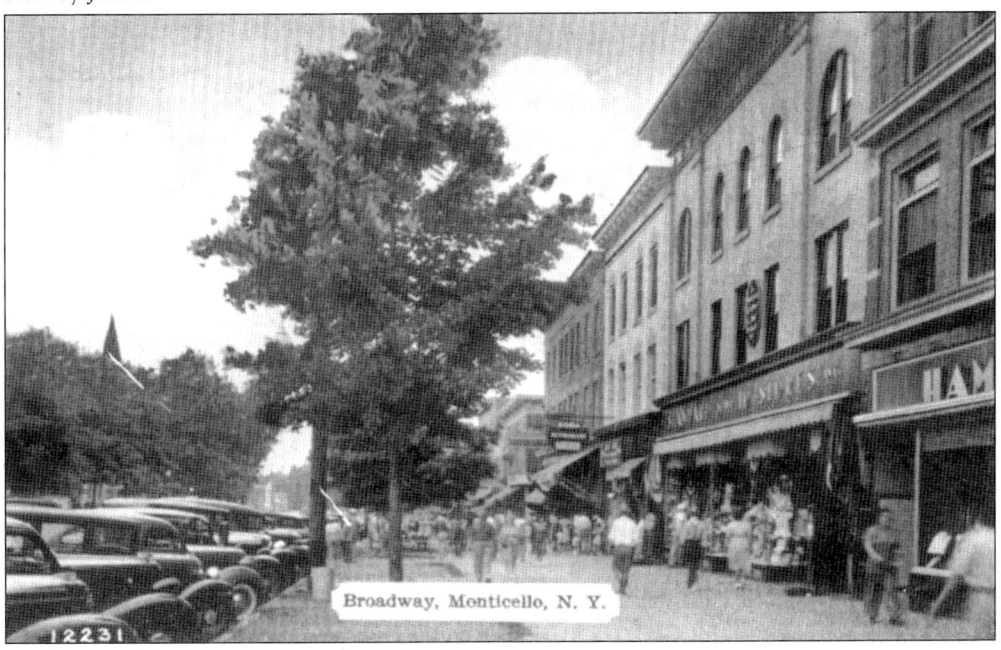

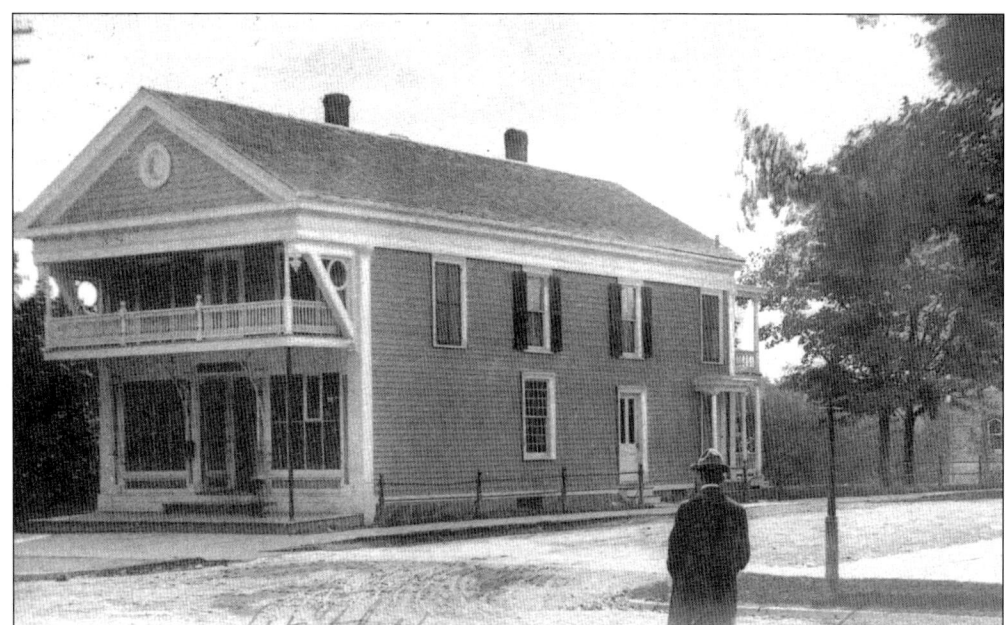

The Monticello Post Office was housed in a handsome Greek Revival building (above), which was spared by the fire of 1909 thanks to the quick work of the volunteer fire company. The post office later moved into its present Colonial Revival building (below), built under the Works Projects Administration in the 1930s.

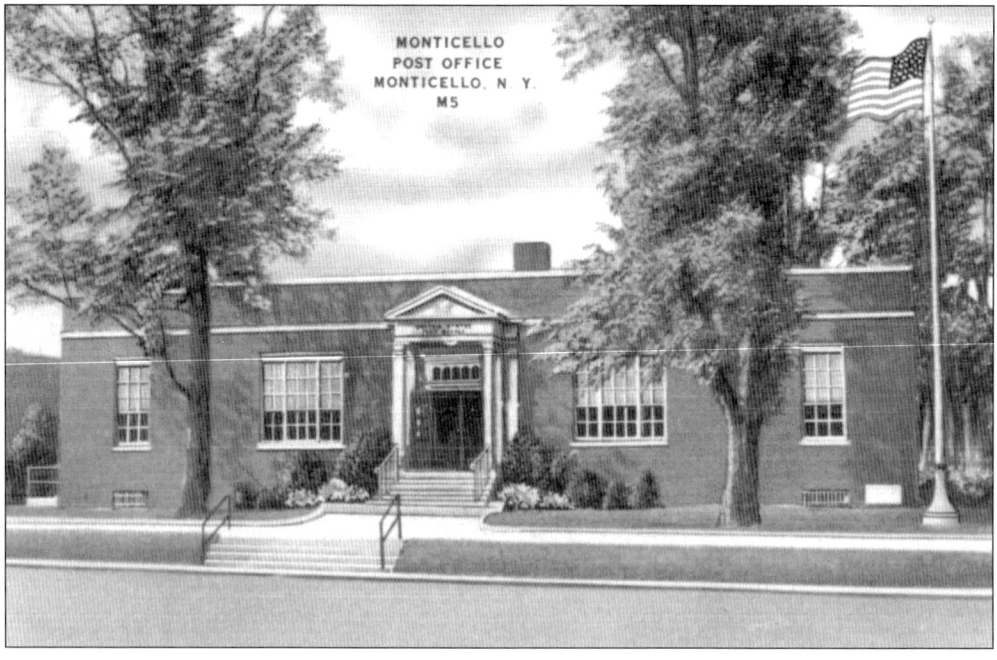

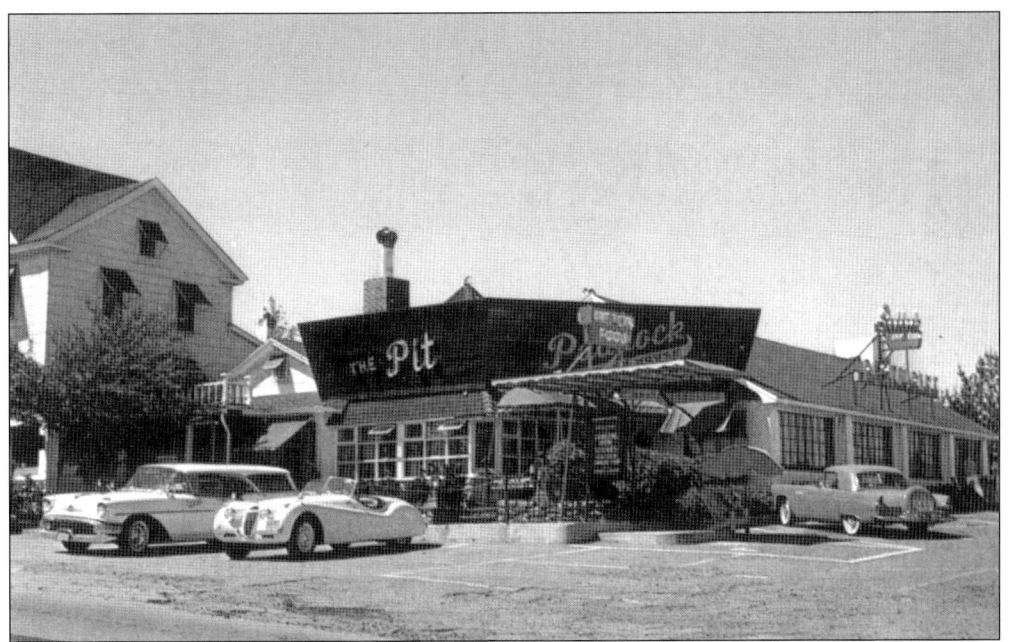

For many years, the Paddock, a mile east of Monticello, was a popular steakhouse. Its phone number was Monticello 2065. The late model cars, especially the sporty ones, were obviously chosen to mark the restaurant as the place to be.

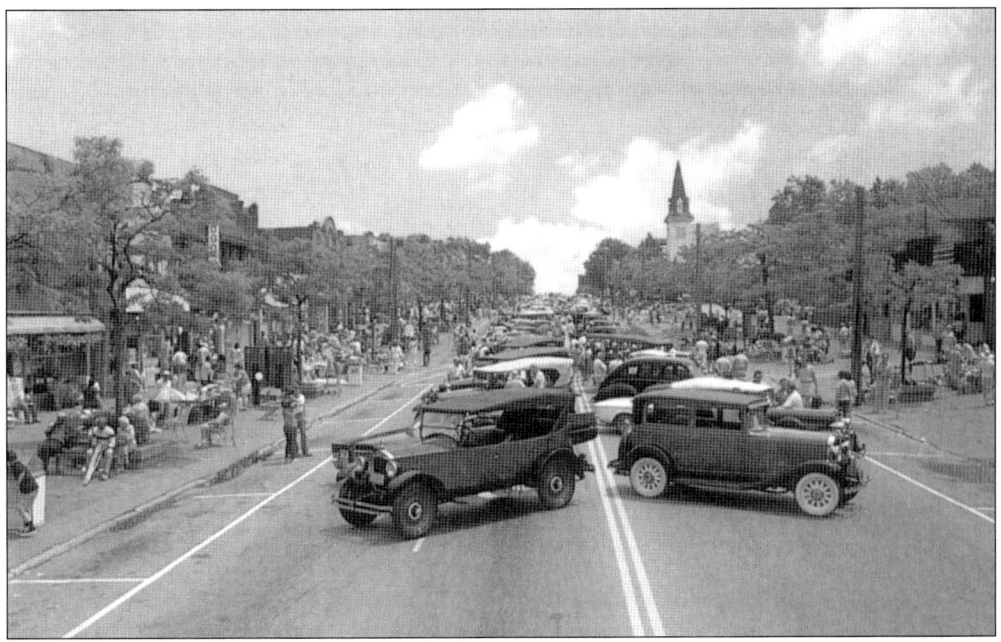

By the 1960s, the bloom was starting to fade from the resort rose and the region was showing signs of decline. The Monticello Action Committee busied itself by bringing myriad events to town, including the Annual Antique Automobile Show and gigantic garage sale held in the middle of Broadway.

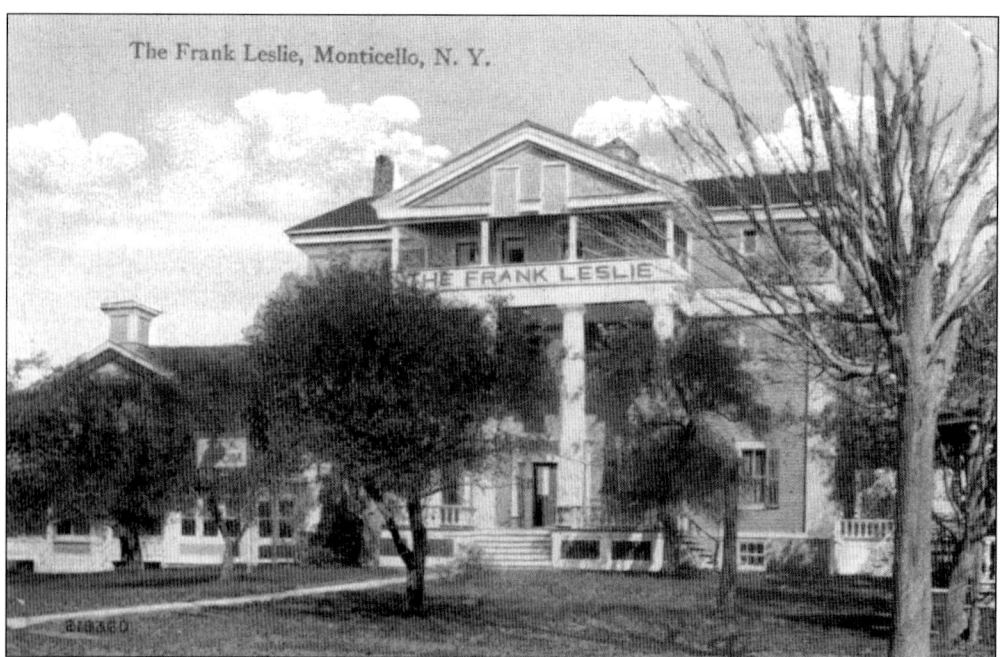

The Frank Leslie, Monticello, N. Y.

The Frank Leslie, above, was one of the more refined hotels scattered through the village of Monticello. In summer, it held croquet and tennis tournaments. After its decline, it was eventually torn down to provide parking spaces for Sullivan County legislators. More raffish and long lasting was the Monticello Inn, below. In the 1920s, it was notorious as a speakeasy. In 1946, "Cookie" wrote to her friend in Pennsylvania, "I'm a hard working girl but having a world of fun." Much altered, a semblance of the Monticello Inn still exists.

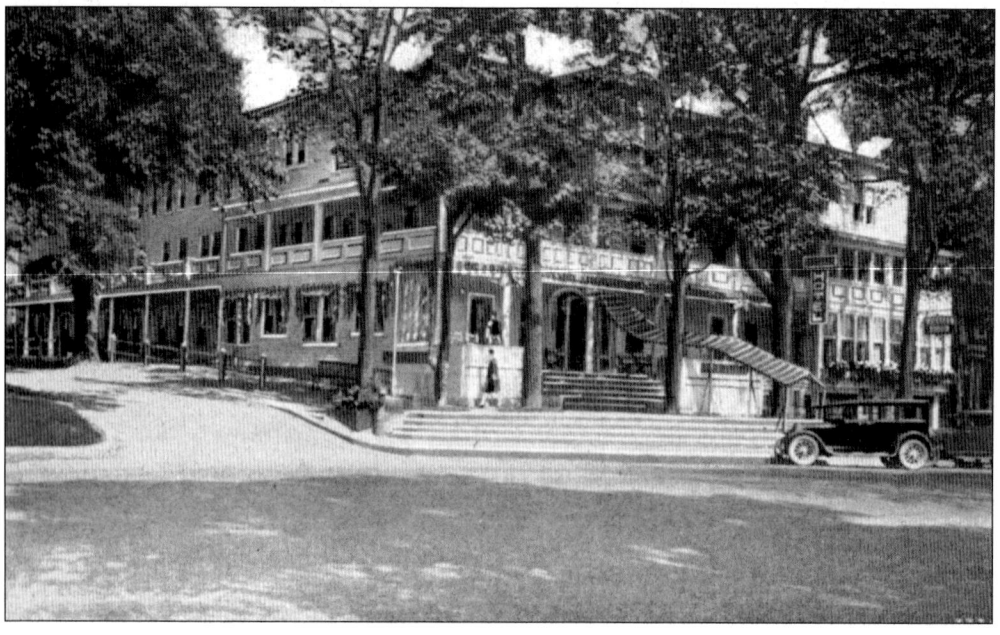

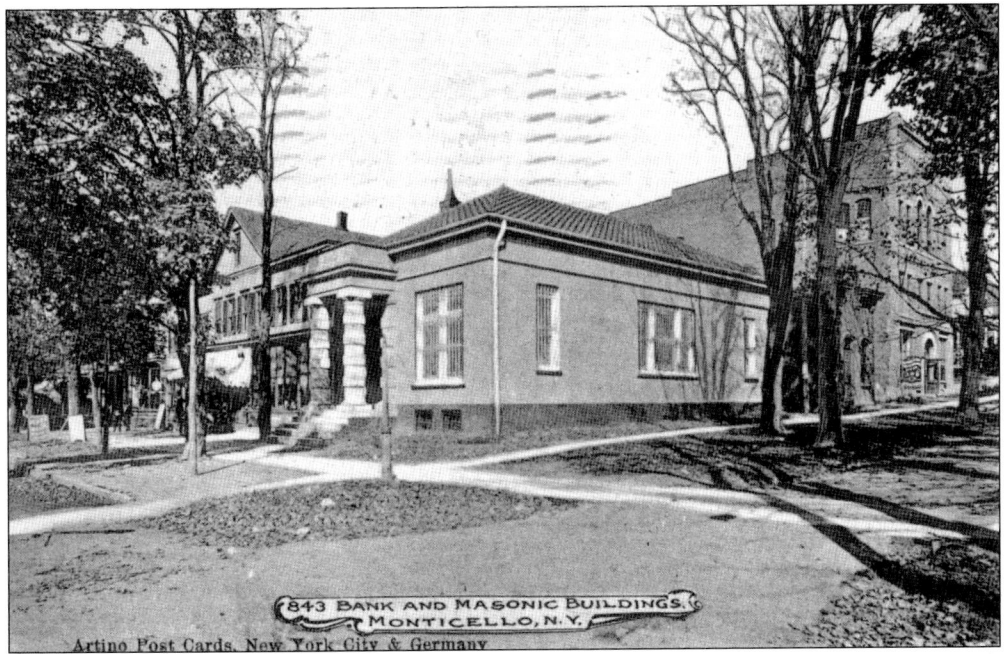

All of the buildings shown in this 1907 postcard survived the great fire of 1909. Although much altered, they still stand across the street from the Courthouse Green.

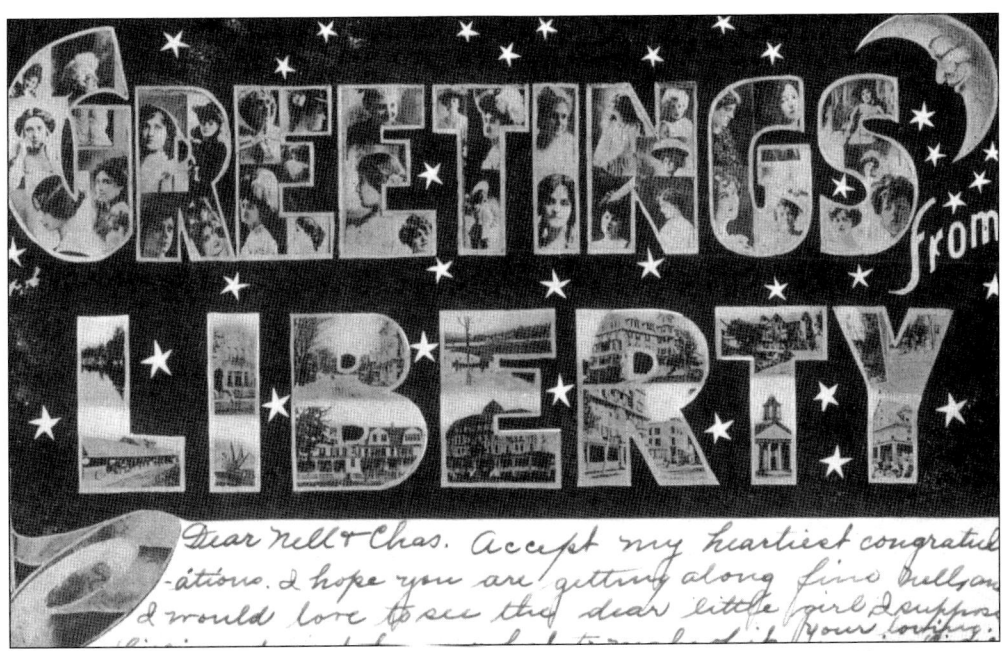

"Greetings from Liberty," mailed in 1907, celebrates Sullivan County's second largest town. The word "greetings" is made up of snippets of images of beautiful and famous women. In the left side of the T, one can make out the image of Alice Roosevelt Longworth, the daughter of Pres. Theodore Roosevelt. "Liberty" has vignettes of the town itself. In the bottom of the letter L is the railroad station.

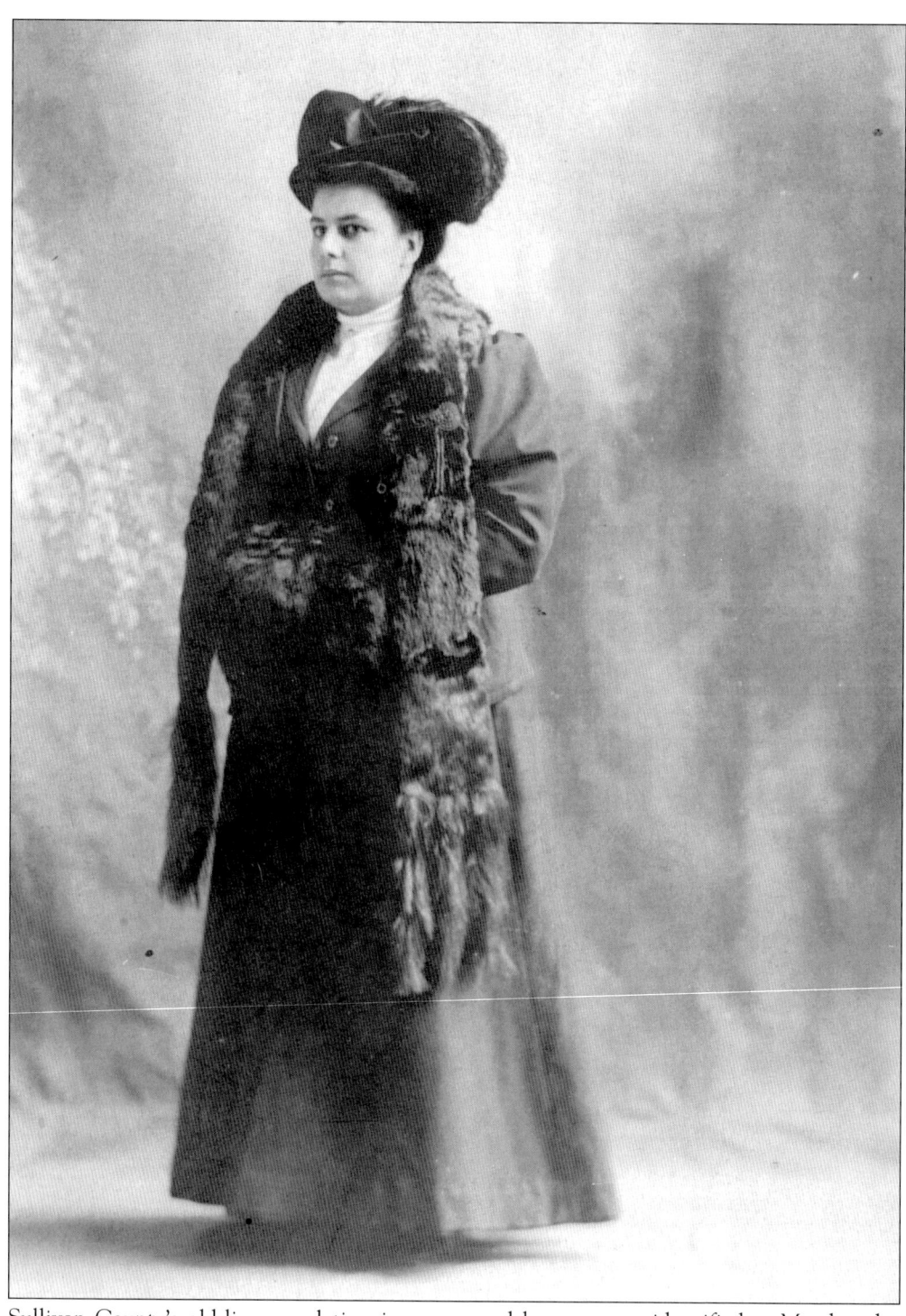
Sullivan County's old-line population is represented by a woman identified as Maude, who went to Otto Hillig for her portrait and, in the fashion of 1910, had it made into a postcard. She sent this image to Mable Kniffin in Youngsville: "I wish you both a merry exmas and a happy new year."

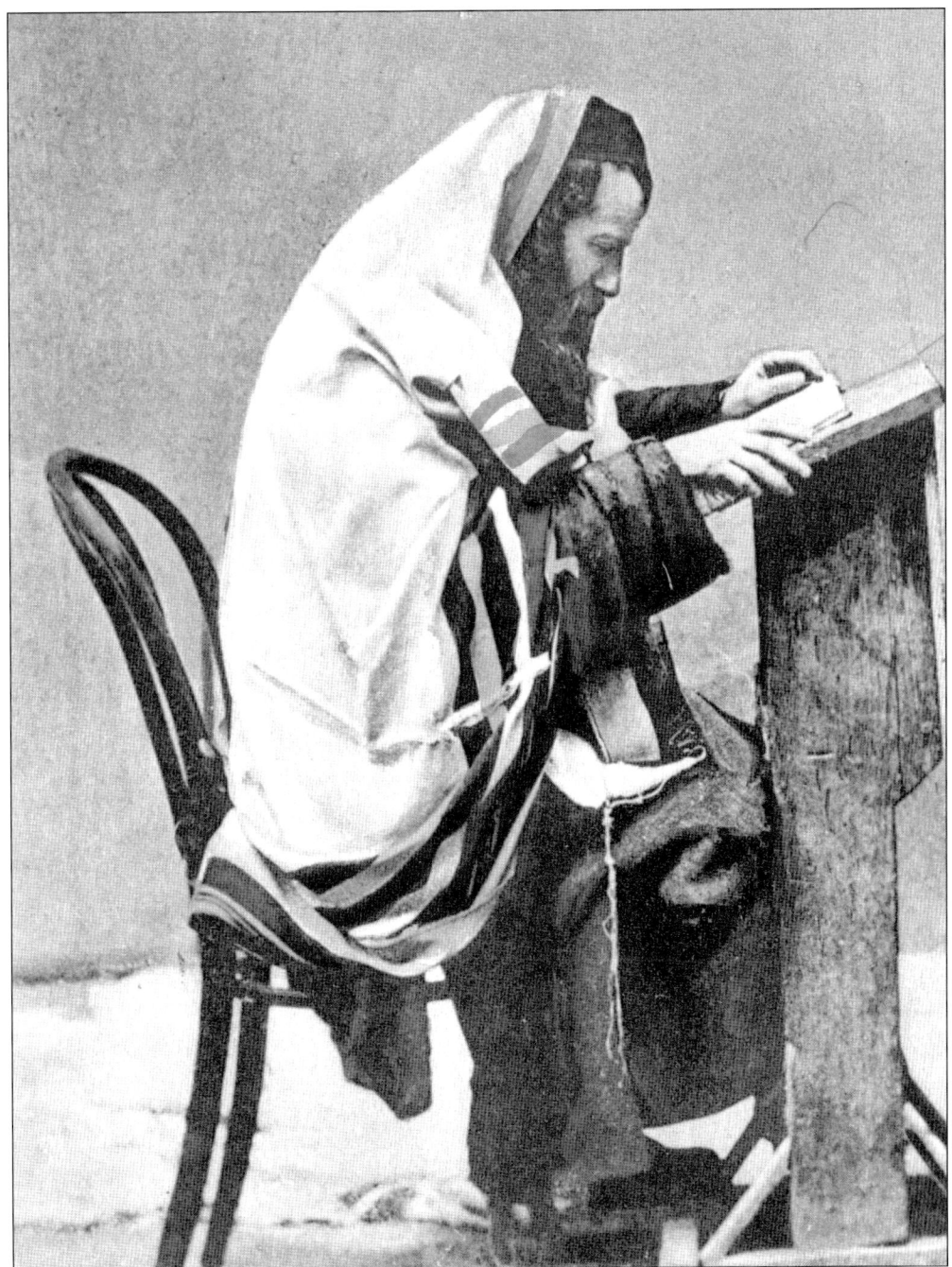

Sullivan County's newer population is represented by this Jewish New Year's postcard, mailed to a Monticello resident in 1907 from a friend or relative in New York City. Created for the American market, this greeting was printed in Germany.

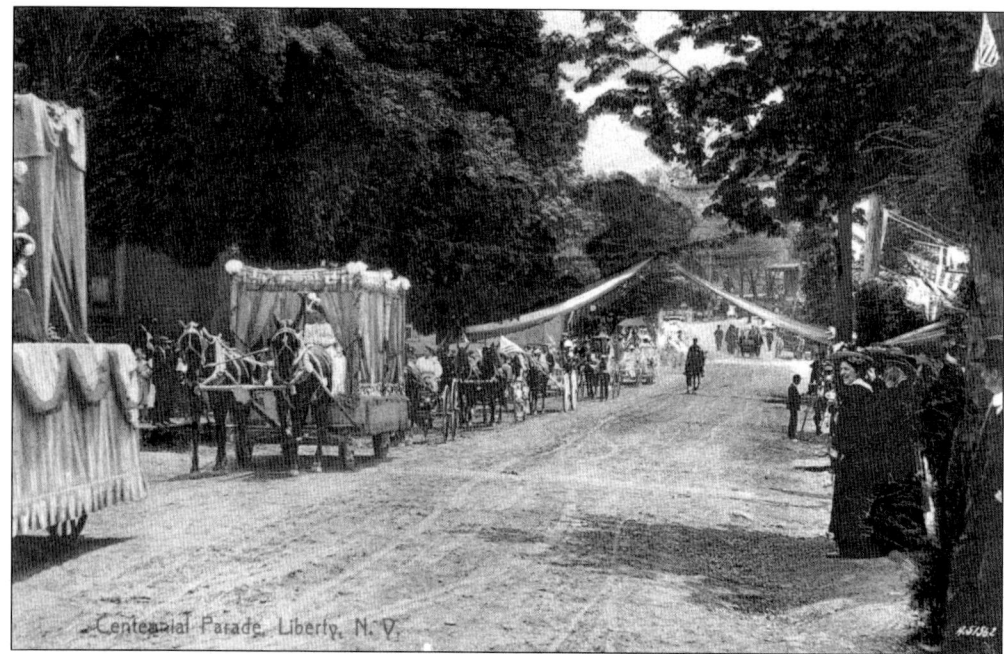

On June 10 and 11, 1907, Liberty, which was founded during the presidency of Thomas Jefferson, celebrated its centennial. The highlight was a grand parade down the town's unpaved Main Street. There were horse-drawn floats and a baby parade. Note the Japanese lanterns strung across the street high above the paraders below.

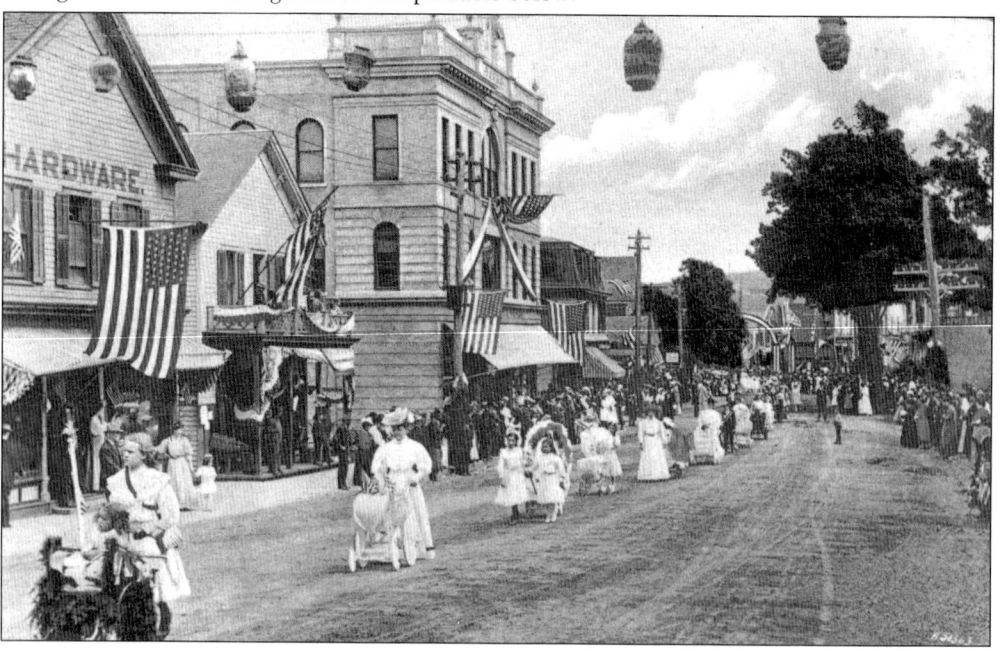

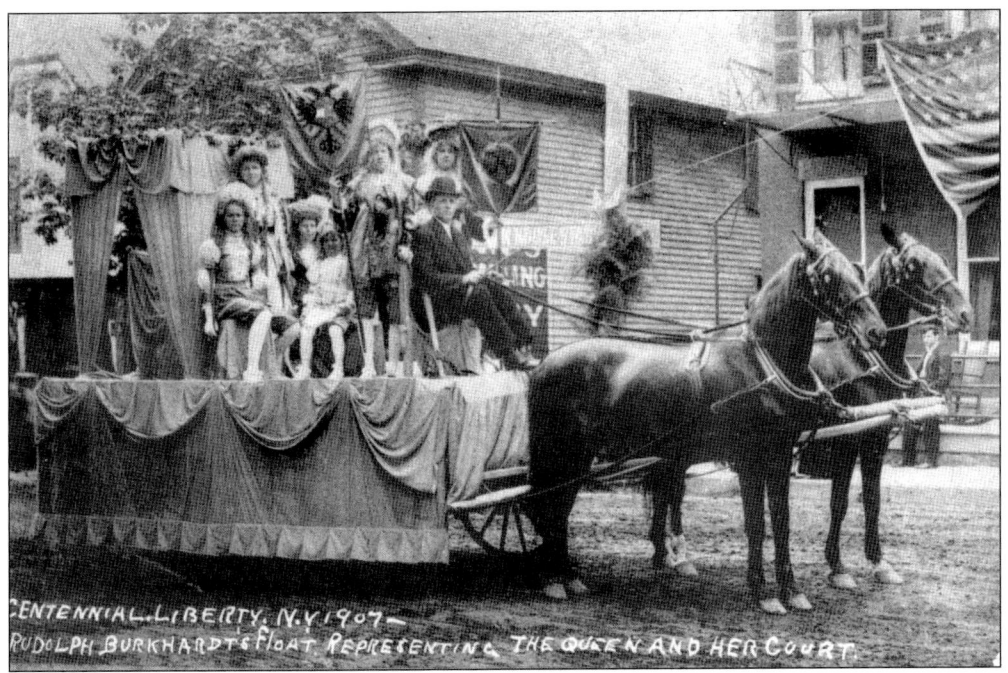

CENTENNIAL LIBERTY, N.Y. 1907 — RUDOLPH BURKHARDT'S FLOAT REPRESENTING THE QUEEN AND HER COURT.

What would a grand event be without a king, a queen, and a grand triumphal arch? Merchant Rudolph Burkhardt's float carried the queen and her court. Continuing a tradition dating from the period of the American Revolution, a grand but temporary triumphal arch was erected across Main Street.

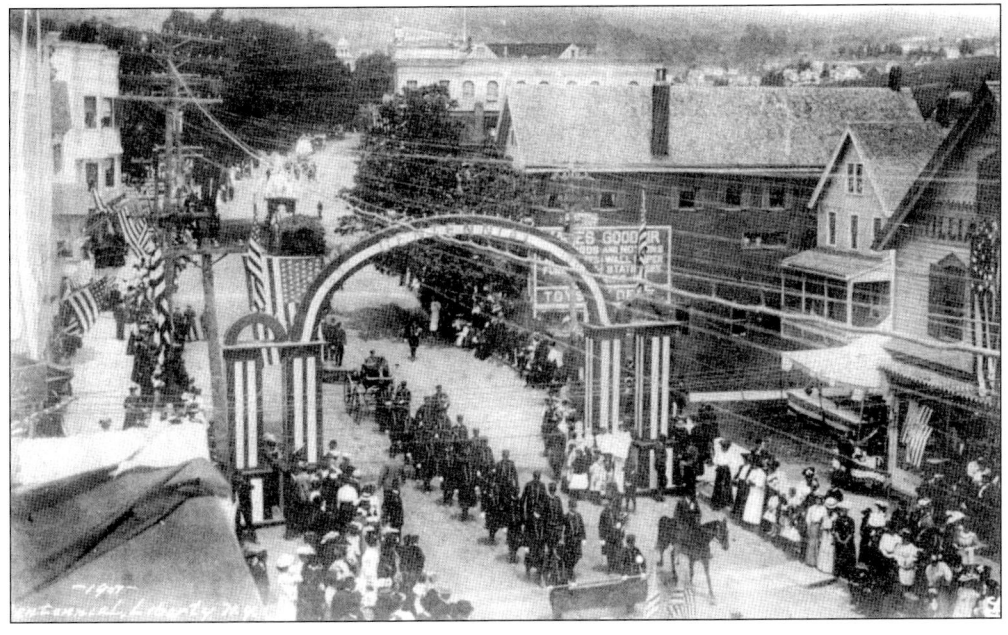

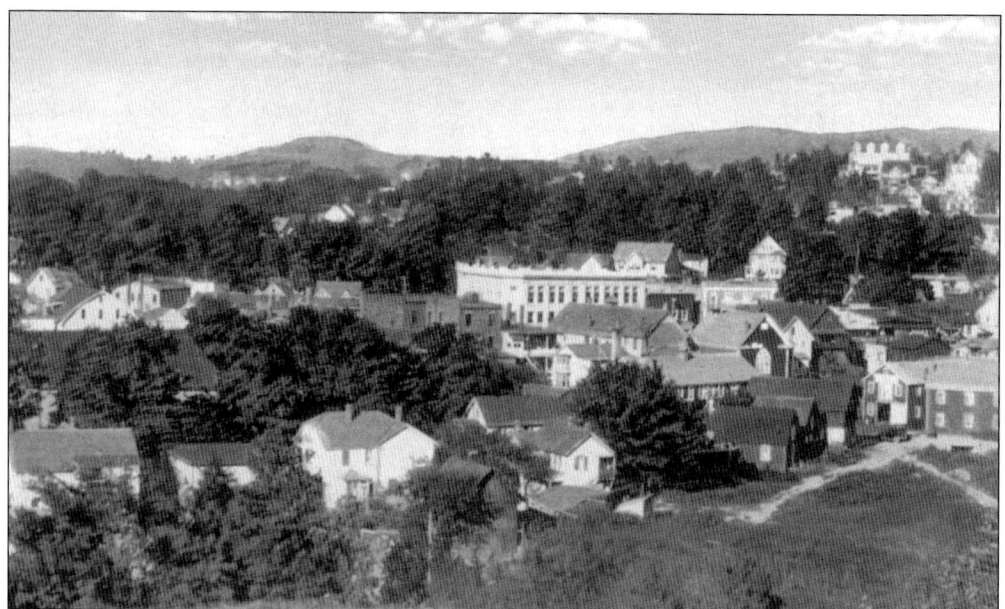

Liberty was a prosperous community by the 1920s, even if all of its residential streets were not yet paved. On the reverse of the postcard showing Wedemeyer Terrace, below, Fred writes to Miss Hayes in Newtown, Pennsylvania, on May 6, 1922, "Very cold and rainy, the wild cherry trees are just starting to come out in bloom. The place here looks just the same only it is full of Jews."

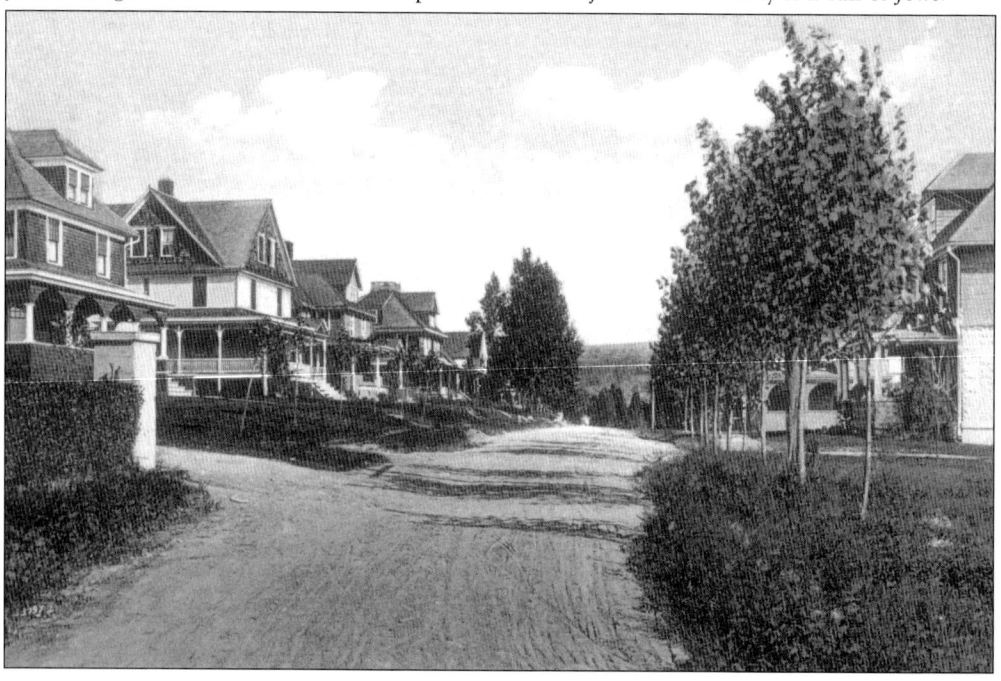

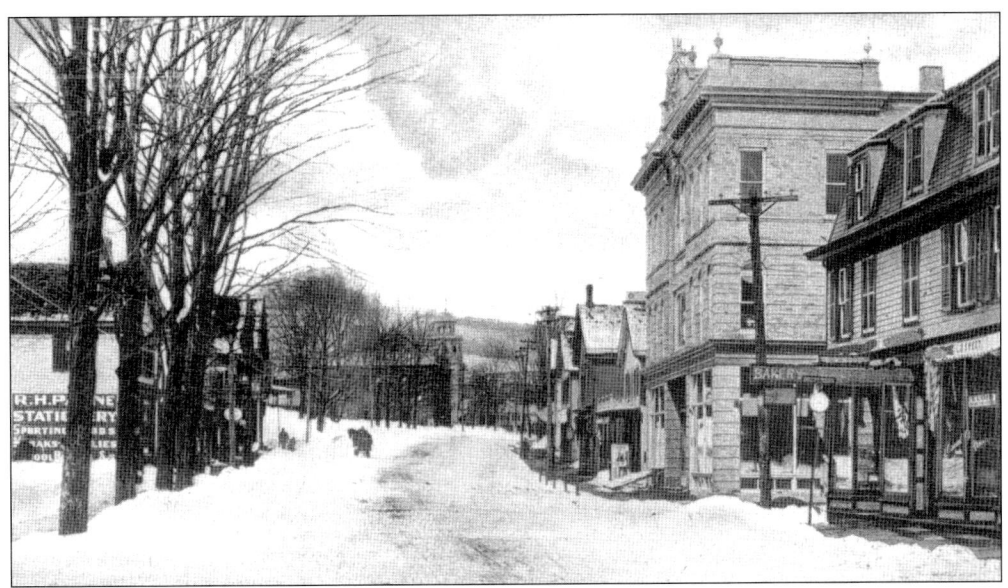

This snow scene of Liberty, above, was printed in Germany c. 1910. The bakery on the right has become a garage in the view below, taken by Otto Hillig in the 1920s. The later view of Main Street shows Liberty in transition from the age of the horse and buggy into the age of the automobile. The man on horseback is the village's first police officer, Harry Swanson.

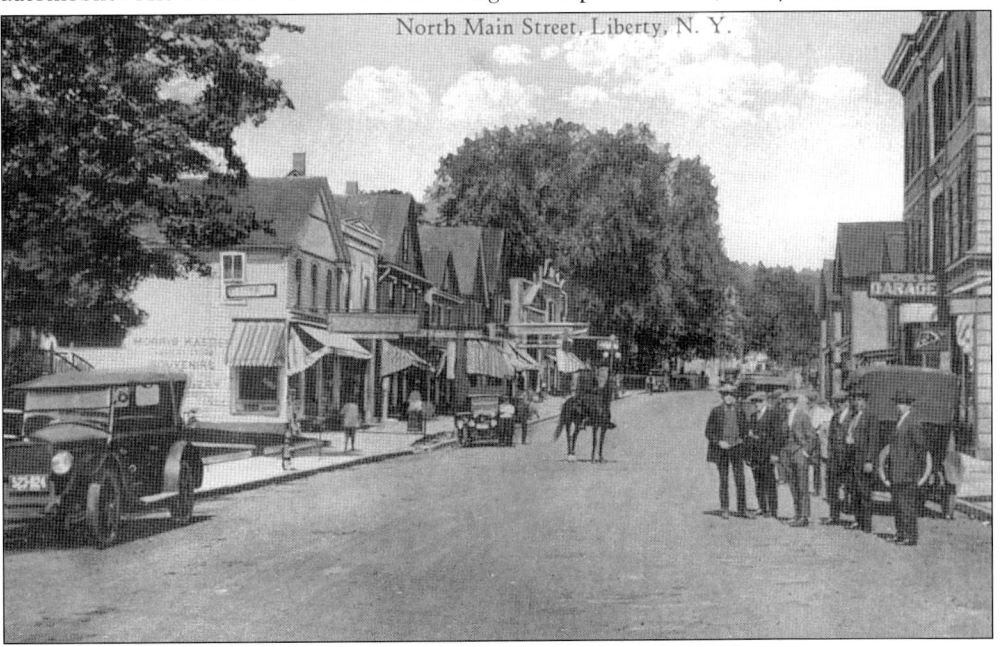

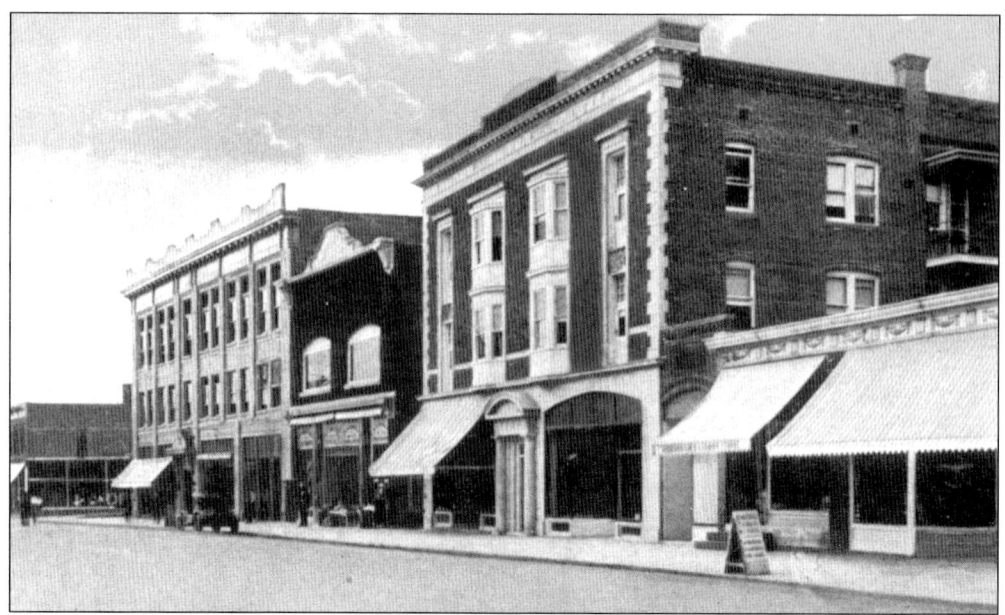

By the 1920s, Liberty had a modern center of commerce and entertainment thanks to the 1913 fire that destroyed half of the business district. The new Liberty Theatre was the town's pride, built in the style that reflected a blend of neoclassicism and the Chicago school. Still a movie house today, the much changed structure has been converted into a multiscreen facility.

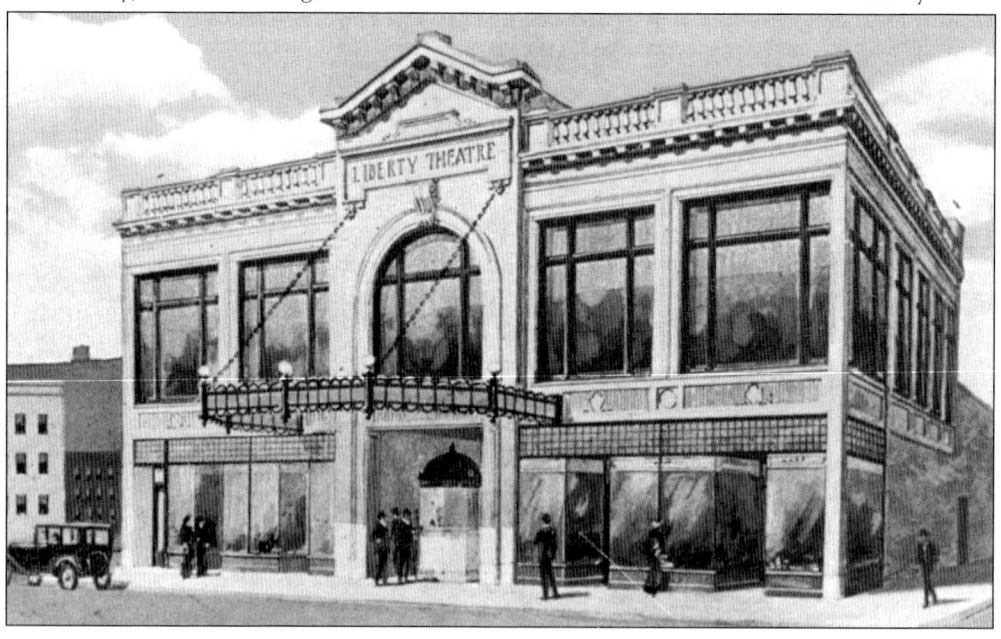

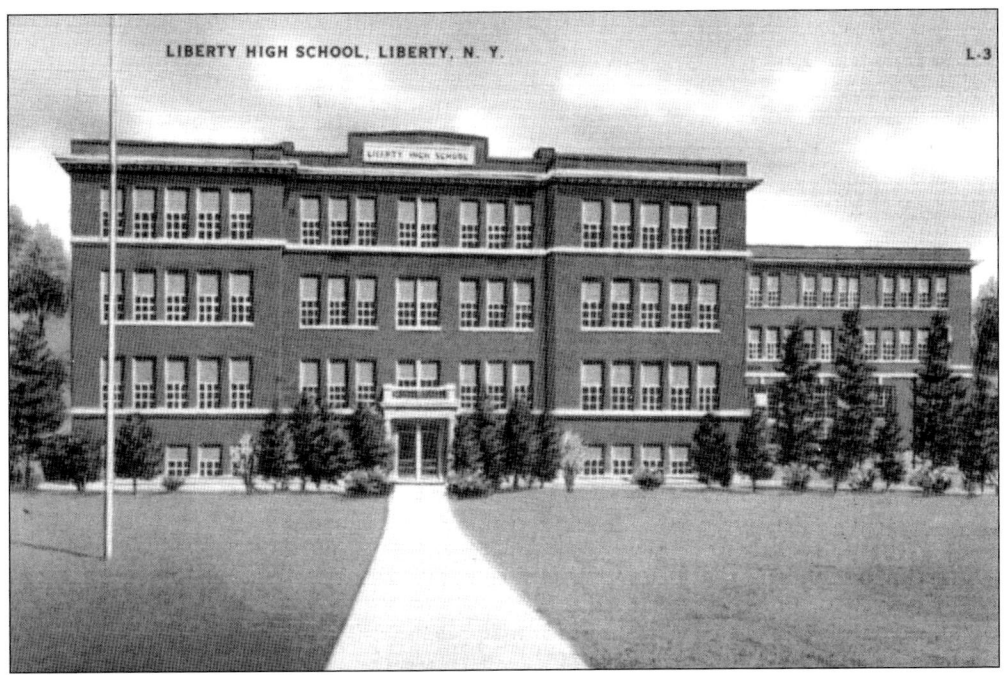

By the start of World War II, Liberty had a lot to boast about. Liberty High School was a reflection of the area's growing population and healthy tax base, as was the new Art Deco–style municipal building, which also served as the firehouse. Liberty's volunteer firemen were seen as heroes, especially after the great fire of 1913.

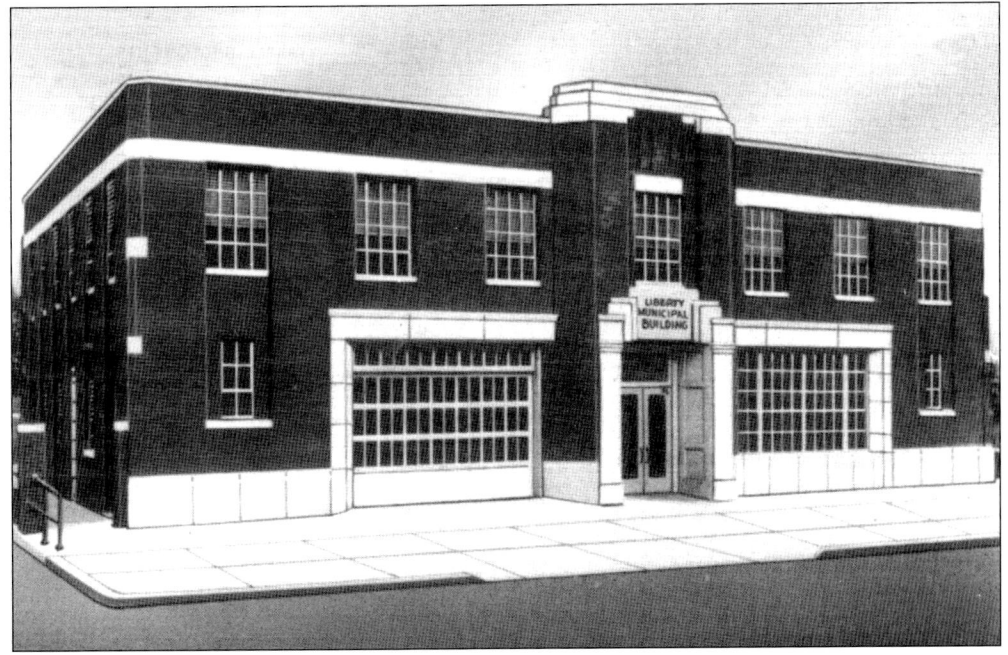

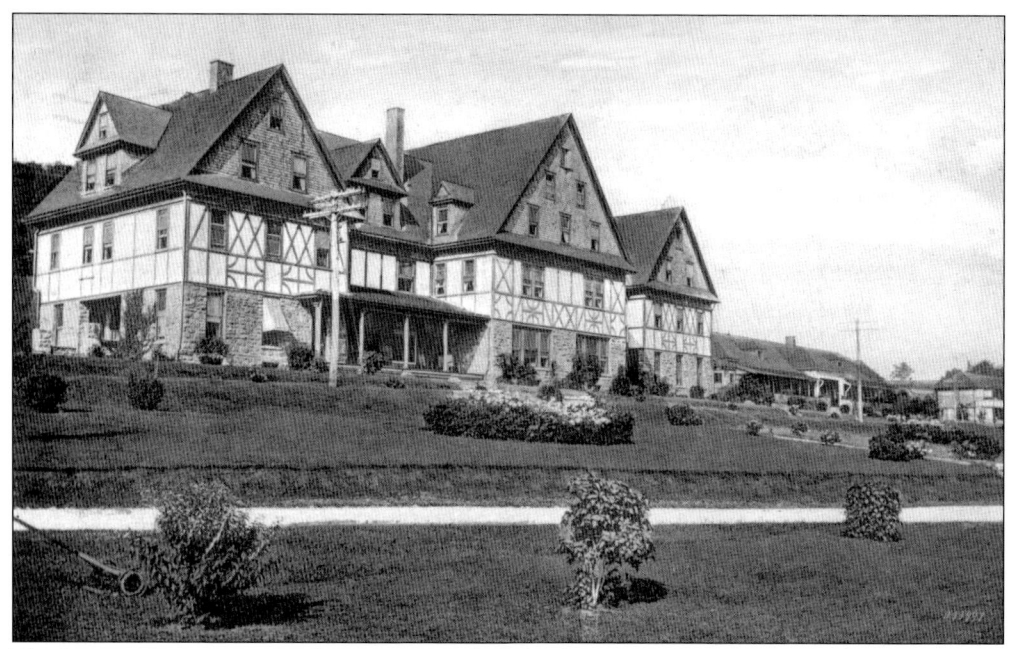

The Loomis Sanatorium for the treatment of tuberculosis was Liberty's most famous institution. Founded in 1895 by Dr. Alfred L. Loomis (1831–1895), it was opened the next year under the auspices of the Episcopal Church. The rate for each patient was $5 per week for board and medicine. A Christian-only establishment, it became a favorite charity of many wealthy New Yorkers who paid for facilities like the homey Casino, below. Emma, writing to Maria Francesconi in Brooklyn in January 1909, notes, "I feel much better since I am up here. Like very much to sleep out doors." In the pre-antibiotic days, fresh air (even in January) was believed to be the best cure for tuberculosis.

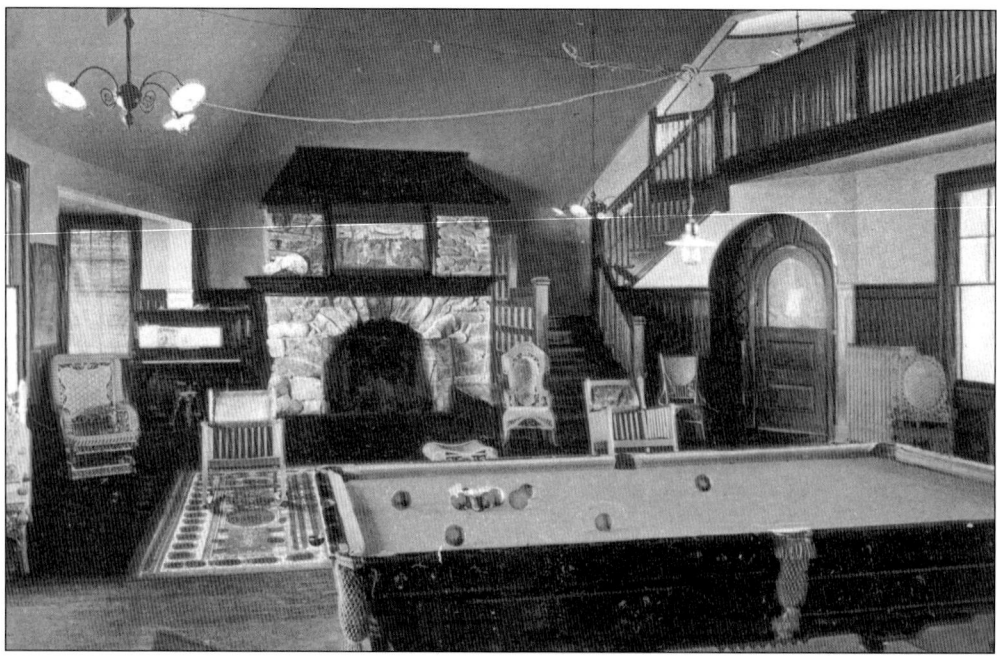

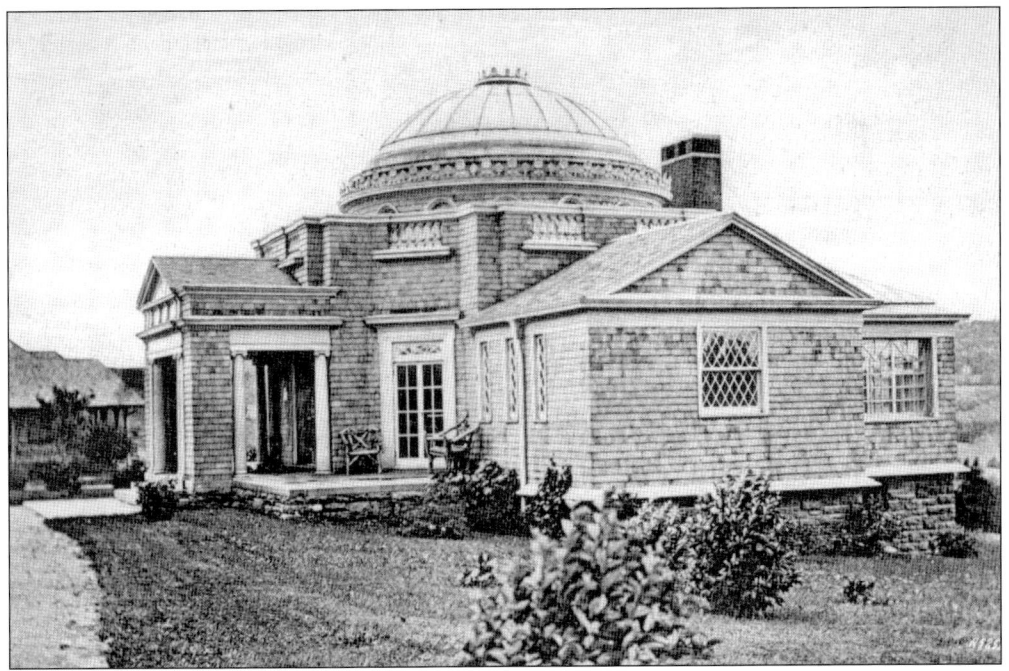

It was thought that culture and refinement were needed to elevate the condition of many tuberculosis patients. The Edson-Aldrich Library at the Loomis Sanatorium was a testimony to this policy. The message on the back of this postcard, mailed on September 2, 1909, is intriguing: "I heard P.H. Mc has jumped his bail on that case that Hadley wrote me about. This is the place where I get my reading when I want any."

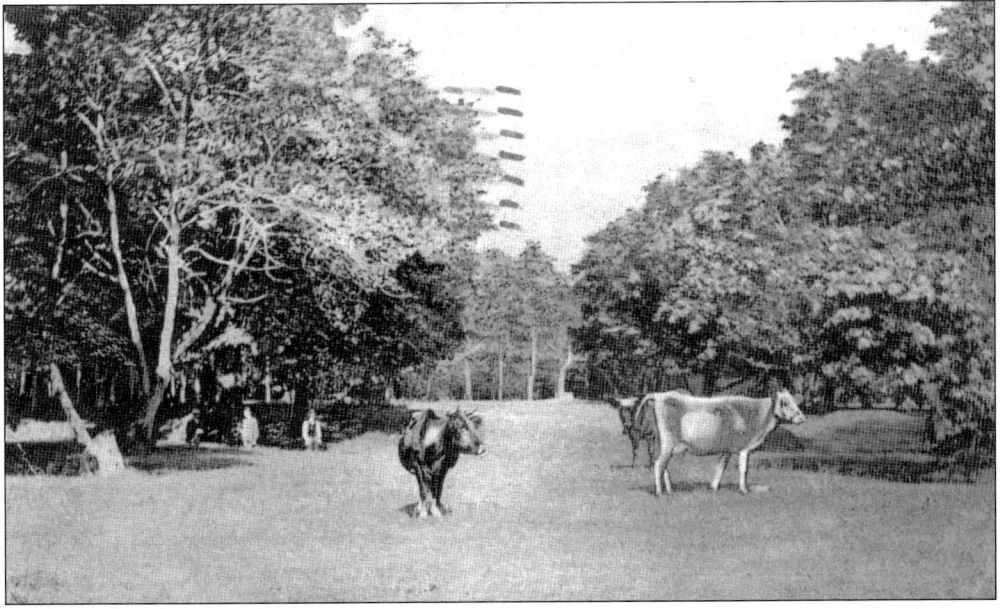

Although Liberty had some fine buildings, it still had a bucolic air. Writing to his daughter Estelle, her father notes on this postcard, "Aunt Annie has some nice cows up here." Beneath peaceful Liberty's surface, there were great tensions visible on the signs placed in the windows of many shops well into the 1920s. One such sign read, "No Consumptives or Hebrews allowed."

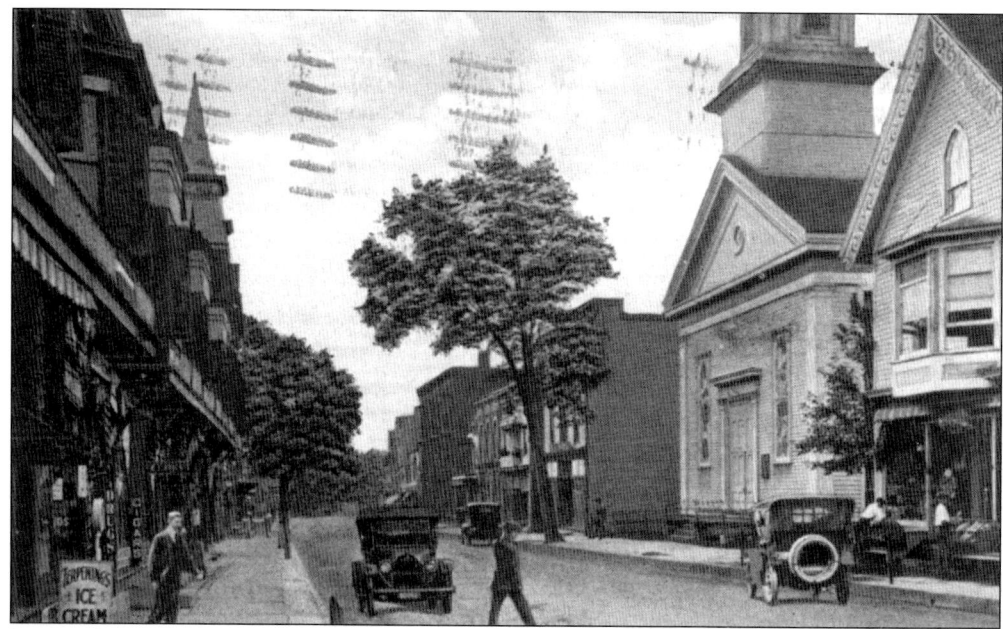

Ellenville, in southern Ulster County, was the region's third largest town. It had been a stop on the Delaware and Hudson Canal, hence the name of its main thoroughfare, Canal Street, which proudly displayed two churches and a paved surface in the 1920s, as seen above. In the railroad age, Ellenville was first served by the New York, Ontario, and Western Railroad and then by the Ellenville and Kingston Railroad. The message on the bird's-eye view below reads, "Dear Grandfather, I thought this nice view of Ellenview might interest you. You will note that the railroad occupies the old canal bed. This picture was taken from the mountain east of Ellenville."

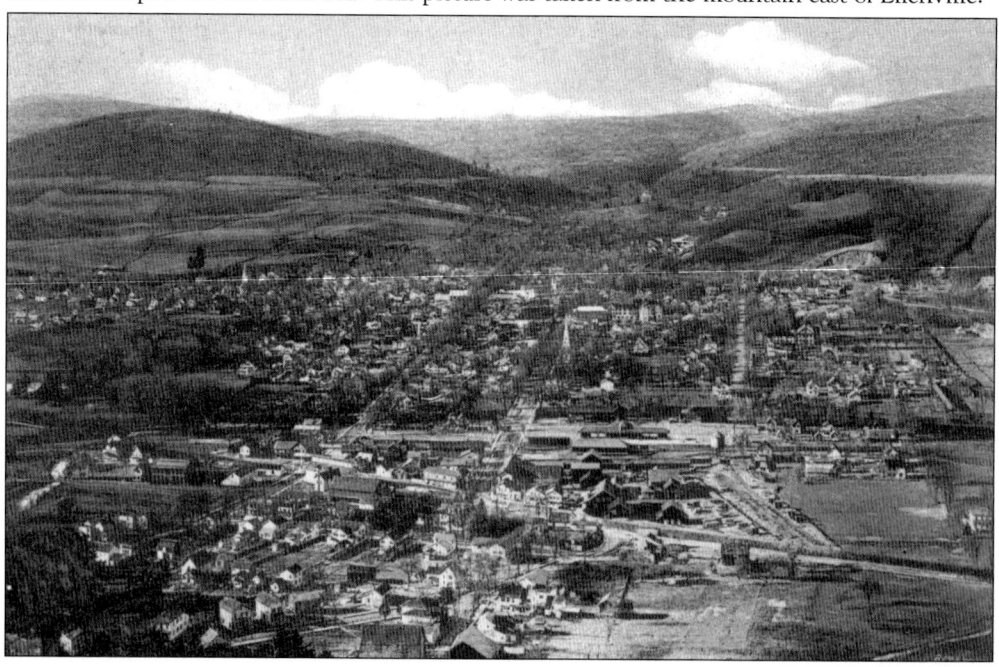

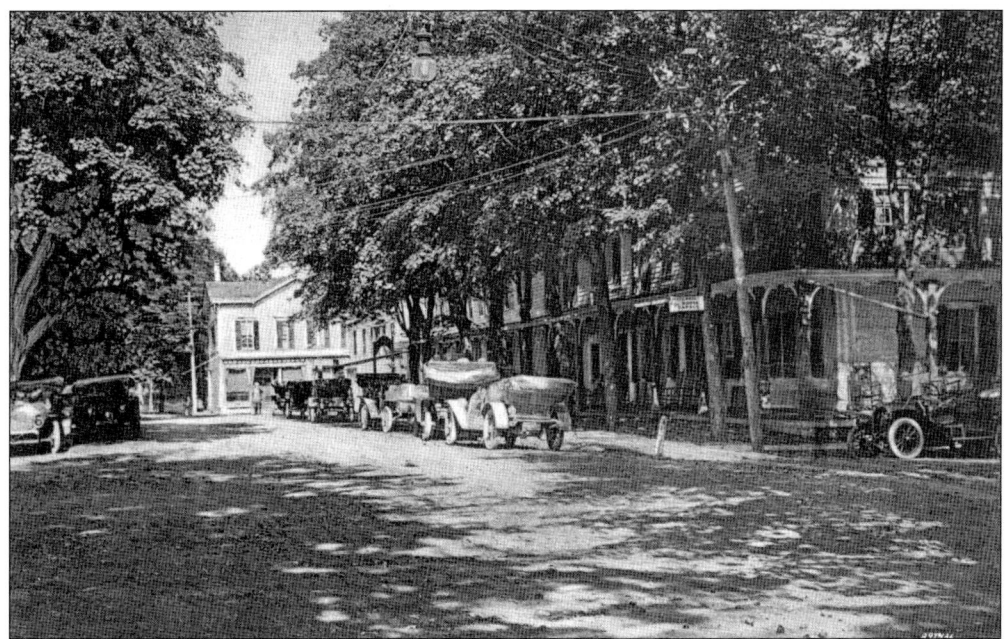

Like Liberty and Monticello, Ellenville had several in-town hotels that had originally been Christian-only establishments but were becoming Jewish resorts by the 1920s. The Mitchell House, above, was typical of the late-19th-century rambling wooden hotels that were often fires waiting to happen. By the end of World War II, Liberty Square, below, had become an "attractive spot in the center of the business district" according to this card. Liberty Square looks the worse for wear today.

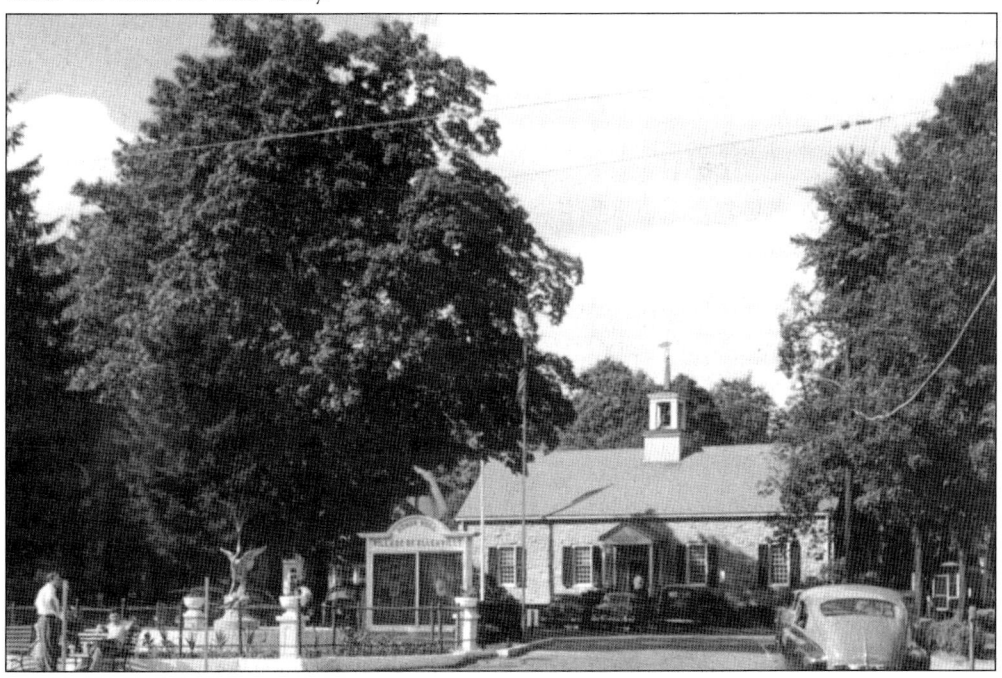

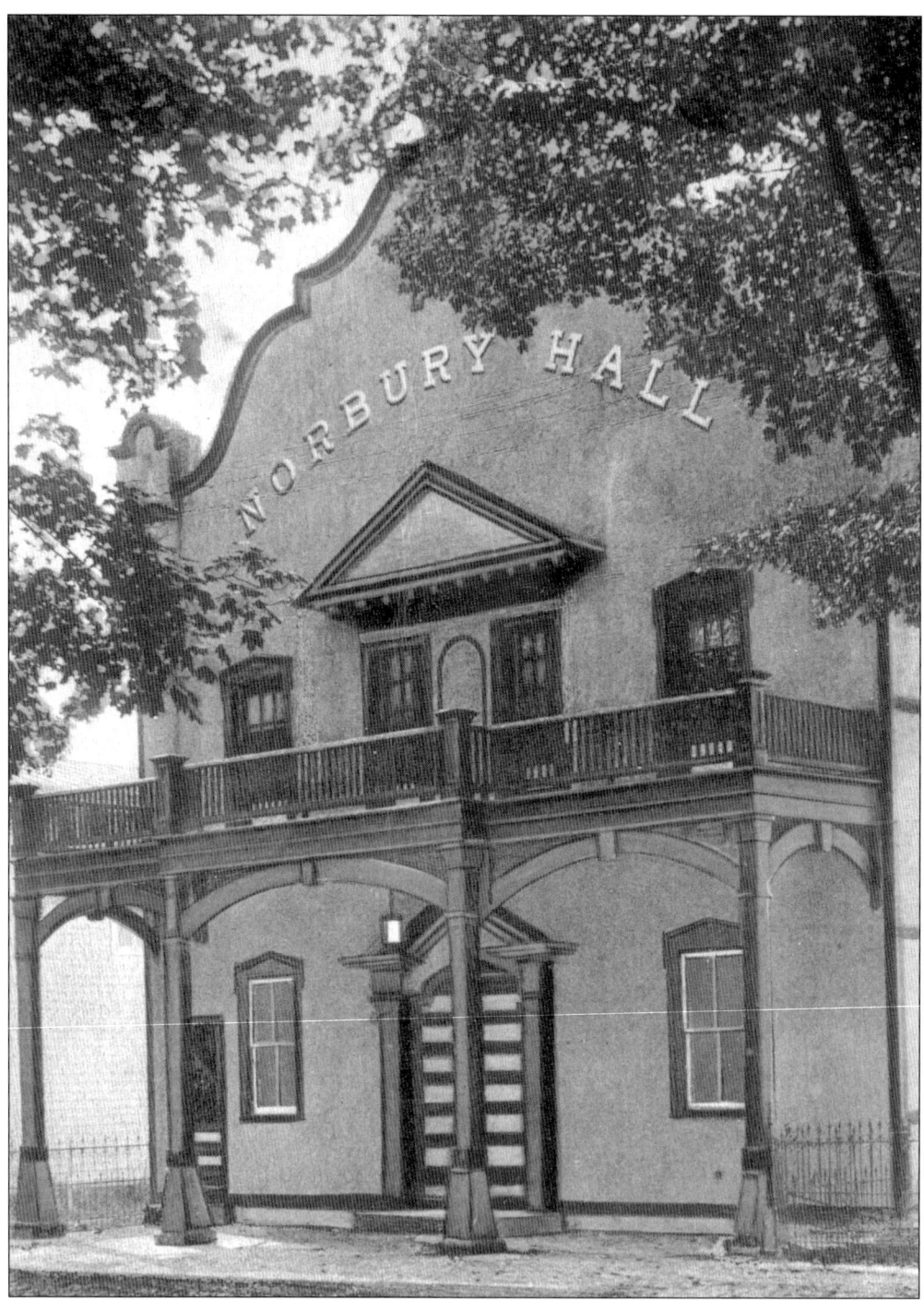

Norbury Hall had been Ellenville's community center for shows and indoor athletics before being turned into a motion picture theater in the 1920s. Very much altered, it still stands. On this 1911 postcard, R.L., who had recently moved to nearby Napanoch "in sight of the reformatory," writes to family back in Monticello, "Yes, I was to the basketball game at Ellenville. This is a postal of the hall where they had it."

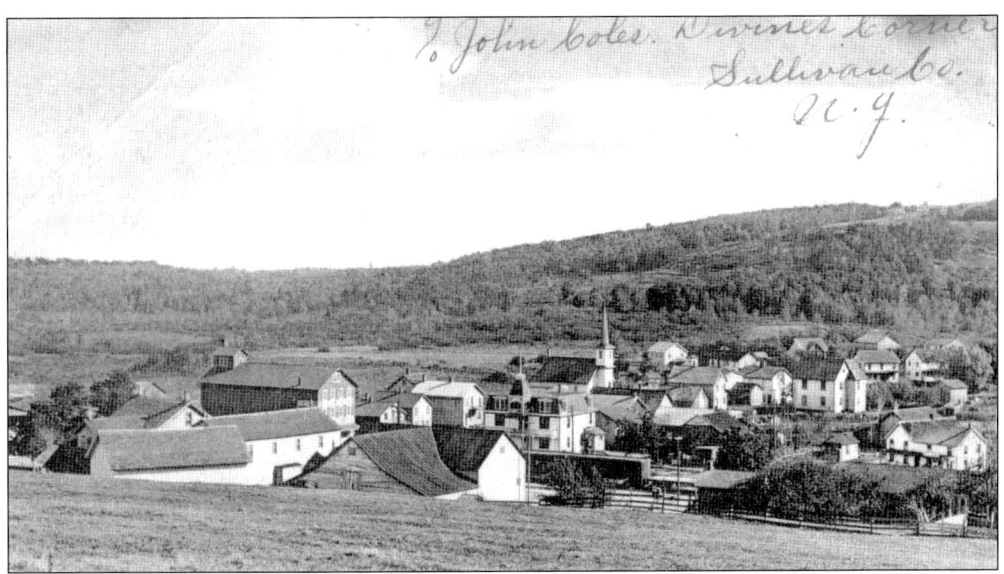

The New York, Ontario, and Western Railroad felt that "Luzon Station" was a classier name for a town it was promoting through its publication *Summer Homes*. Village residents welcomed the railroad but kept the name "Hurleyville." In 1907, about the time these postcards were published, there were 34 resorts listed in Hurleyville. Mrs. M. Brophy's Mountain View House was considered especially colorful. Known as "Brophy's Madhouse," it catered to New York City firemen and policemen who "let their hair down when they went to the mountains." The building burned in 1910, but Brophy's Road still exists.

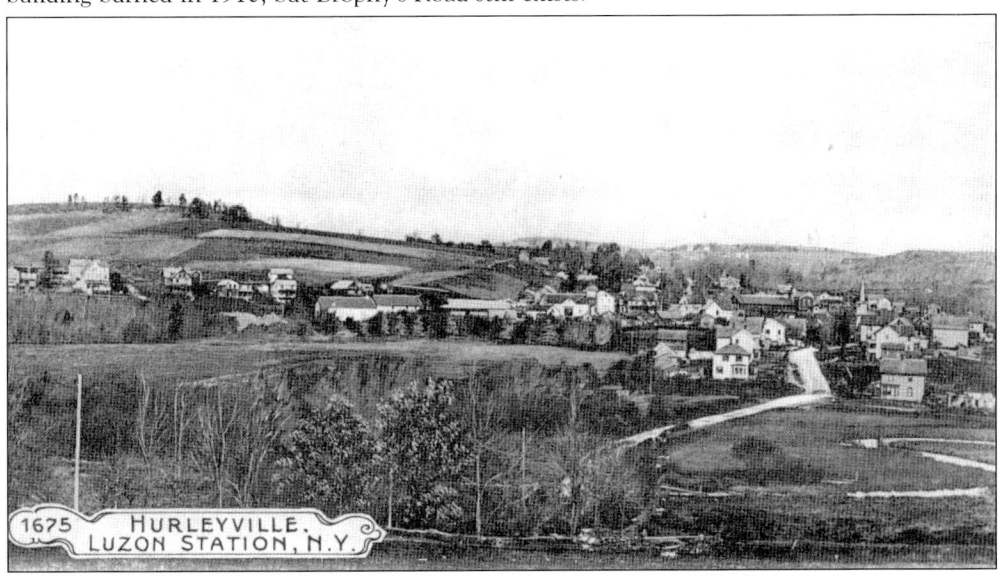

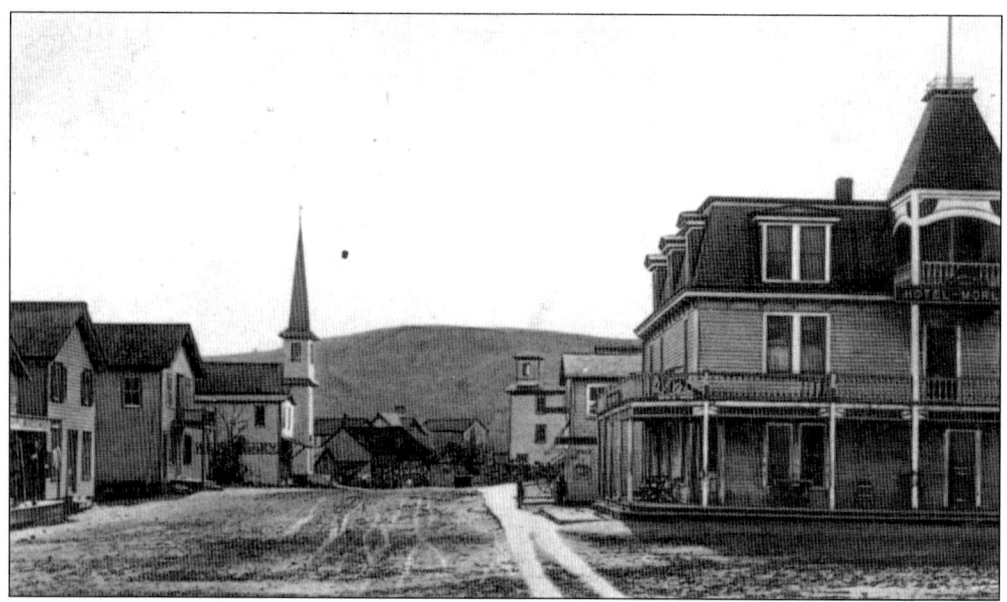

Hurleyville's Christian resorts were being acquired by Jews at around the time this postcard of South Main Street was mailed in 1908. The street is unpaved and mostly devoid of trees. A typical mansard-roofed hotel is to the right, with no one on its large porch. The photograph was probably taken in the early spring.

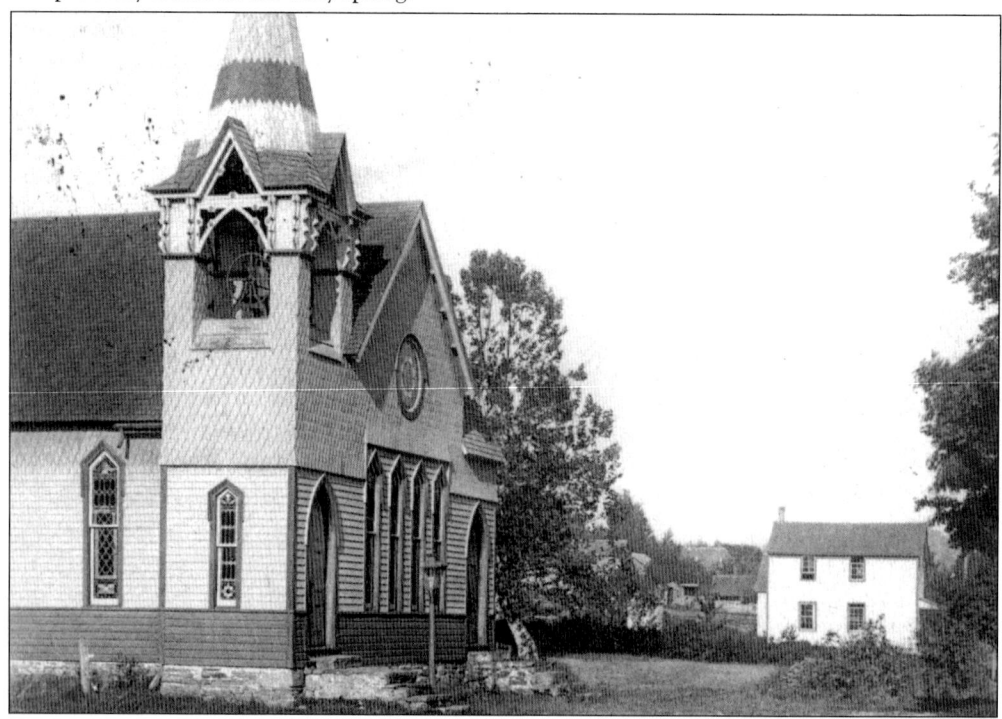

Centreville, just miles from Glen Wild (where Jana Gershon opened the first Jewish boardinghouse), was a small crossroads village before the railroads came. Yielding to the New York, Ontario, and Western Railroad, Centreville changed its name to the more evocative "Woodridge." The church faced on Centreville's main street, colorfully named "the Bowery."

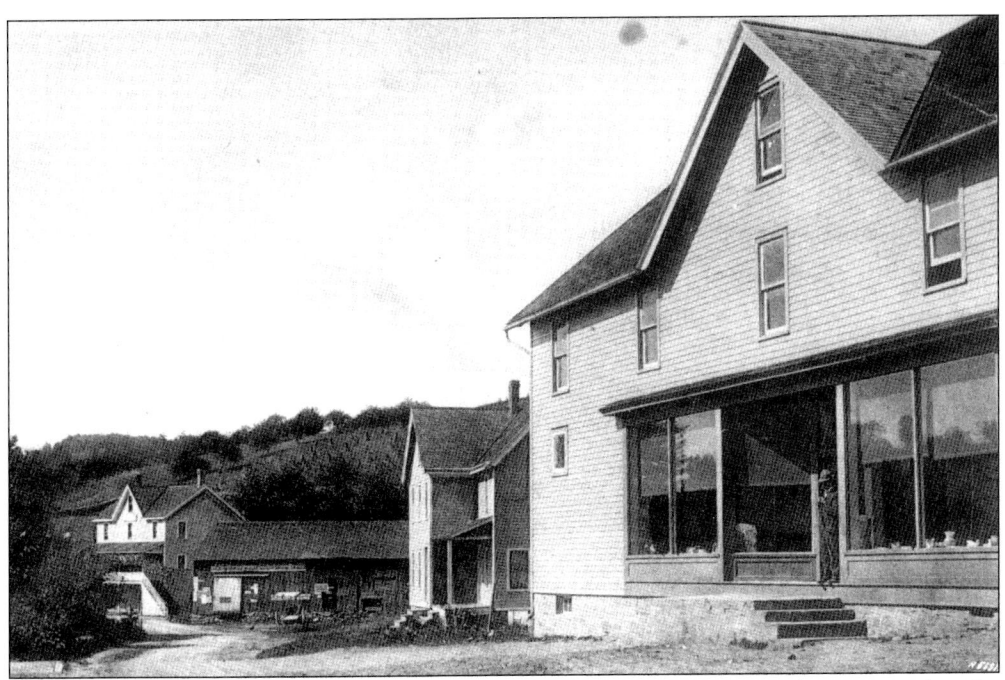

Ferndale was originally named Liberty Falls. The town gladly changed its name (at the suggestion of the New York, Ontario, and Western Railroad) to disassociate itself from Liberty, which had become associated with tuberculosis sanitariums. In a town well known locally for its gristmill, Manion's store was the quintessential country store of 1910. Twenty years later, Ferndale would also have a kosher butcher shop.

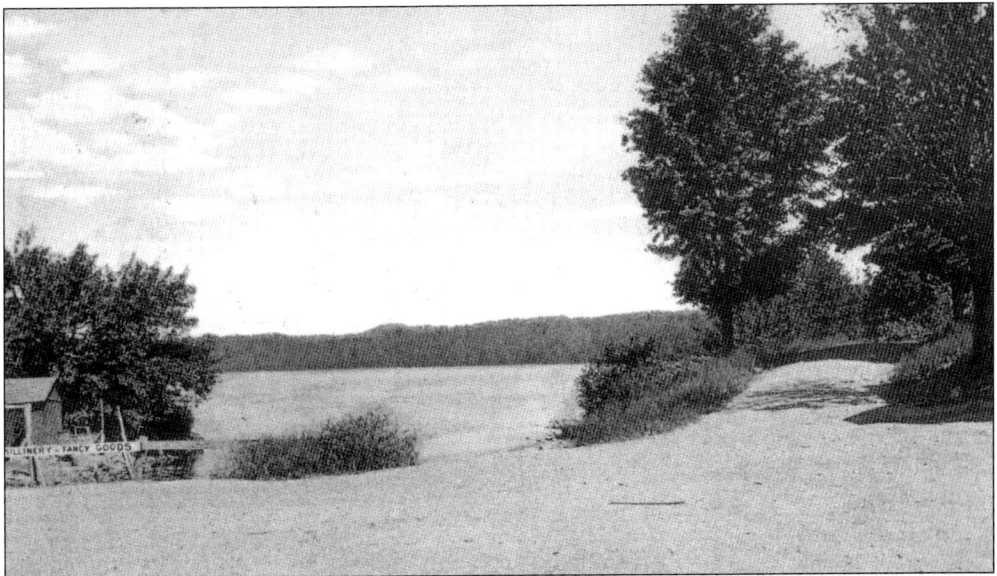

What is now New York Route 52 passes Ferndale and leads to Loch Sheldrake and then on to Woodbourne. At the "Parting of the Ways" at Loch Sheldrake, you could (and can) take a back road that leads to the hamlet of Hasbrouck. Crossroads appear on many postcards of the early 1900s. On the reverse of this postcard, H.S. seems positive about Loch Sheldrake: "I like it here all right guess I will stay."

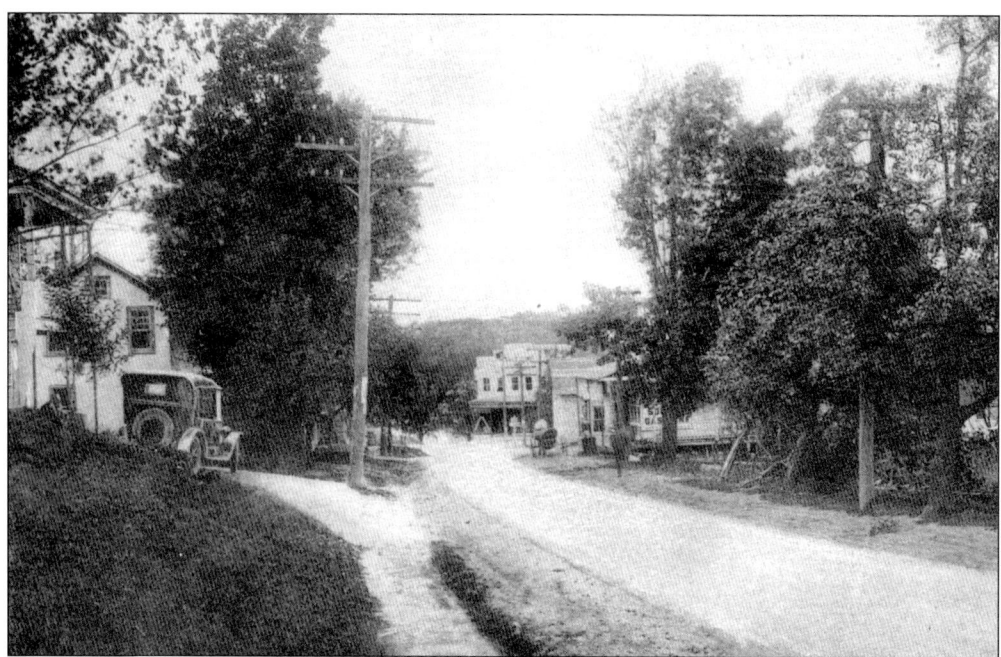

Before the railroads came, Sheldrake was a little farming village. Because of its lakeside setting, it was rechristened Loch Sheldrake. Sheldrake Pond became Loch Sheldrake Lake—a redundant phrase since "loch" is Scottish for "lake." The town soon developed as a lively resort. The sign in the lower postcard directs you to the Loch Sheldrake Casino. The town's 1920s movie house, once the Strand and now the Hippodrome, still shows films. Like most Sullivan County towns, Loch Sheldrake was at its peak in the 1950s. At that time, Herbie's Restaurant was packed with people looking for the restaurant's famed Chinese roast pork sandwich, made with garlic bread. Similar to the New York egg cream, the sandwich is a regional specialty.

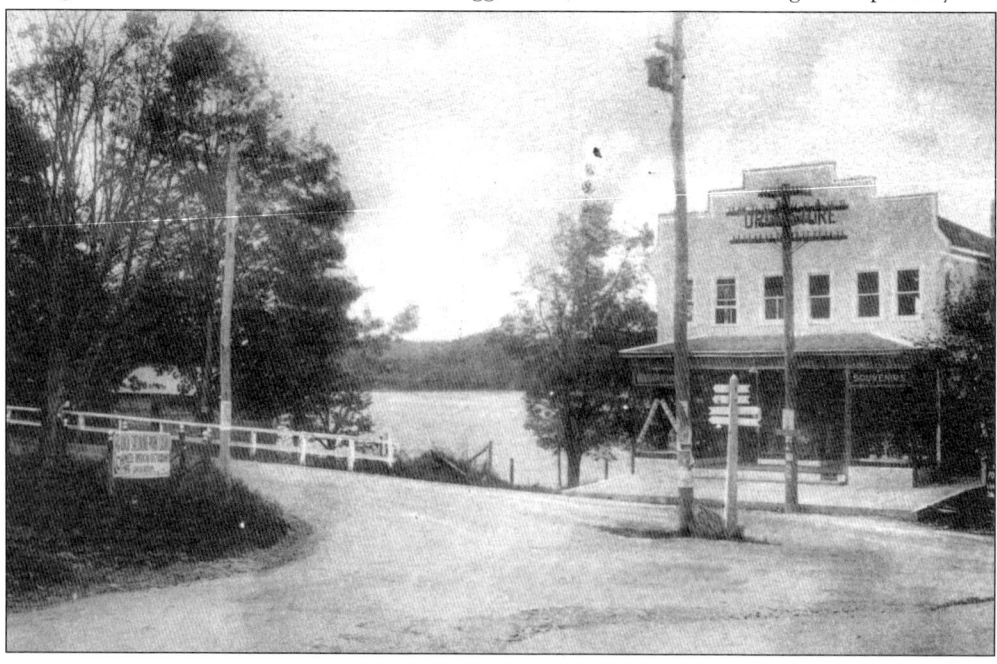

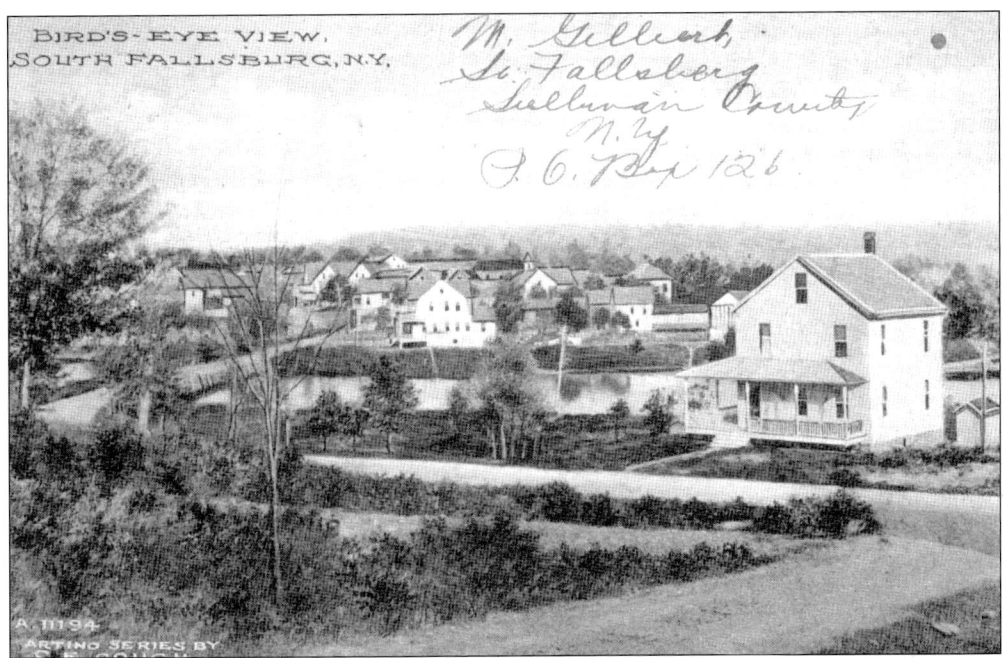

In 1912, South Fallsburg was a quiet farming and mostly Christian resort town. Marion, writing to her friend Bella Roth, reports on the above postcard, "I taught a summer session for six weeks. I am here since Sunday with mother and brother and enjoy it immensely." Shown below, tree-shaded Main Street would soon change its character completely. The obverse of the lower postcard has a wonderfully enigmatic message: "Dear Dick, Mr. Slater wants you to come up Sat. night and stay on Sun. A couple of queens will be here. Herb."

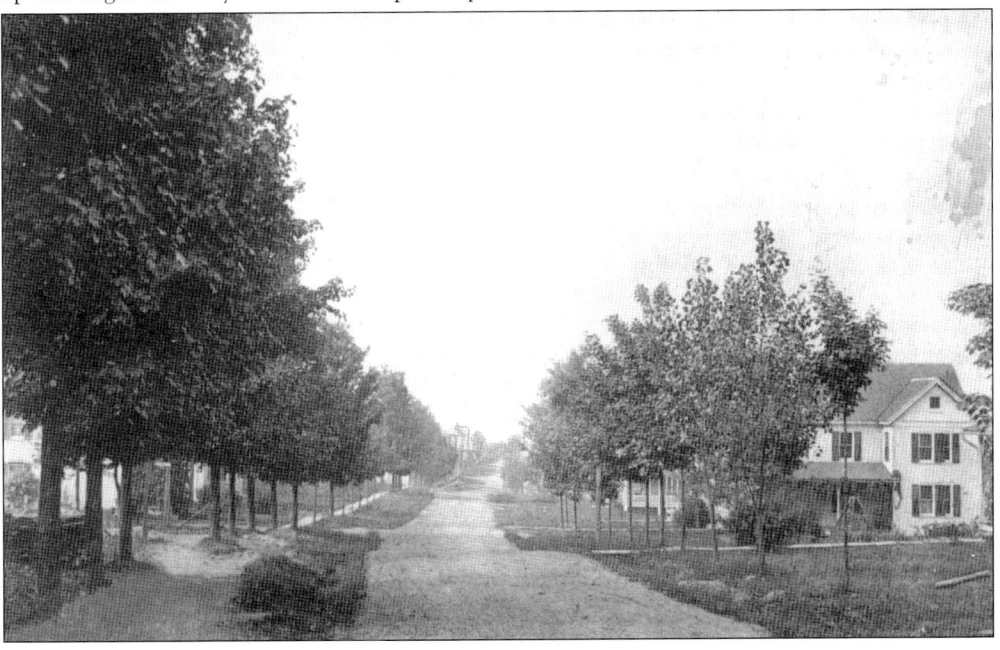

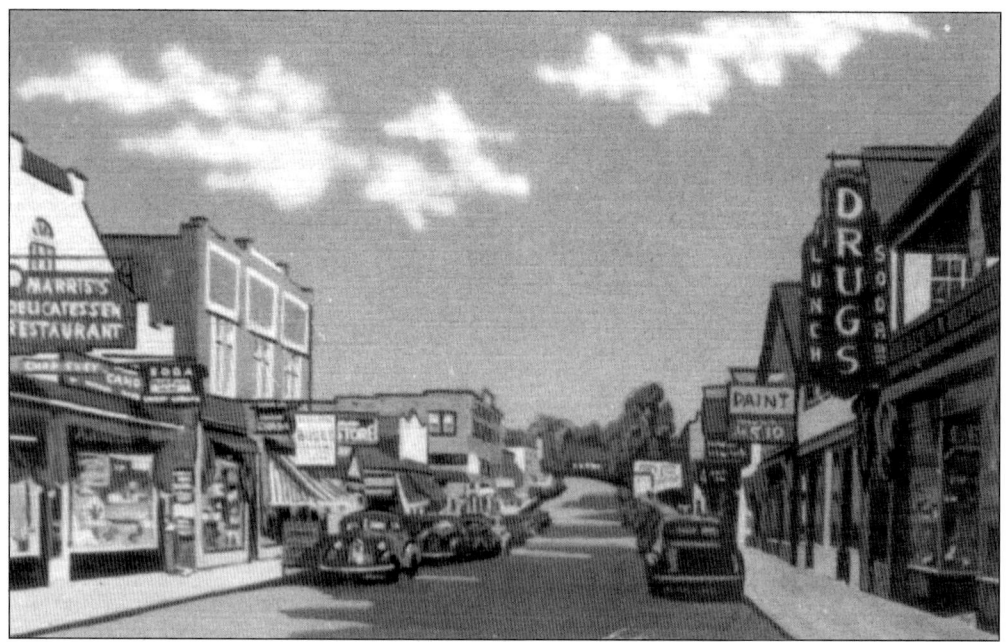

South Fallsburg had blossomed into one of the most active Borscht Belt towns by the time of this 1930s postcard. On the left, Marris's Delicatessen has added a sign stating that it serves chop suey. There is a well-known affinity that American Jews hold for Chinese food. In the distance on the left is the Rivoli Theatre, which is now a performing arts center.

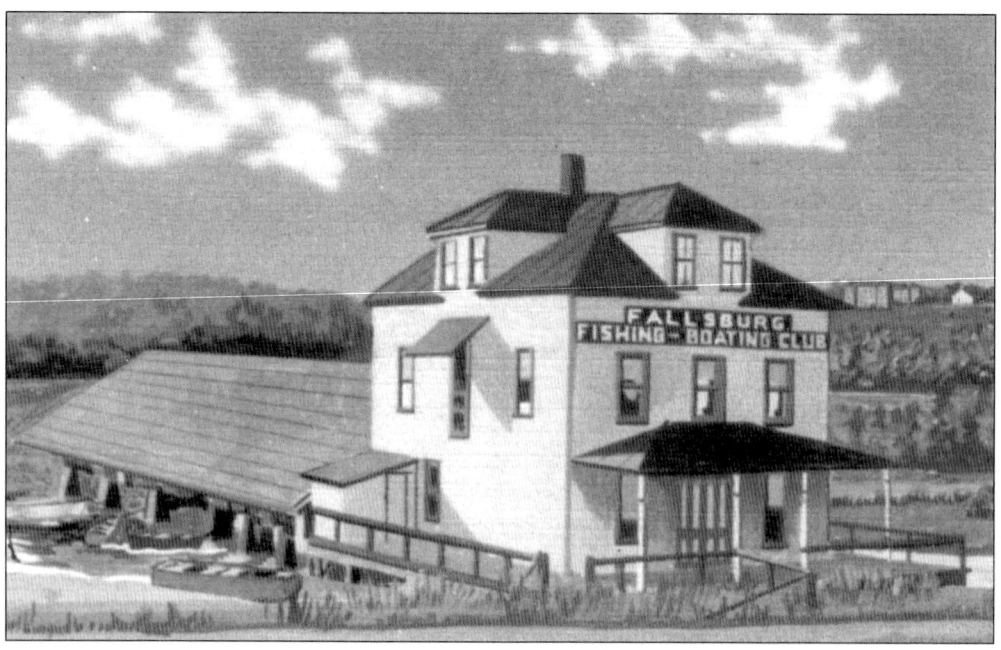

The Fallsburg Fishing and Boating Club was located on a small lake in South Fallsburg. Housed in an Arts and Craft–style building, it is shown in one of the series of postcards published by M. Glusker and Son in Ellenville. A hotel stands atop the hill in the background.

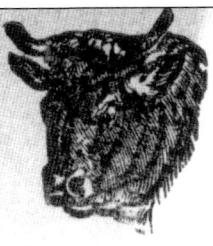

Tel. Fallsburg 227

HENRY W. BLEICHER

"HANKS" CHOICE MEATS & PROVISIONS

Hotels and Bars Supplied   SO. FALLSBURG, N. Y.

As resorts developed, so did the businesses that supplied and serviced them. South Fallsburg wholesale merchants served many of the small towns nearby, including Woodbourne and Loch Sheldrake. Butcher Henry W. Bleicher also had a retail store in South Fallsburg with the short telephone number of 227. Telephone exchanges were so small, there was no need to use a number at all. Just asking the operator for Hank's Meats was enough.

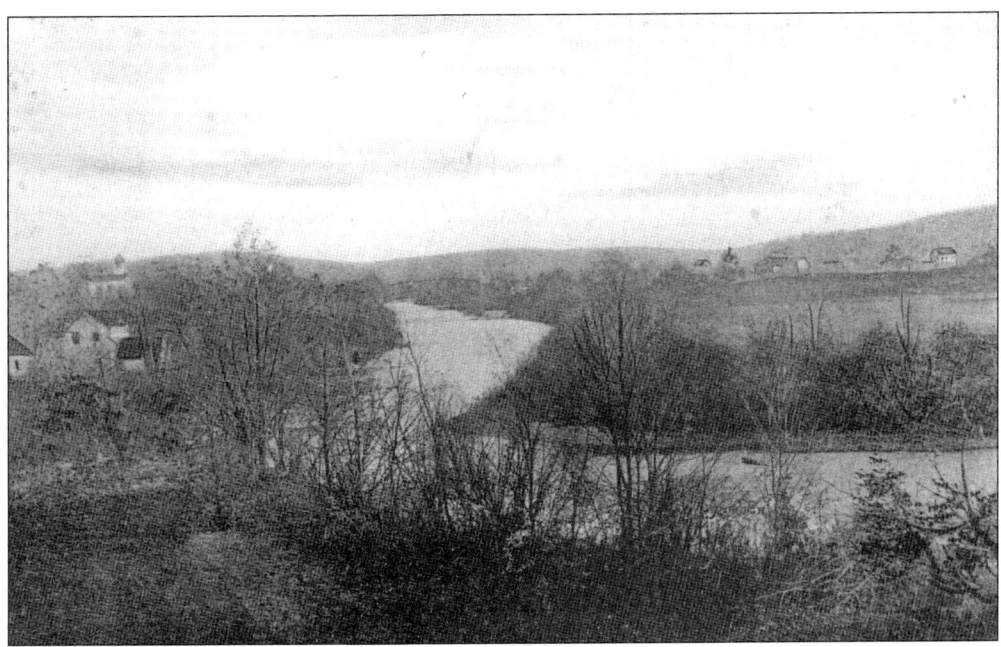

Woodbourne is in the Neversink Valley near the town of Fallsburg. The tallest building in this 1913 view is the Dutch Reformed church on the left. The Woodbourne Correctional Facility, which has dominated the landscape since 1930s , was later built on the rise to the right.

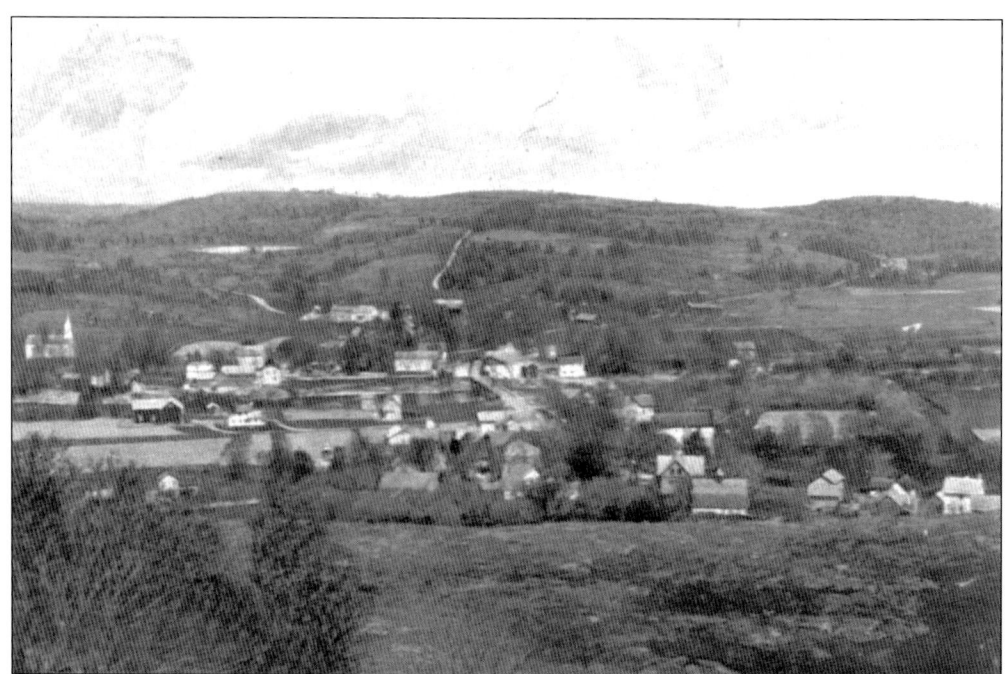

In 1906, the New York, Ontario, and Western Railroad produced more than 100,000 postcards to promote its service area. Shown is one of the railroad's publicity pieces. Like Fallsburg, Woodbourne was founded as a tannery town, in this case, built around the enterprises of one Austin Strong.

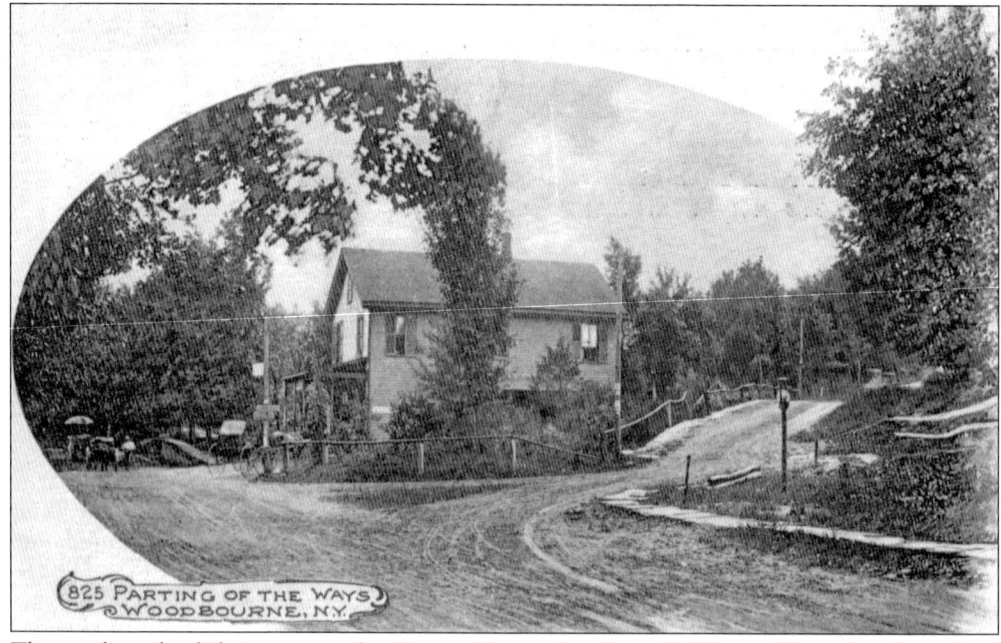

The road to the left is present-day Route 42, coming from Fallsburg. The other branch of Woodbourne's "Parting of the Ways" is present-day Route 52, going toward Loch Sheldrake and Liberty. In 1903, the Liberty *Register* reported, "Hebrews have turned their attention toward Woodbourne and are buying up the purchasable farms in that section."

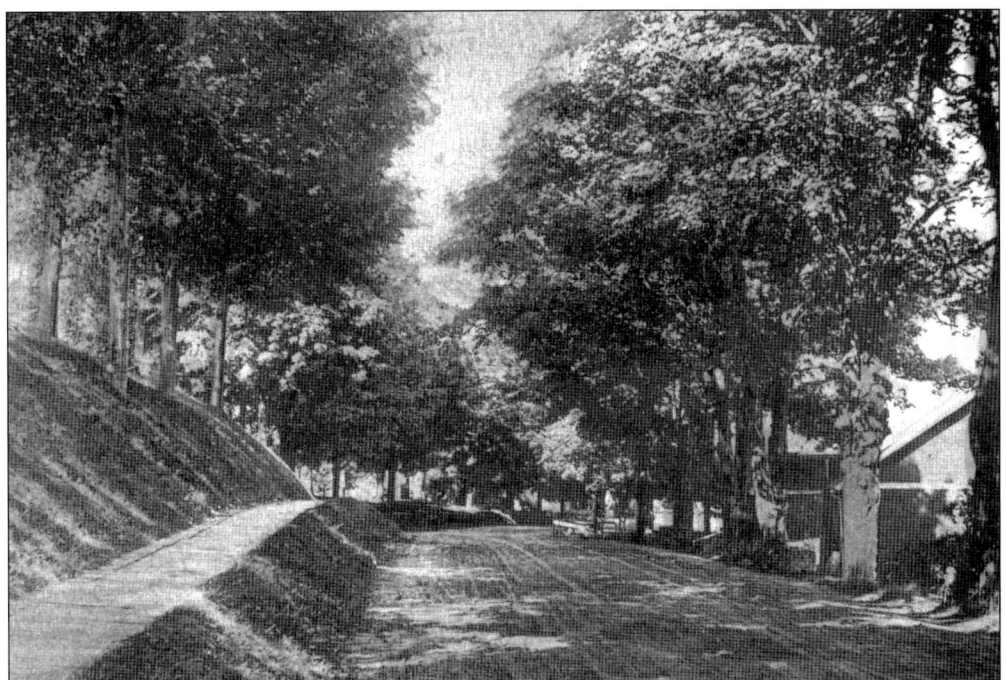

Lover's Walk, above, was a popular spot for the romantically inclined. On this 1909 postcard, Clara is very enthusiastic about Woodbourne's many activities: "Having a fine time roller skating, dancing, bowling, etc. We have a very lively crowd at the house." She was obviously staying at a local boardinghouse and spending a lot of time at the local casino. Writing from the Maple Crest House, below, Madelin reports, "We are all well and having a fine time. The house we are stopping at is very nice. The meals are excellent and we get plenty. The proprietor is nice and the boarders receive a lot of privileges which make it pleasant."

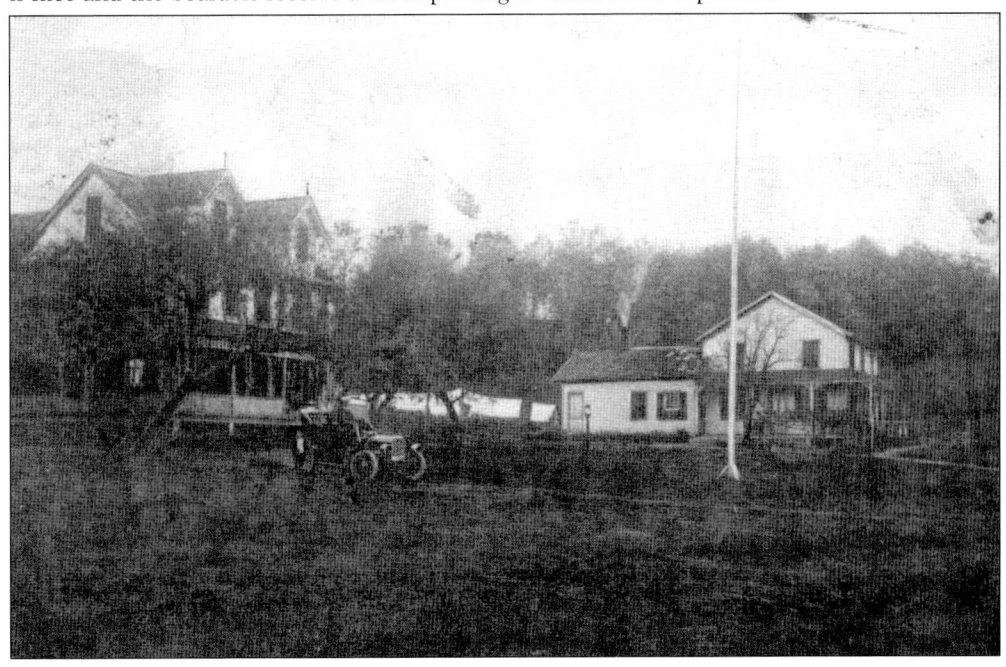

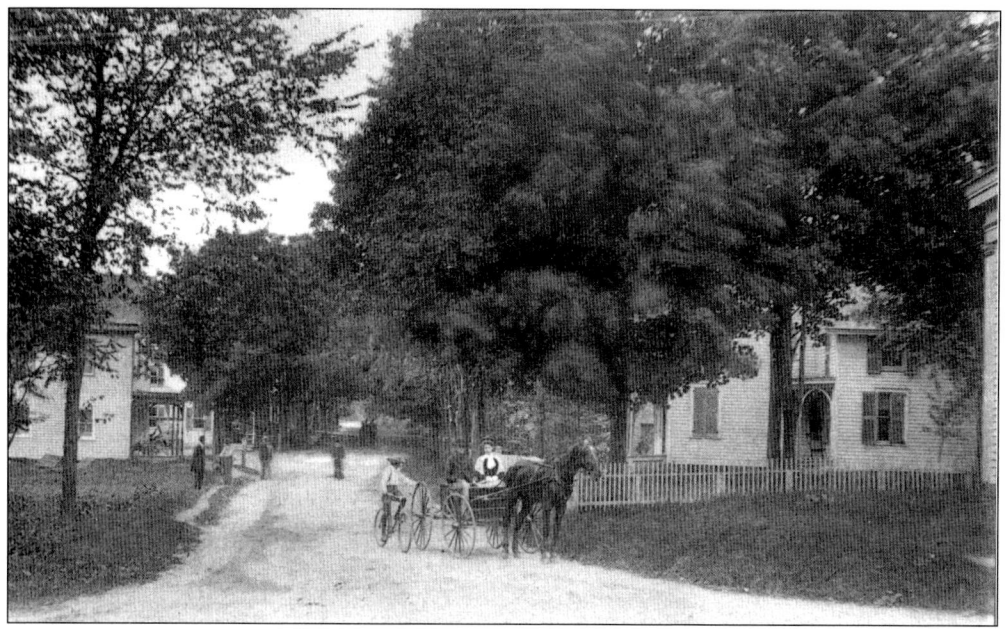

Woodbourne was quite literally a one-horse town in 1906. Maple Street is present-day Route 42. The post office is at the extreme right. The resort owned by the author's family was a half mile from this point, where Route 42 heads toward Grahamsville. All of the buildings in this view are now gone.

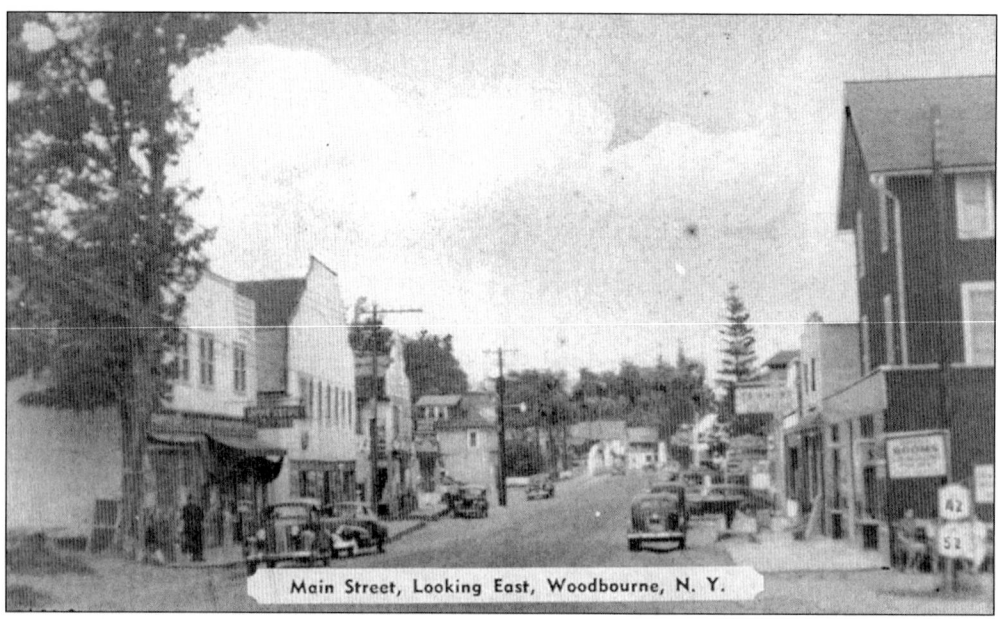

Woodbourne was a vibrant, small town that had year-round businesses and also catered to vacationers. A disastrous fire in 1964 destroyed many of the buildings shown in this 1950s view. On the left are Kanowitz's Dairy, Bernstein's Five-and-Ten, Lebed's Drug Store, and Smiley's Bar. The building with the shed dormer on the roof, housed Dominion's Barber Shop, which survived the fire, only to be destroyed in 1998 by a runaway garbage truck.

Woodbourne Correctional Facility Exhibit

Woodbourne Correctional Facility is unique among New York State prisons for its wealth of architectural detail. Because the facility was built as a WPA project in the midst of the 1930's Depression, many skilled craftsmen were available for the labor pool. Master bricklayers, stonemasons, concrete workers, metal workers, and cabinetmakers combined their efforts to create motifs that reflected the penological theories of the day.

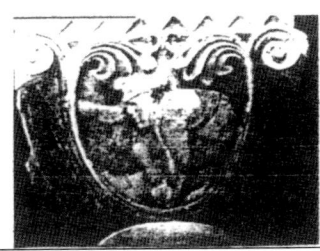

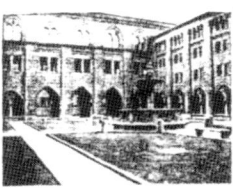

The design of the facility was said to be adapted from the plan of a Spanish monastery. At the center of the administration building is a courtyard surrounded by beautifully engraved columns depicting a safecracker, a policeman, a judge, and an inmate shackled to his ball and chain; plus columns engraved with *Lex*, the written law; alpha and omega, the beginning and the end linked by chain and held in open scissors, the hourglass of time; and the scales of justice mounted on a sword.

It is impossible to include a description of all the elements the builders included in the design and construction, but everywhere you look in the facility, there is a surprisingly executed construction detail that reflects both the original craftsman's commitment to quality workmanship and the unique nature of the Woodbourne Correctional Facility's environment.

In June 2000, the Woodbourne Correctional Facility—popularly called "the Woodbourne Prison" or facetiously "Hotel Woodbourne"—was the subject of an exhibition at the Sullivan County Historical Society. The show made an attempt to demystify the huge structure, which has loomed over Woodbourne for almost 70 years.

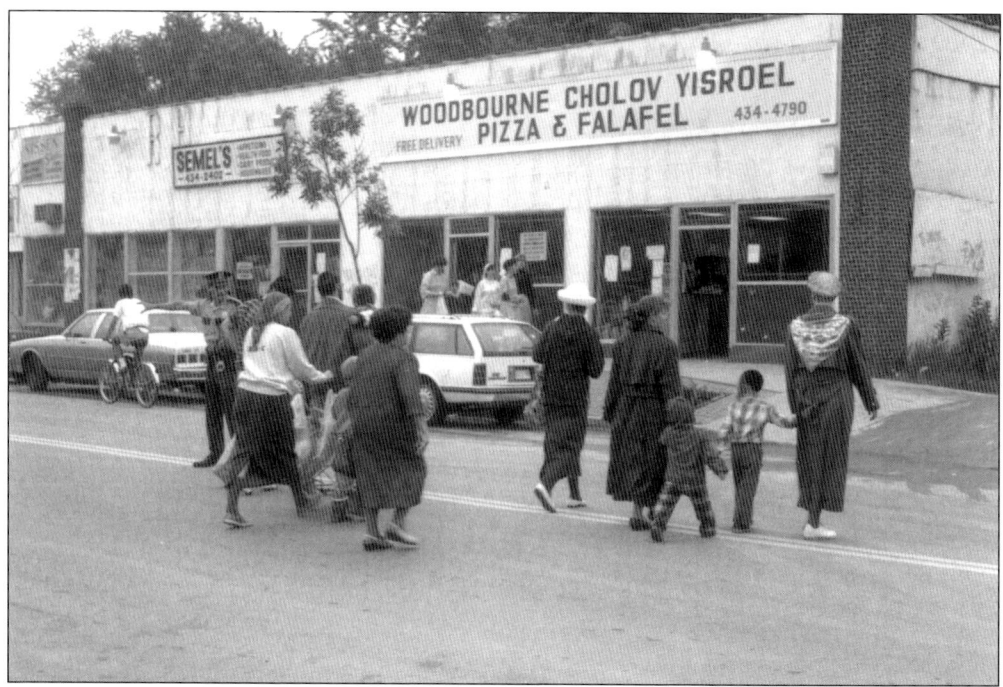

Woodbourne, like many of the other small resort towns of the Borscht Belt, has changed. Vacationers are seldom normative, secular Jews but rather the modern Orthodox and the Hasidim. Above, Orthodox women and children cross the street in front of the stores built after the fire of 1964. Semel's was a branch of a Brooklyn market. Across the street, the building that had once been Lebed's Drug Store became the Pita Mountain, shown decked out in wall murals below. It is now a kosher Chinese restaurant.

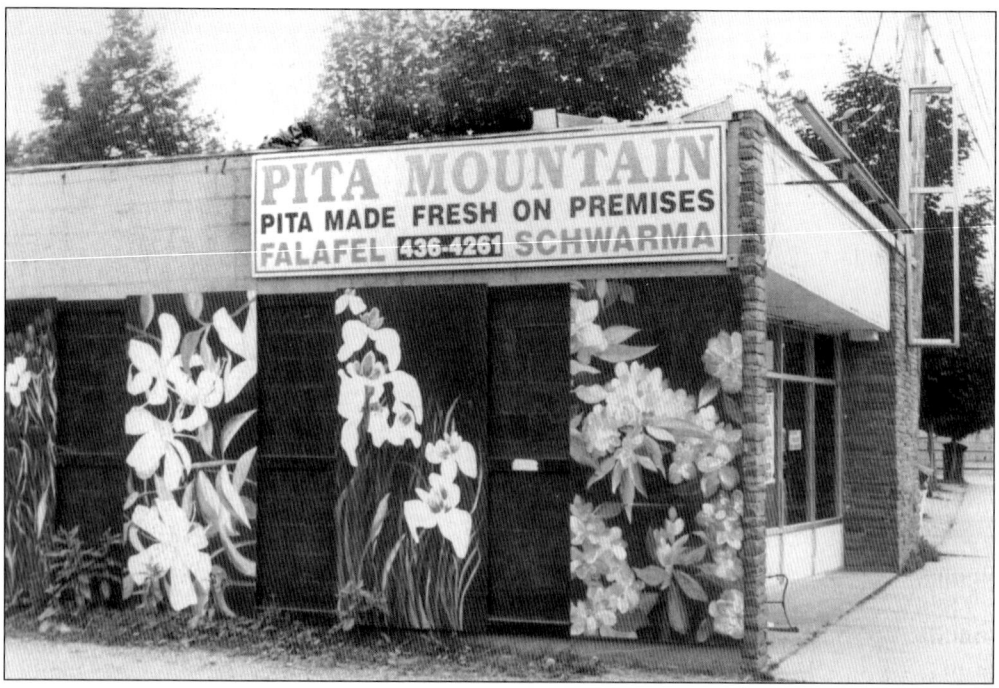

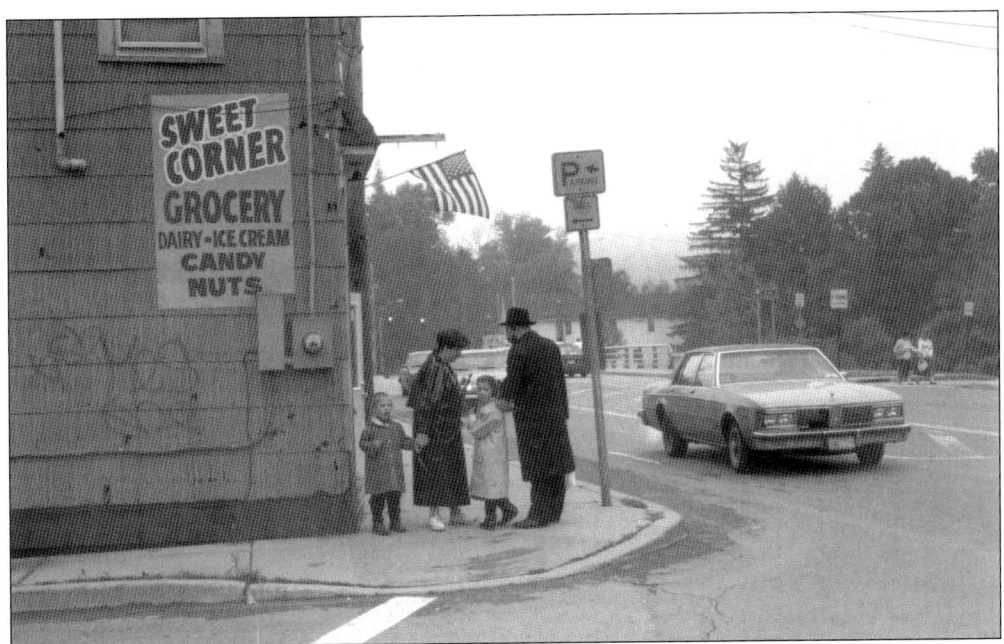

Woodbourne is the most observant of Sullivan County towns. On the Sabbath, the streets are empty except for people strolling after synagogue services and lunch. Locals usually avoid coming to town, where most businesses are shuttered. In the above view, traffic is passing through the town on Route 52. Sweet Corner, housed in what had been the local barbershop, was demolished after a garbage truck hit it in 1998. Beginning at about 10:00 on summer Saturday nights, the Orthodox came out to play at the conclusion of the Sabbath. The Game Room, below, is a popular spot for the younger crowd. Notice the *yalmukes* on the men. The man in the center, playing pinball, is wearing *tsitsis*.

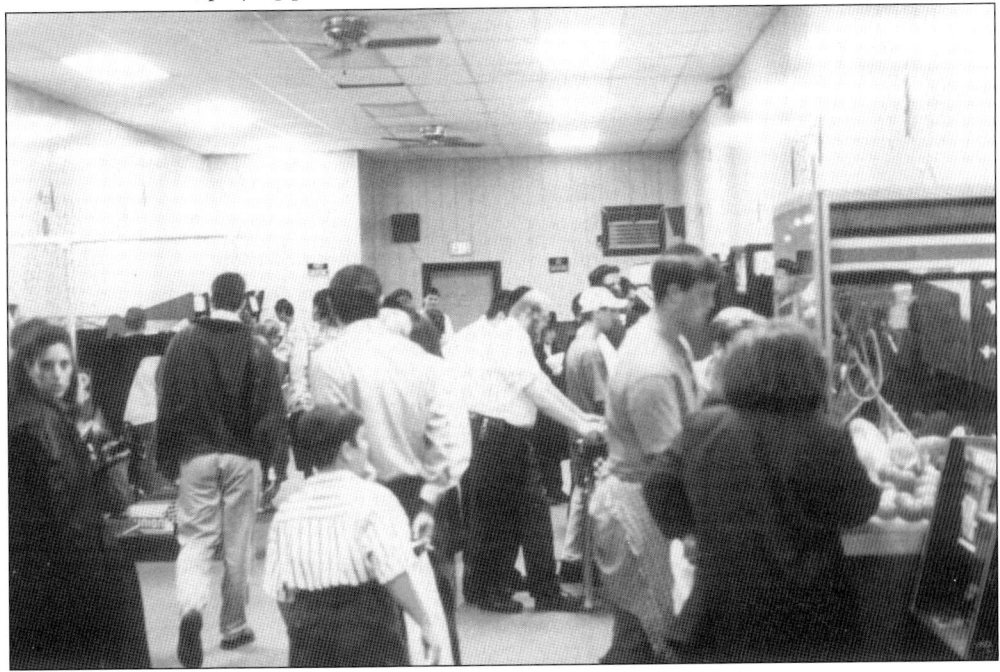

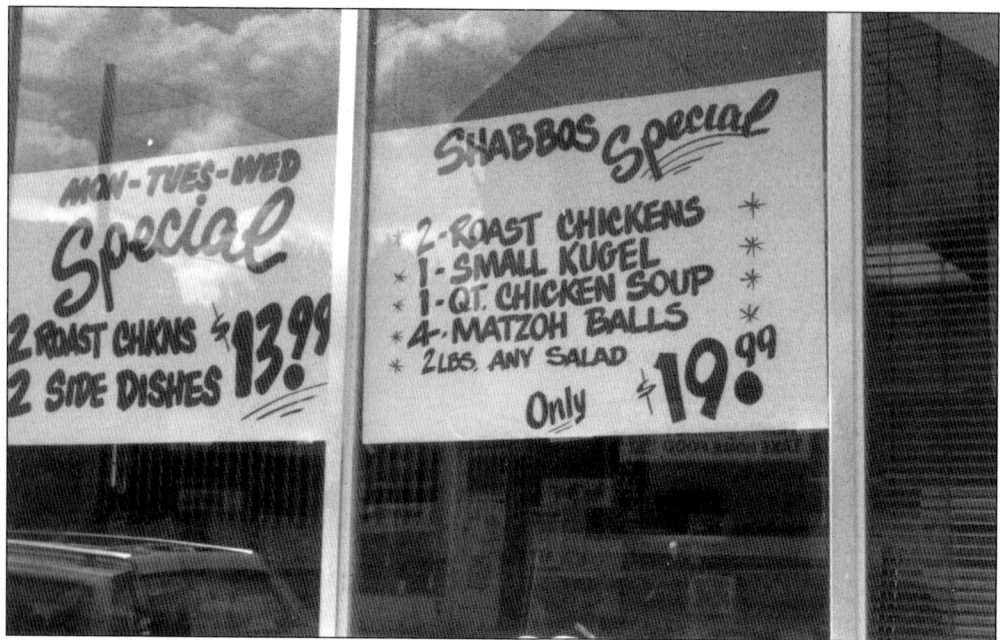

Modern Orthodox Jewish women may be just as observant as their mothers, but they often cook less. As advertised in the window of Woodbourne's Glatt Spot in the 1990s, you could buy your *Shabbos* (Sabbath) dinner or your weekday feed when the husband is away. Down the street, the kosher Chinese restaurant now offers similar deals.

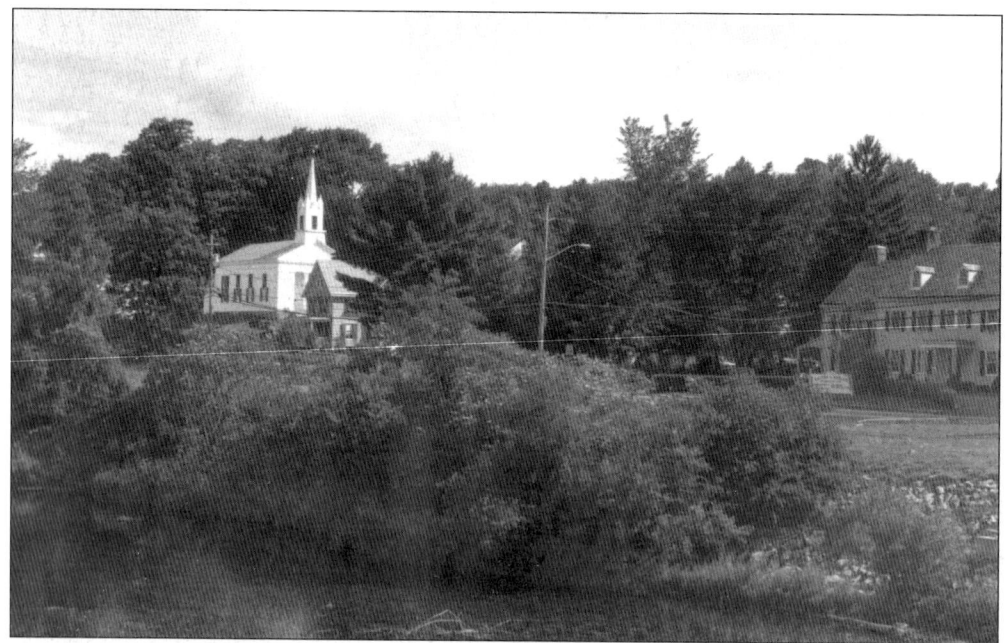

While summer days might give the impression that Orthodox Jews dominate the Catskills, they do not. Even in the halcyon days of the 1950s, Jews were a minority in Sullivan County, as they are today. They are the most distinctive and, among the Hasidim, the most noticeable of the county's residents. This serene scene, taken in 1993 from the bridge crossing the Neversink in Woodbourne, suggests a different, parallel world.

Three
KUCHALEINS AND BUNGALOW COLONIES

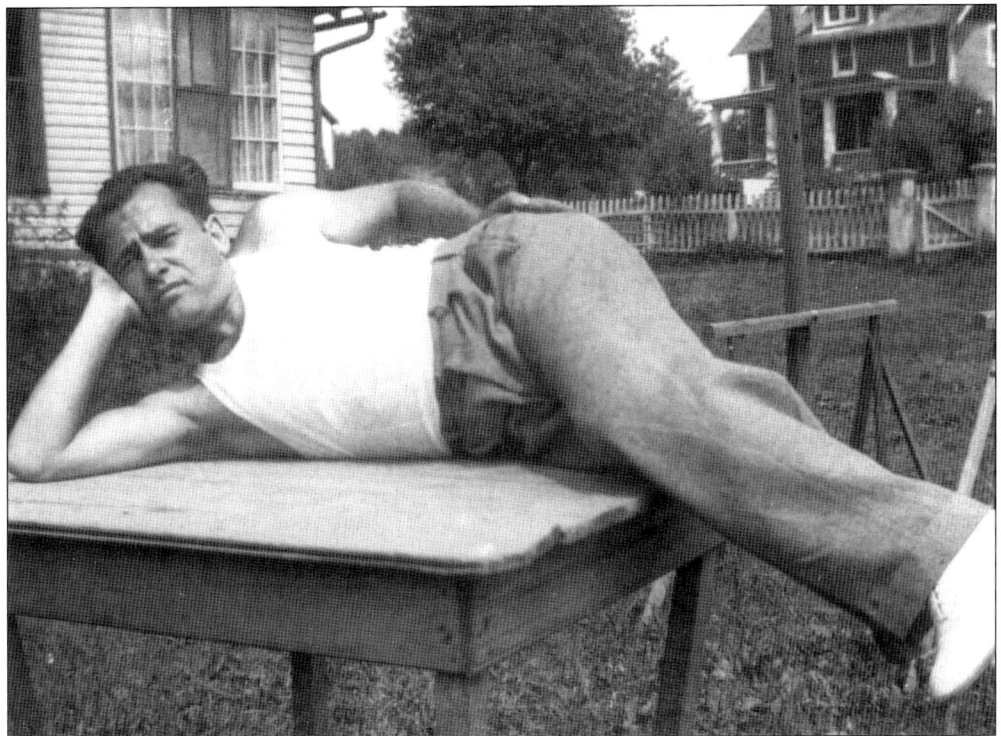

Few *kuchalein* (rooming house) male tenants had sports clothes in the 1920s and 1930s. Their time in the mountains was brief, as few men had their whole weekends free. This picture, taken at Reddish's *kuchalein* in Woodbourne in 1935, also speaks volumes about the sparsity of lawn furniture at that period.

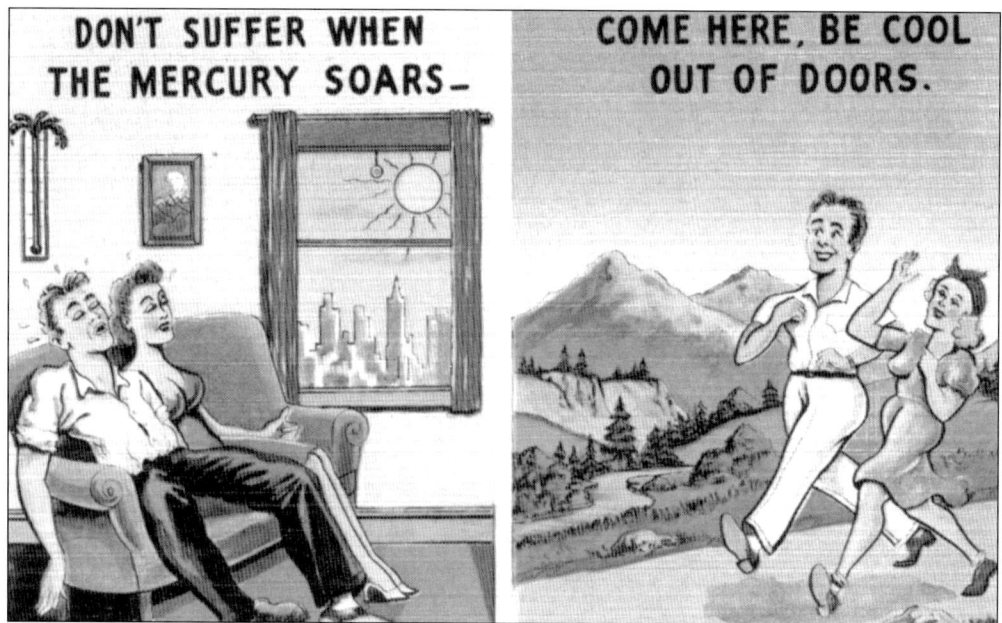

Why go to Sullivan County? This postcard answers the question. New York's skyline is clearly visible through the window. Note the thermometer shaped like a palm tree. Alas, the gentle southern Catskills look like the Rockies.

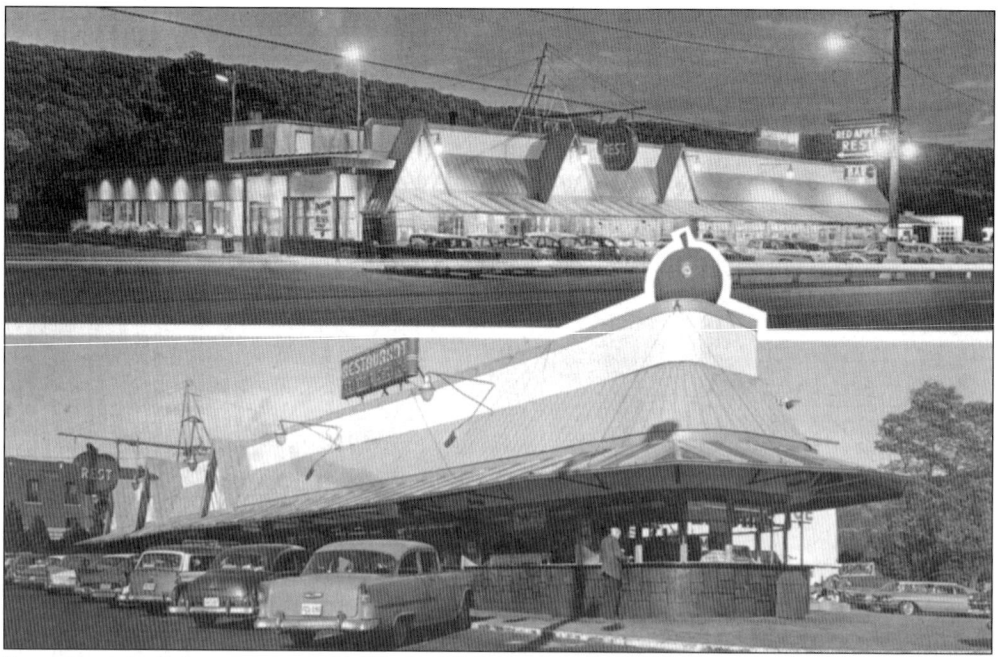

Every Borscht Belt vacationer who traveled by car or bus from New York City stopped at the Red Apple Rest, located on Route 17 in Southfields. Its hot dogs were legendary, and it was a great bathroom stop, halfway to Sullivan County. On the way back, many stopped at Orseck's, a similar place on the other side of the highway.

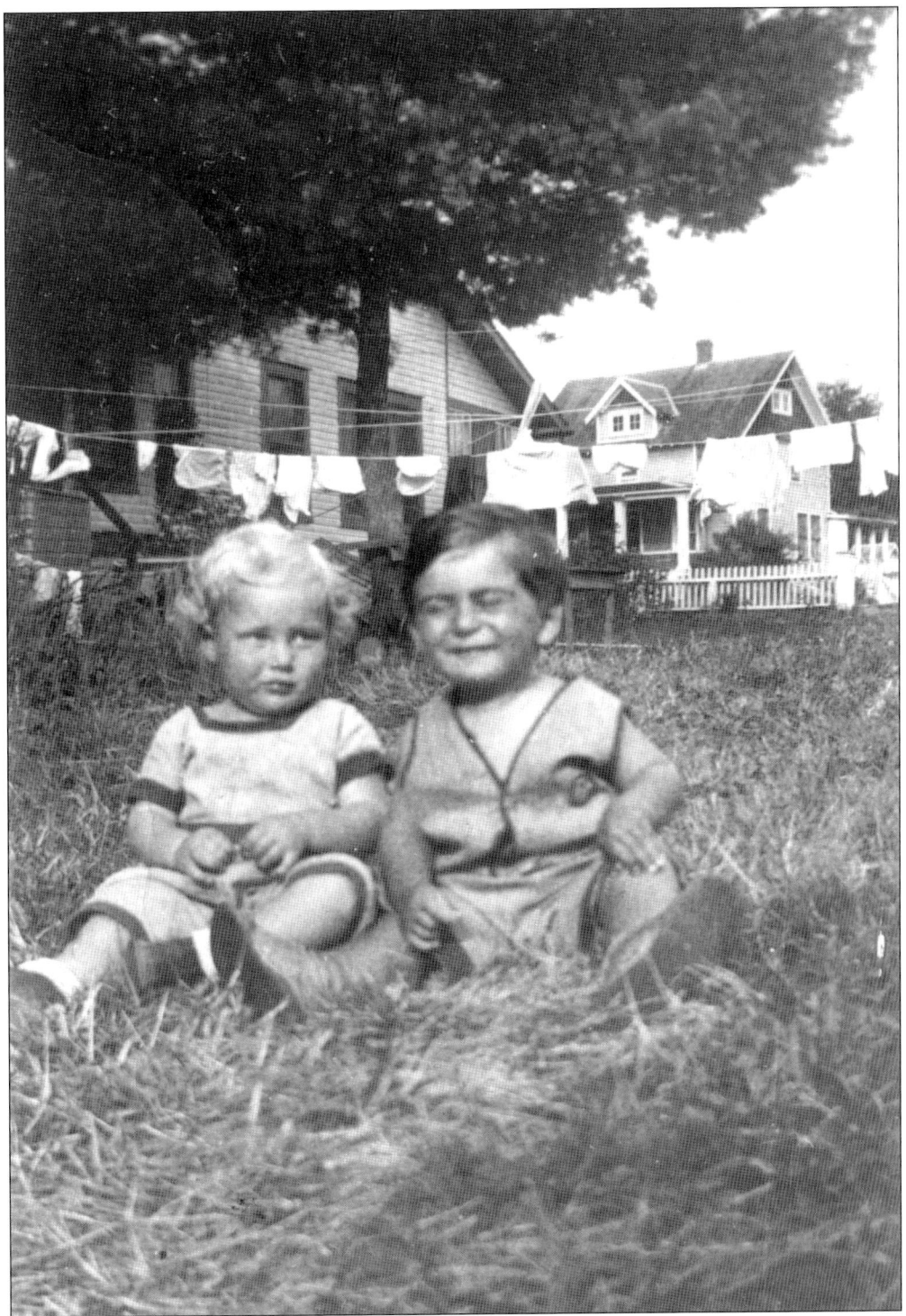

Two toddlers sit on the rough-cut grass of a *kuchalein* in Woodbourne in the mid-1930s. Clothes hang like signal flags on the clotheslines. Women devised strategies to get first access to the best clotheslines—those in full sunlight hanging over level ground.

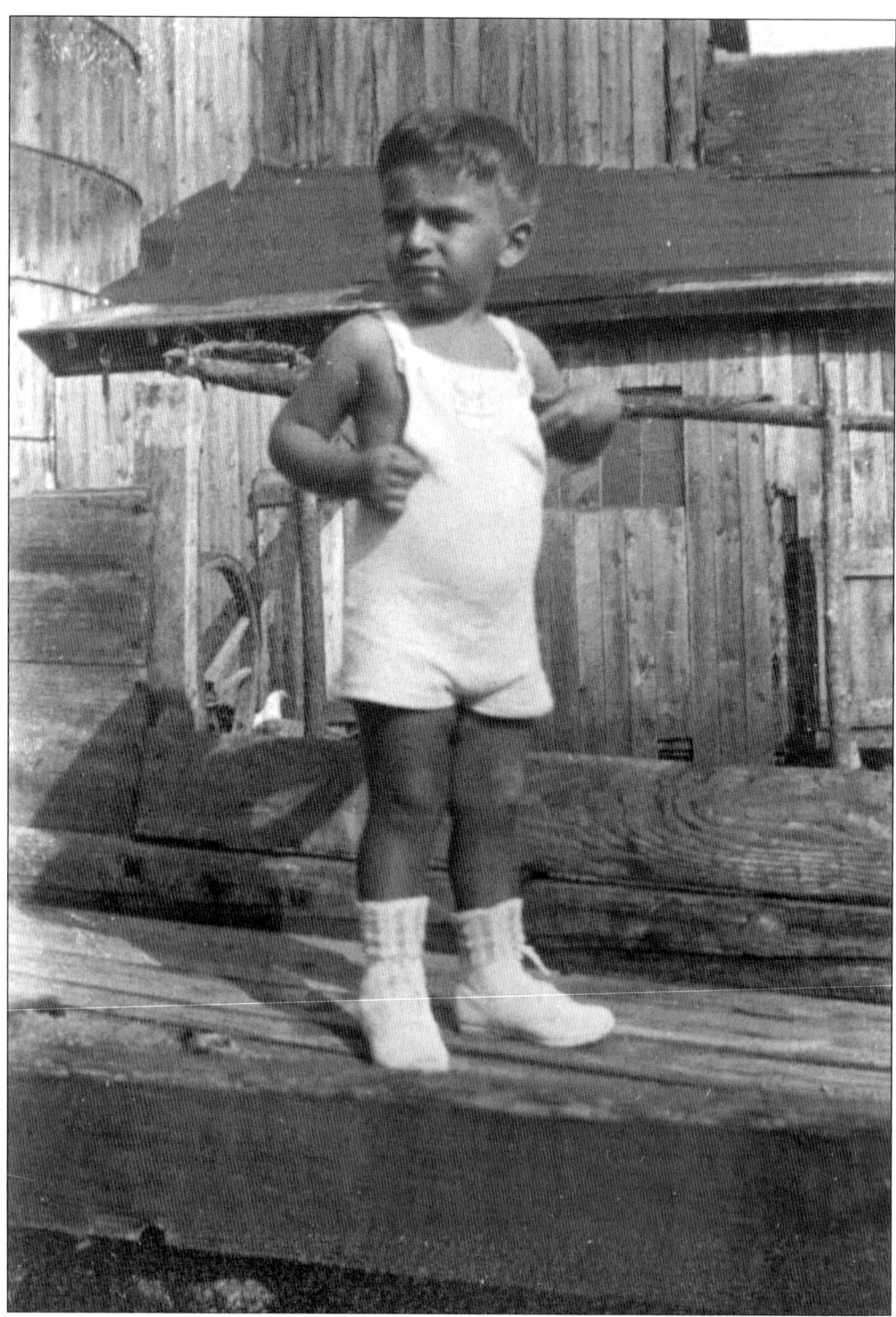
Many *kuchaleins* were started by farmers. Sullivan County had many Jewish farmers, but the generally poor soil of the area turned them into resort owners. In this 1930s image, Seymour Richman, a tenant's son, poses in front of the barns at Rosenshein's Farm.

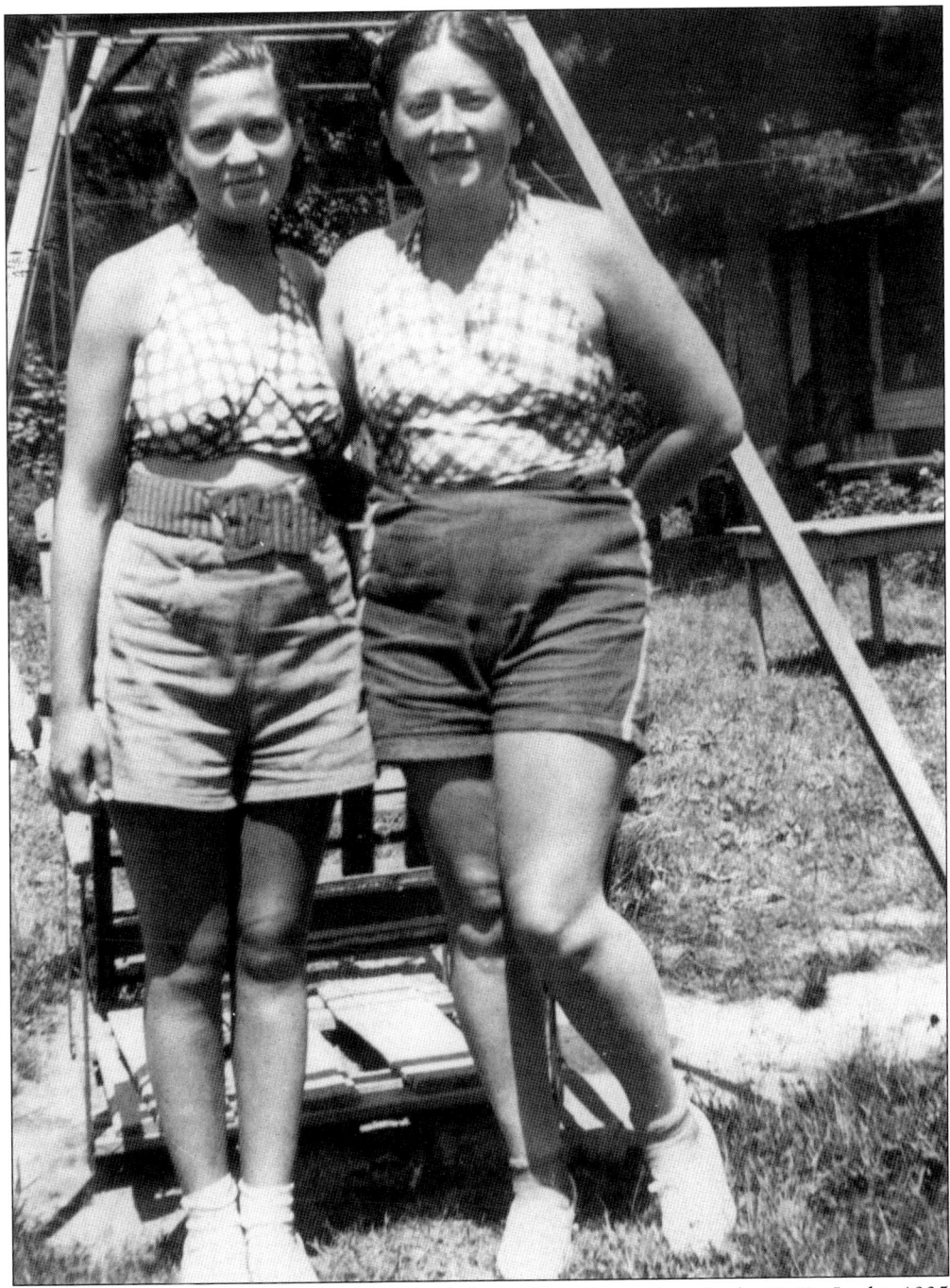

Lawn gliders were a must at almost every *kuchalein* or bungalow colony in the 1930s. In this 1935 image, Lena Storcheim and Bertha Richman proudly pose in front of the glider at Reddish's, a small, up-to-date *kuchalein*. Reddish's had flush toilets, although they did not always work. The resort also had an outhouse for back up.

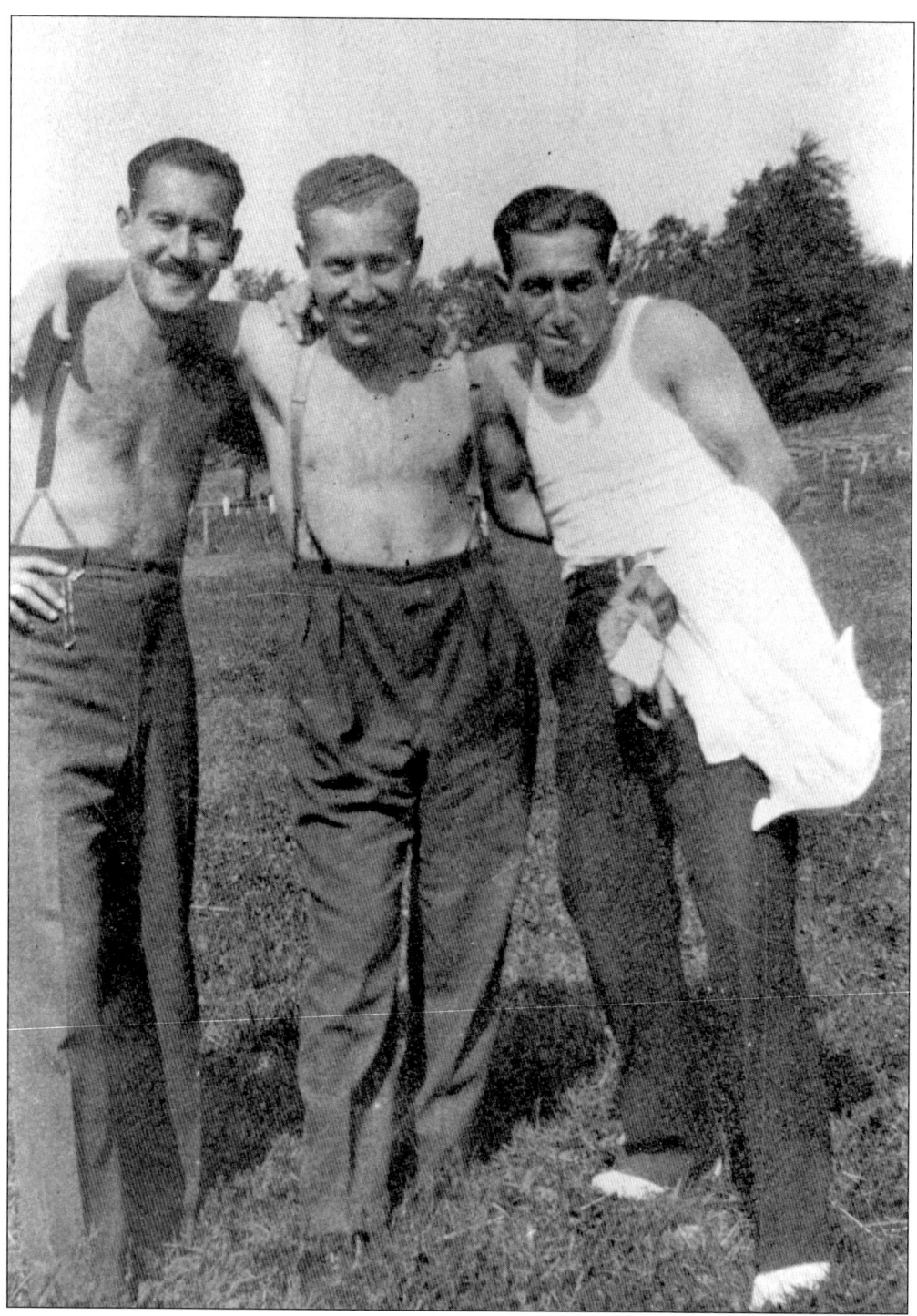

Three men mug for the camera in this *c.* 1932 photograph, taken at Rosenshein's *kuchalein* near Woodbourne. They are wearing street clothes at a time when suspenders were common. The barefoot man holding his shirt and tie probably just arrived from New York City for his day or two in the country. Single-sex pictures like this one were popular in the 1930s.

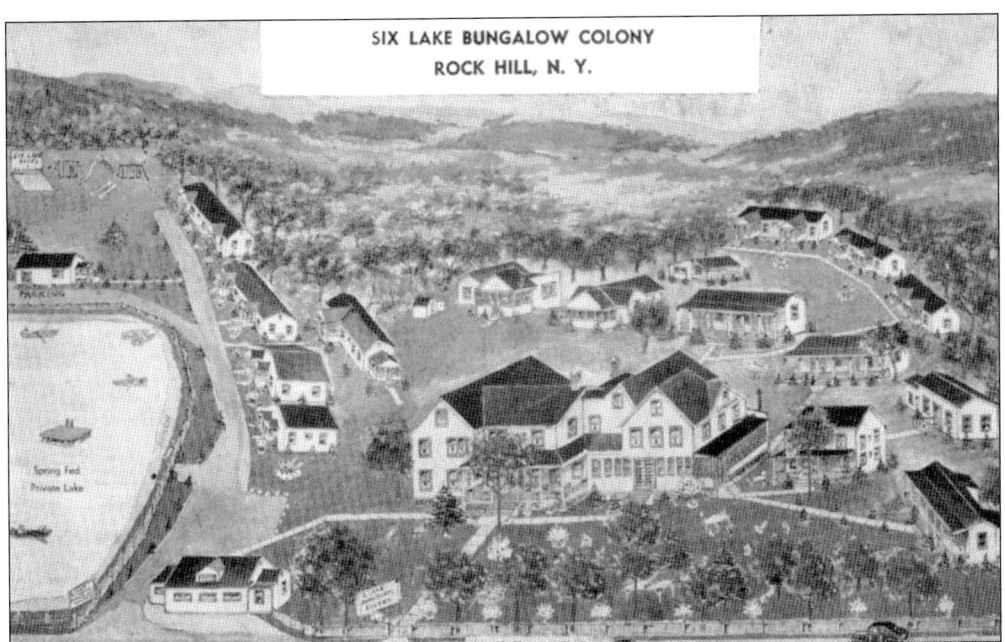

Postcards of bungalow colonies, perhaps Sullivan County's most distinctive resort, are rare. The above view shows the Six Lake Bungalow Colony in Rock Hill with a variety of accommodations. In the foreground is the main house, which probably started as a farmhouse before being converted into units (as rooms, apartments, and bungalows were called). The telephone number of the resort was Monticello 1807. Below, six young folks are having fun at a bungalow colony at Shandelee Camp in Livingston Manor.

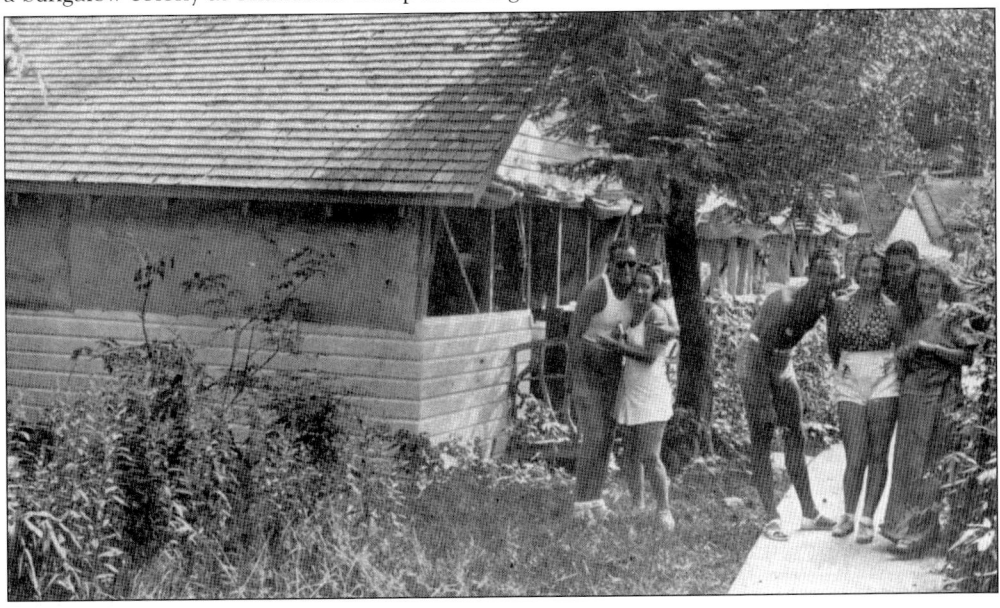

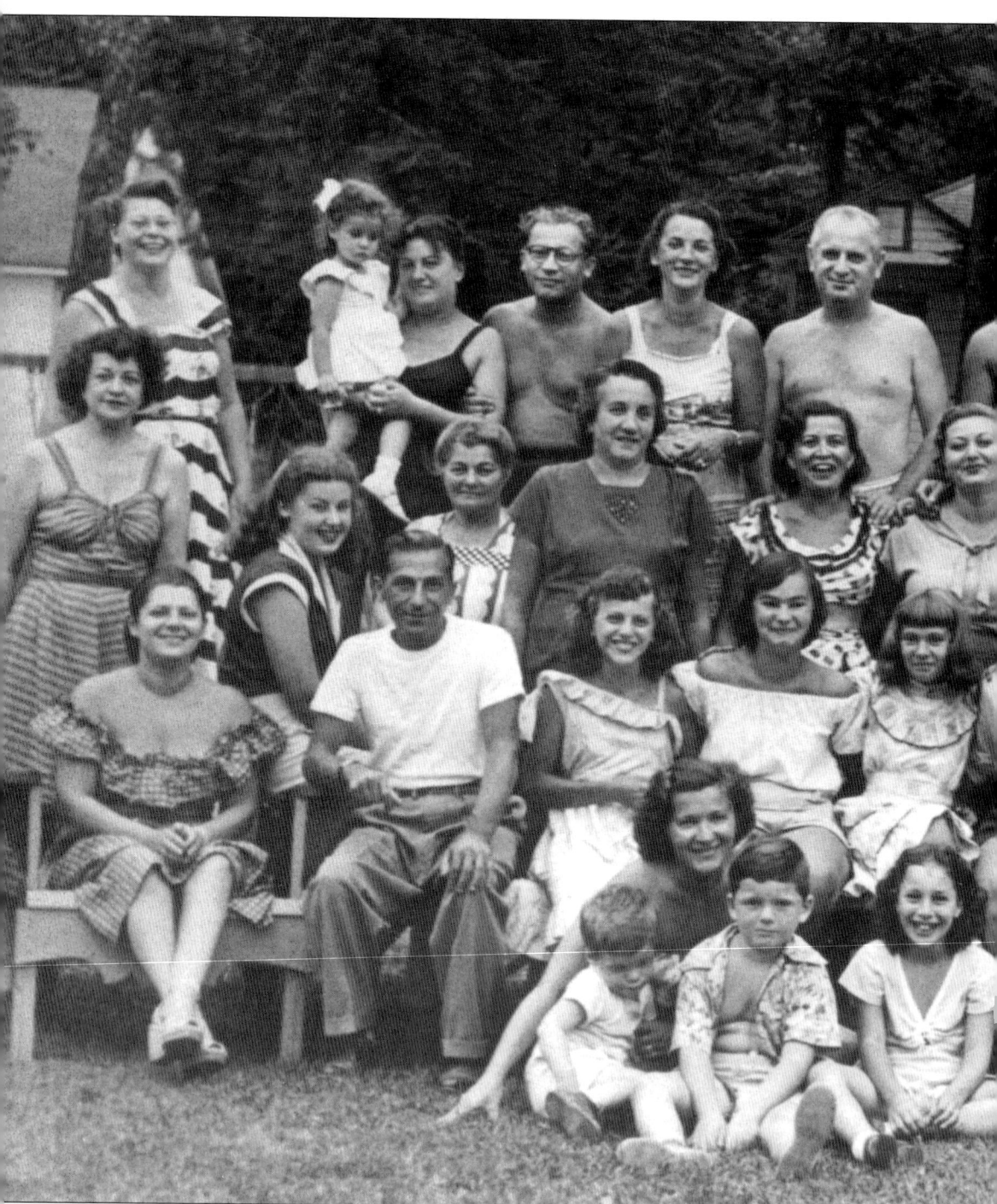

"Watch Harry's belly button go in and out," said Jack Cowan (back row, fifth from right) just before this photograph was taken. Professional photographer Harry Stern, Cowan's brother-in-law, took this 1951 photograph at the A. Richman Bungalow Colony in Woodbourne as a gift for the landlords. Cowan was the proprietor of an elegant Manhattan dress shop. His stylish wife and business partner, Eve, sits in the Adirondack chair on the far

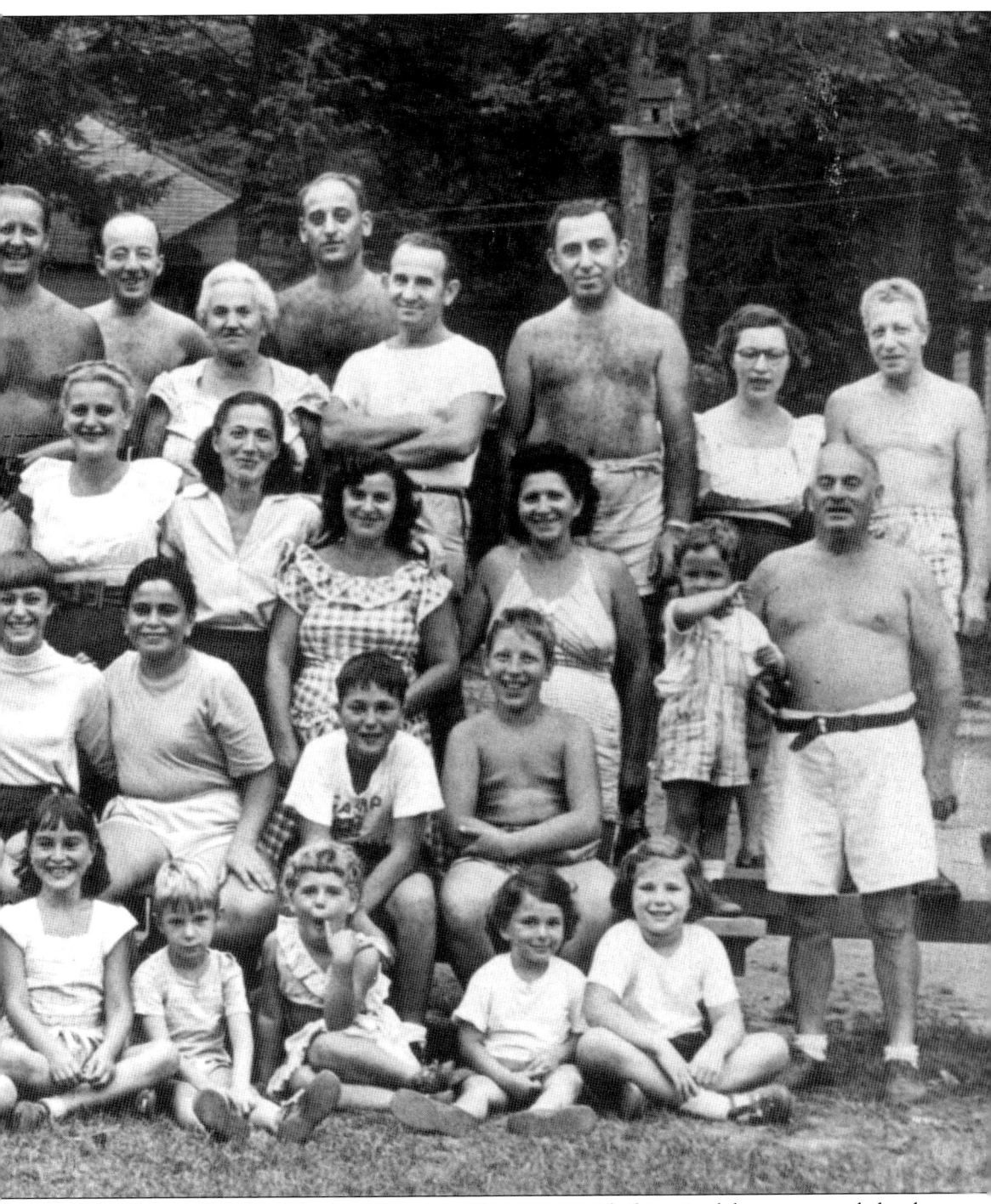

left. The crowd was middle class to upscale. The woman with the striped dress two rows behind Eve was the Manns' maid. Lou and Kate Mann (holding their daughter) owned a chain of ladies' specialty shops in Brooklyn. Because this picture was taken on a Saturday in August, several Sabbath-observant guests are absent.

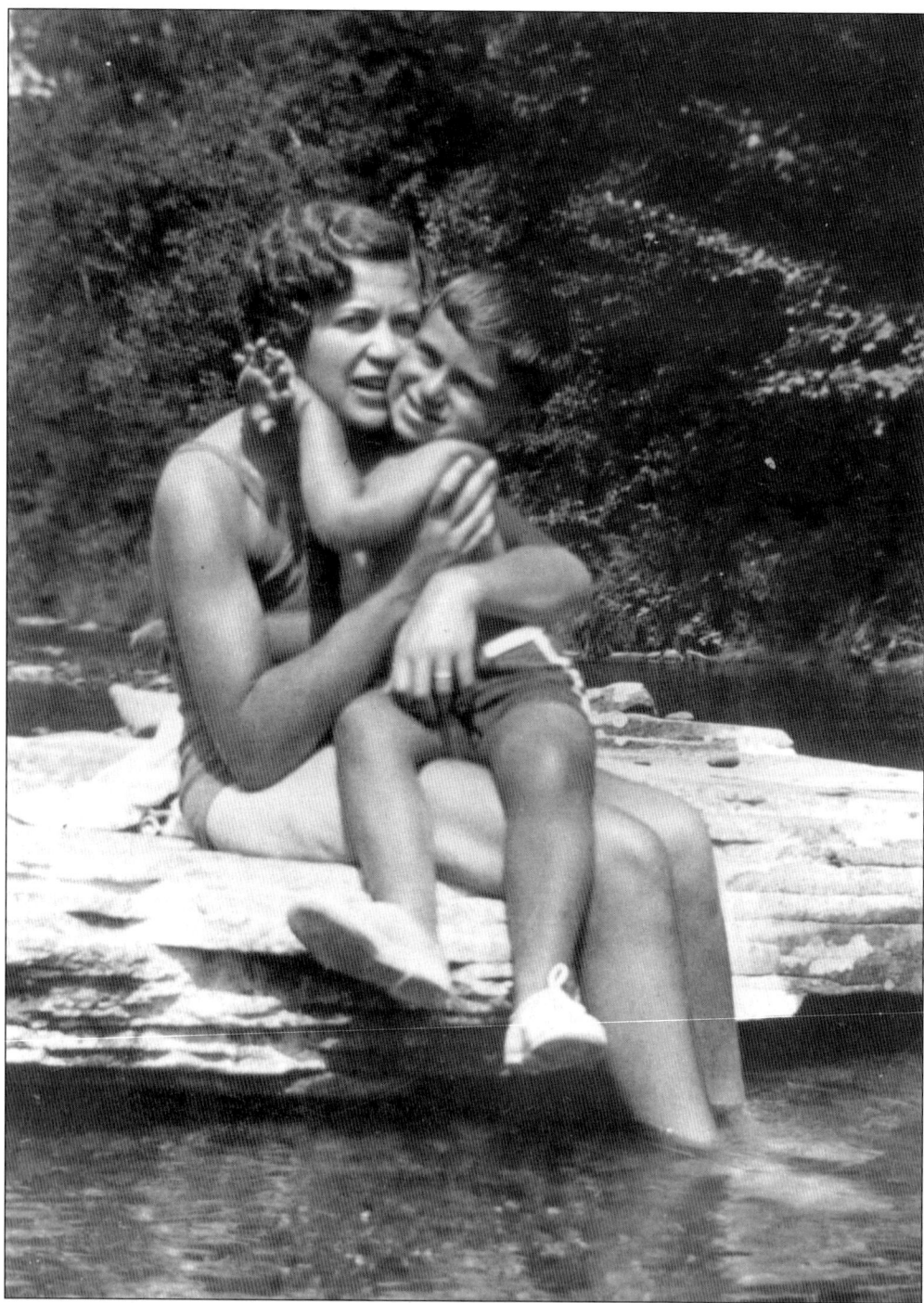

There are very few beaches on the Neversink River. The most celebrated natural one is at Hasbrouck. Like most Neversink beaches, including the sarcastically named "Sandy Beach," the beaches are made up mostly of river stones. Some hotels, like the Levbourne, brought in sand to make their own beaches. Most *kuchaleiners* and bungalow colony folks used the many boulders that dot the river as their beaches. This photograph was taken in the 1930s.

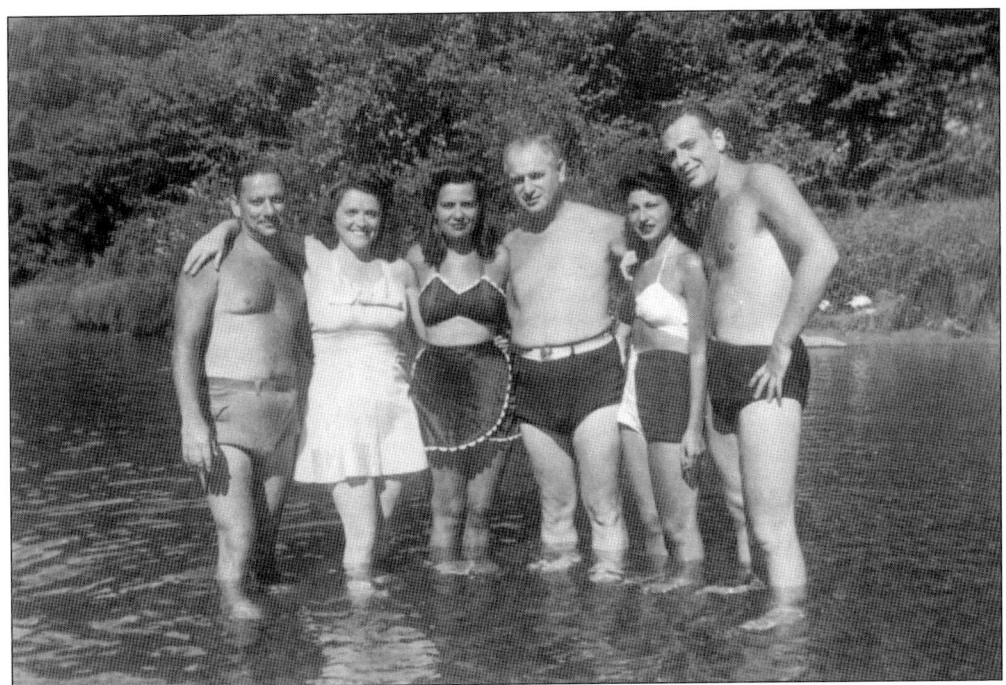

All resort-goers prized a choice place on the Neversink River. The ideal spot had shallow and deep water and a group of large boulders to lounge on. River photographs were extremely popular. Posing c. 1945 in the above picture are, from left to right, Frank Roth, Zena Roth, Bertha Richman, Alexander Richman, Hilda Kagan, and Harry Kagan. Below, a group of bungalow colony kids, including the author (front row, left), poses in slightly deeper water.

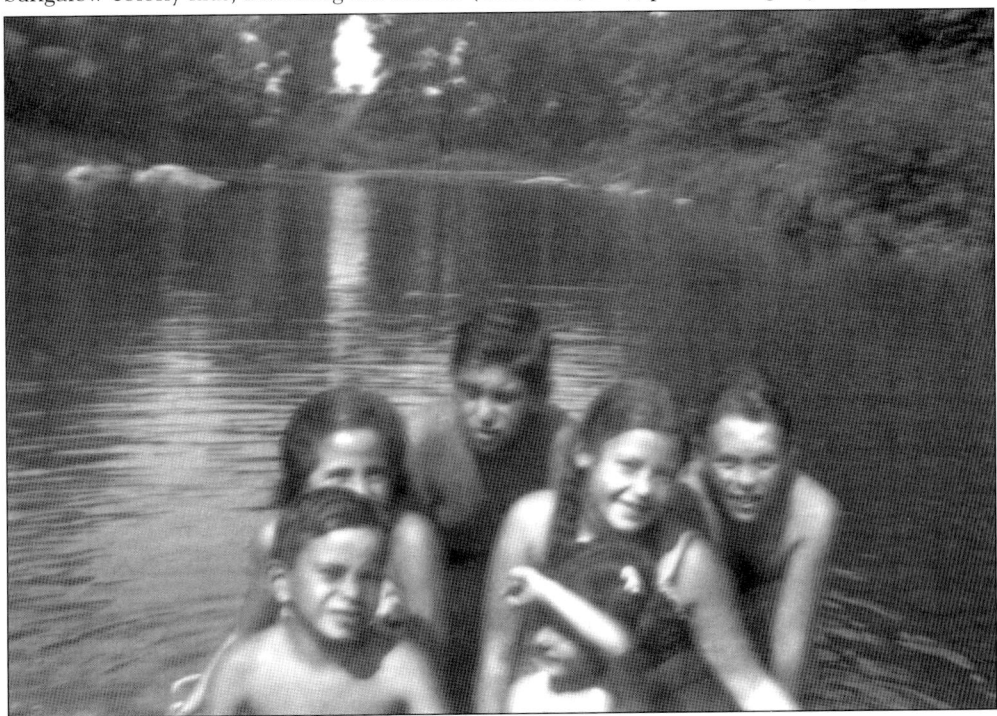

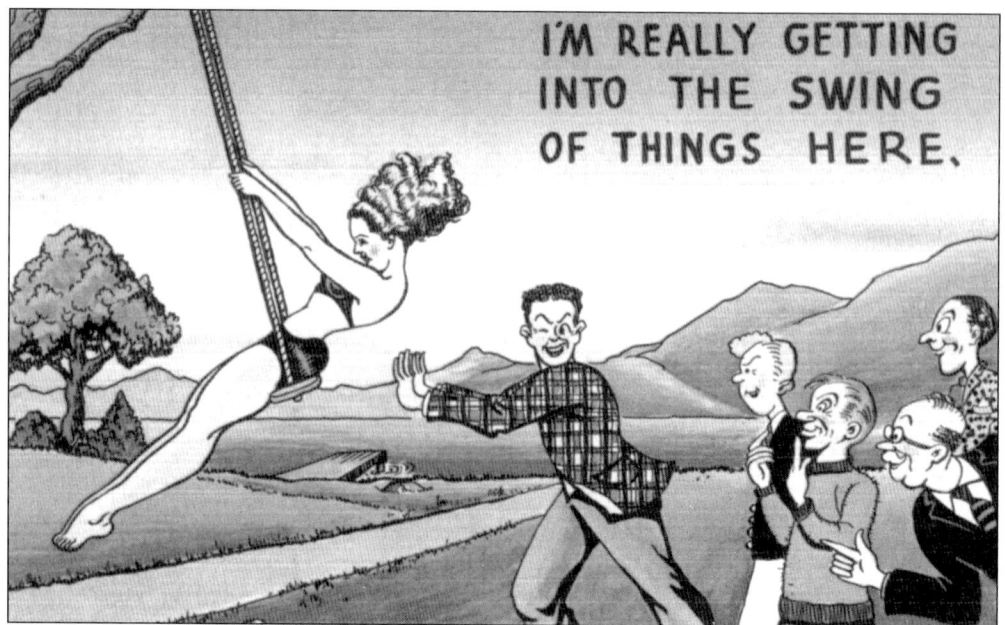

Romance was always in the air in the mountains—or it was supposed to be. Many comic postcards attested to this. Every Sullivan County drug and variety store had racks of them. In this image, the young man is into the action while the older, presumably married men look on enviously.

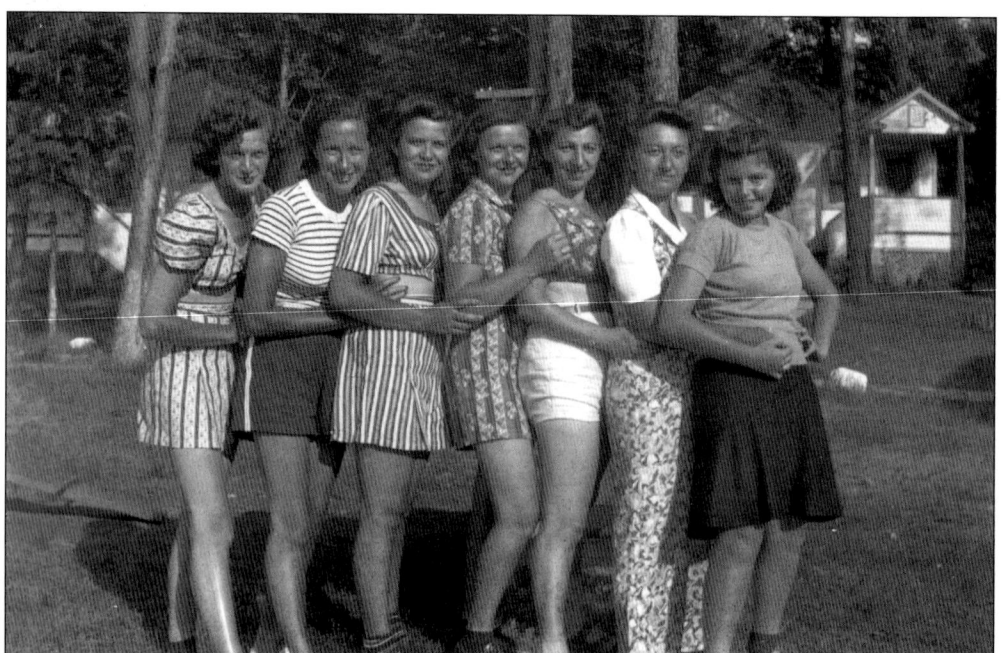

The year was 1945 and the conga, a line dance, was all the rage. They sang, "One, two, three la conga," and kicked off to the side. This is the quintessential Catskill "girl picture" of the 1940s. A wonderful impromptu conga line is re-created in the Woody Allen film *Radio Days*.

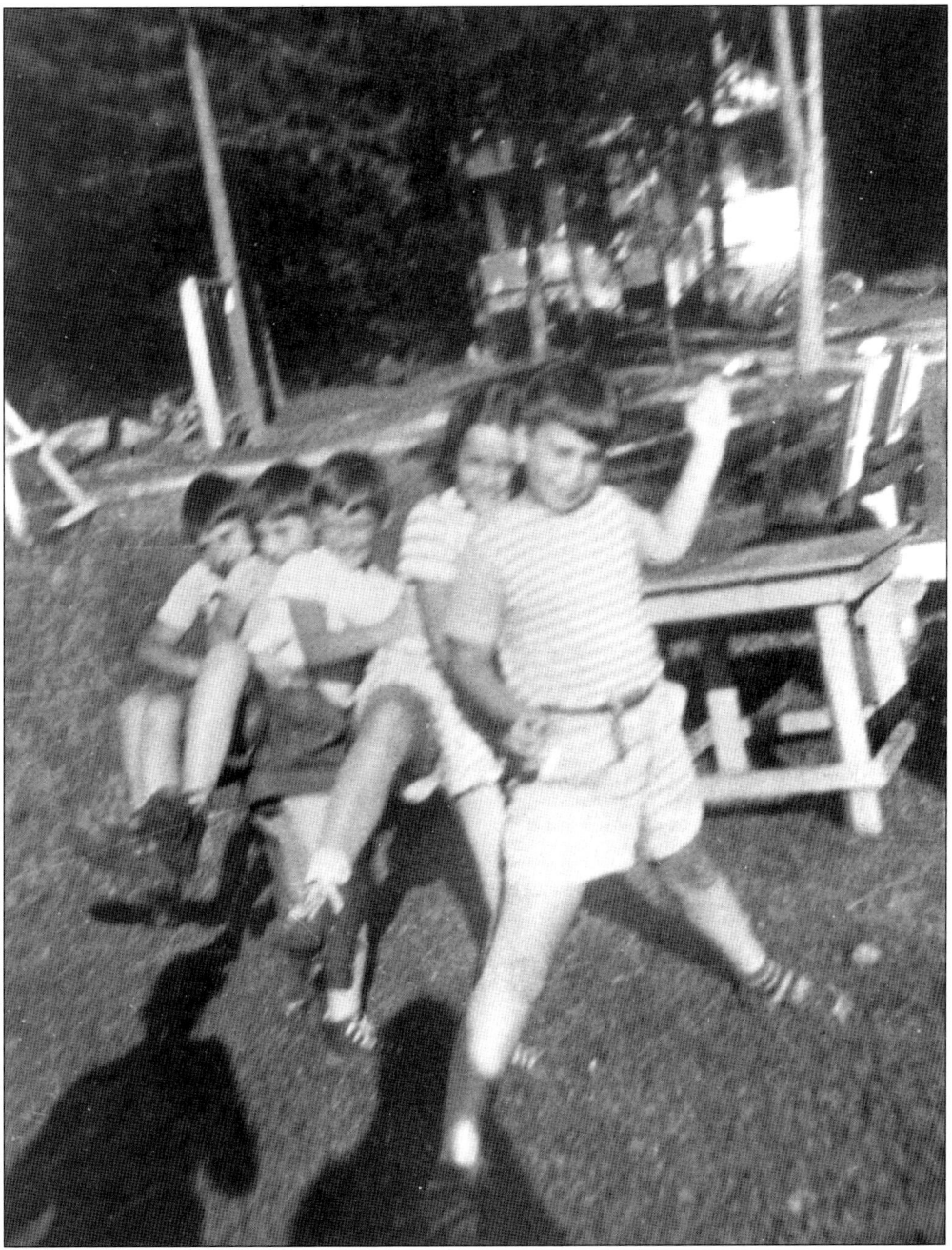

The kids also did the conga, but they were never content to stay still when a picture was being taken. This scene is typical of a bungalow colony in the 1940s. Note the homemade table and the Adirondack chair, common lawn furniture of the period.

NOTE: This list is derived from the Yellow Pages for Sullivan County as published by the New York Telephone Company. It therefore may not be complete. Since many operators work only on a seasonal basis, and are not on premises at all times, it is advisable to either be persistent in attempts to call bungalow colonies or to rely on written communication.

BUNGALOW COLONIES

ANDRESKY'S BUNGALOWS Hurleyville	434-6514
AVON RIVERSIDE BUNGALOW COLONY South Fallsburg	434-9110
BARRONS COTTAGES Fallsburg	434-9503
SAMUEL BERNHARD South Fallsburg	434-9712
CALVIN'S BUNGALOW COLONY South Fallsburg	434-9087
CHAI MANOR BUNGALOW COLONY South Fallsburg	434-9855
CLAUDIO'S VILLAGE Mountaindale	434-9650
COLONY HILL BUNGALOWS South Fallsburg	434-9565
COOPER'S BUNGALOWS Fallsburg	434-9551
CORNYN'S ROADSIDE COLONY South Fallsburg	434-9504
CUTLER'S SUMMER HOMES South Fallsburg	434-9662
DELMAR COLONY Fallsburg	434-9602
WILLIAM DESAPIO Mountaindale	434-9897
DOCTOR LOCKER'S BUNGALOWS Mountaindale	434-9203
EDDIE'S BUNGALOW COLONY Loch Sheldrake	434-9567
ELM SHADE COLONY Route 42 South Fallsburg	434-4545
EVE SHERMAN'S COTTAGES South Fallsburg	434-9771
FISCHER'S SUNSHINE BUNGALOW COLONY Woodbourne	434-9190
BARBARA VILLA Mountaindale	434-9708
ANCEL BERKOWITZ Mountaindale	434-9362
BORRELLO'S SHADY MAPLES Hasbrouck Rd. Woodbourne	434-9879
BROOKSIDE BUNGALOW COLONY South Fallsburg	434-9480
CAMP IMPALA INC. Woodbourne	434-9739
CHERVIOK BUNGALOWS Maple Ave. Woodridge	434-9160
THE CLINTON HOUSE Hurleyville	434-9211
COLONY PARK BUNGALOWS Mountaindale	434-9240
COOPER'S COTTAGES South Fallsburg	434-9634
CUTLER'S COTTAGES South Fallsburg	434-6400
DAMESEK'S WOODLAND COLONY Woodbourne	434-9121
DEER MOUNTAIN RESORT COLONY South Fallsburg	434-9182
DISHNER'S BUNGALOWS South Fallsburg	434-9533
EAST POND COTTAGES INC. Fallsburg	434-9773
SAM EISENMAN Woodridge	434-9345
ENGELSOHN'S BUNGALOWS Woodbourne	434-9174
EVERGREEN COTTAGES South Fallsburg	434-9722
FLORIDA BUNGALOW COLONY Woodridge	434-9550
FOUR J'S BUNGALOW COLONY Hasbrouck Road Woodbourne	434-9235
FRIED BUNGALOWS Hurleyville	434-9687
FRIEDA'S BUNGALOWS Woodridge	434-9386
SAM GANZ Divine Corners	434-9123
GENDEN'S BUNGALOWS Russell St. South Fallsburg	434-9025
GLUCKSMAN'S COLONY Woodbourne	434-9709
GOLDEN BELLS South Fallsburg	434-9524
GRAND HOUSE South Fallsburg	434-9193
GREENWALD BUNGALOWS Woodridge	434-9277
GRINE FELDER COLONY Woodridge	434-9356 434-9610
GROSSGOLD'S BUNGALOWS South Fallsburg	434-9845
BEN GULKOW Woodbourne	434-9119
HAPPY HAMLET Hasbrouck Road	434-9045
HECHTS BUNGALOW COLONY Glen Wild	434-9790
HELENA'S BUNGALOWS South Fallsburg	434-9118
HERSKOVITZ MOLVINA Mountaindale	434-9017
HIGH CLIFF BUNGALOW COLONY Mountaindale	434-9361
HILLAIR Route 42 Woodbourne	434-9085
HOLIDAY BUNGALOWS Fallsburg	434-9676
HOMESTEAD COTTAGES Highland Ave. Woodridge	434-9048
DAVID JACOBY South Fallsburg	434-9319
FRANK'S VILLA Woodbourne	434-9103 434-9183
ISAAC FRIED Hurleyville	434-9078
G & S BUNGALOWS Mountaindale	434-9323
GEE-MAR COLONY Fallsburg	434-9506
GLENWOOD RESORT CORP. Mountaindale	434-9044

GOLDCREST BUNGALOW COLONY Loch Sheldrake	434-9249
GOODMAN'S BUNGALOWS Glen Wild Rd. Woodridge	434-9066
GRAYSTONE MANOR South Fallsburg	434-9715
GREENWOOD PARK South Fallsburg	434-9236
I & R GROSS BUNGALOWS South Fallsburg	434-9530
GUILD MANOR BUNGALOW COLONY South Fallsburg	434-9668
H & H MANOR INC. Loch Sheldrake	434-9419
HARTMAN'S BUNGALOW COLONY Woodbourne	434-9800
HECHT'S COLONY Loch Sheldrake	434-9777
MELOCK GROVE ESTATES Mountaindale	434-9169
HIDDEN LAKE COTTAGES Glen Wild	434-9335
HIGHLAND PARK BUNGALOW COLONY Woodridge	434-9570
HODES BUNGALOWS Woodridge	434-9660
HOLIDAY PARK BUNGALOWS Woodbourne	434-9143
JFH BUNGALOWS Fallsburg	434-9512
JACOBY'S COTTAGES INC. Woodbourne	434-9889
JAFRE FIVE STAR COTTAGES Loch Sheldrake	292-9592
GEORGE KWOKA Mountaindale	434-9300
LAKEWOOD COLONY Woodridge	434-9039 434-9787
LANSMAN'S BUNGALOW COLONY Woodbourne	434-9094
LETTER'S BUNGALOW COLONY Woodridge	434-9315
MARSHA'S BUNGALOWS Loch Sheldrake	434-9273
MAYBROOK BUNGALOW COLONY Woodbourne	434-9859
METROPOLITAN BUNGALOWS South Fallsburg	434-9148
MINZER'S HOLLYWOOD BUNGALOWS Mountaindale	434-9317
MOONGLOW INN Loch Sheldrake	434-9627
MOUNT BROOK BUNGALOWS Mountaindale	434-9374
MULBERRY COTTAGES Thompsonville Rd. South Fallsburg	434-9609
NAN-ACRES BUNGALOW COLONY South Fallsburg	434-9405 434-9803
THE NEW VICTORY South Fallsburg	434-9553
PANCREST LODGE South Fallsburg	434-6670
PARADISE COTTAGES Church Rd. Mountaindale	434-9261
PHYL-BOB COLONY Fallsburg	434-9022

By the mid-1960s, as the bungalow business started to go sour, governmental agencies and private organizations did their best to promote resorts. Derived from the telephone directory, this list (only part of which is shown) was printed by the Town of Fallsburg to advertise its motels, hotels, bungalows, and "other attractions." As suggested in the note at the upper left, there were many bungalow colonies that were not listed in the phone book because it cost extra to be included as a business. Many owners simply listed their numbers as being residential. The Grine Felder Colony, included in the brochure, was a famed resort founded by Yiddish-speaking intellectuals.

83

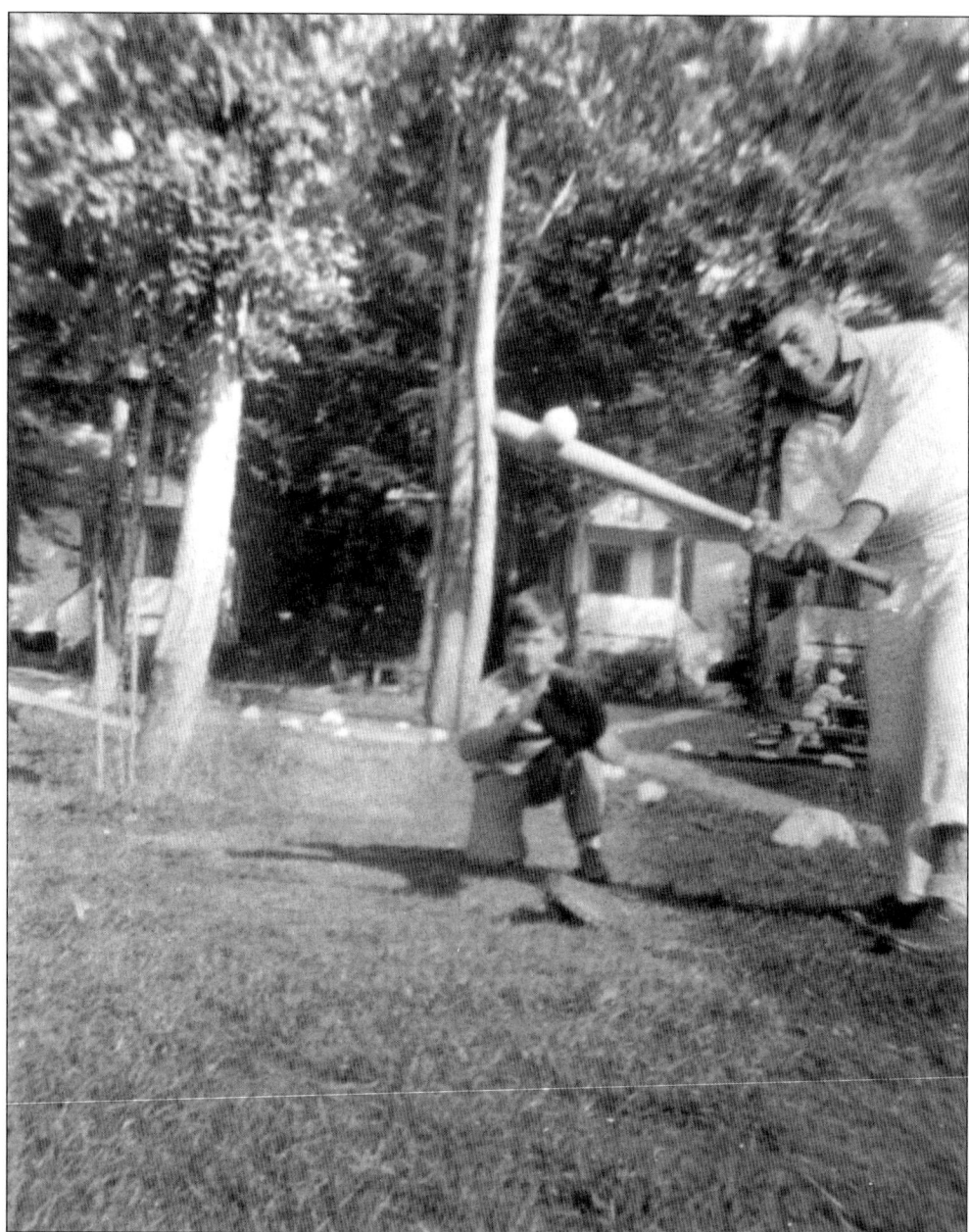

Baseball was an important time filler, as was trick photography. In 1947, with only a simple Kodak Brownie camera to use, you had to pin the ball to the bat for a picture like this. Children were not allowed to play baseball so close to the bungalows. Some large places had ball fields, but others offered only a farm pasture, where kids who wanted to play ball would have to watch out for cow patties.

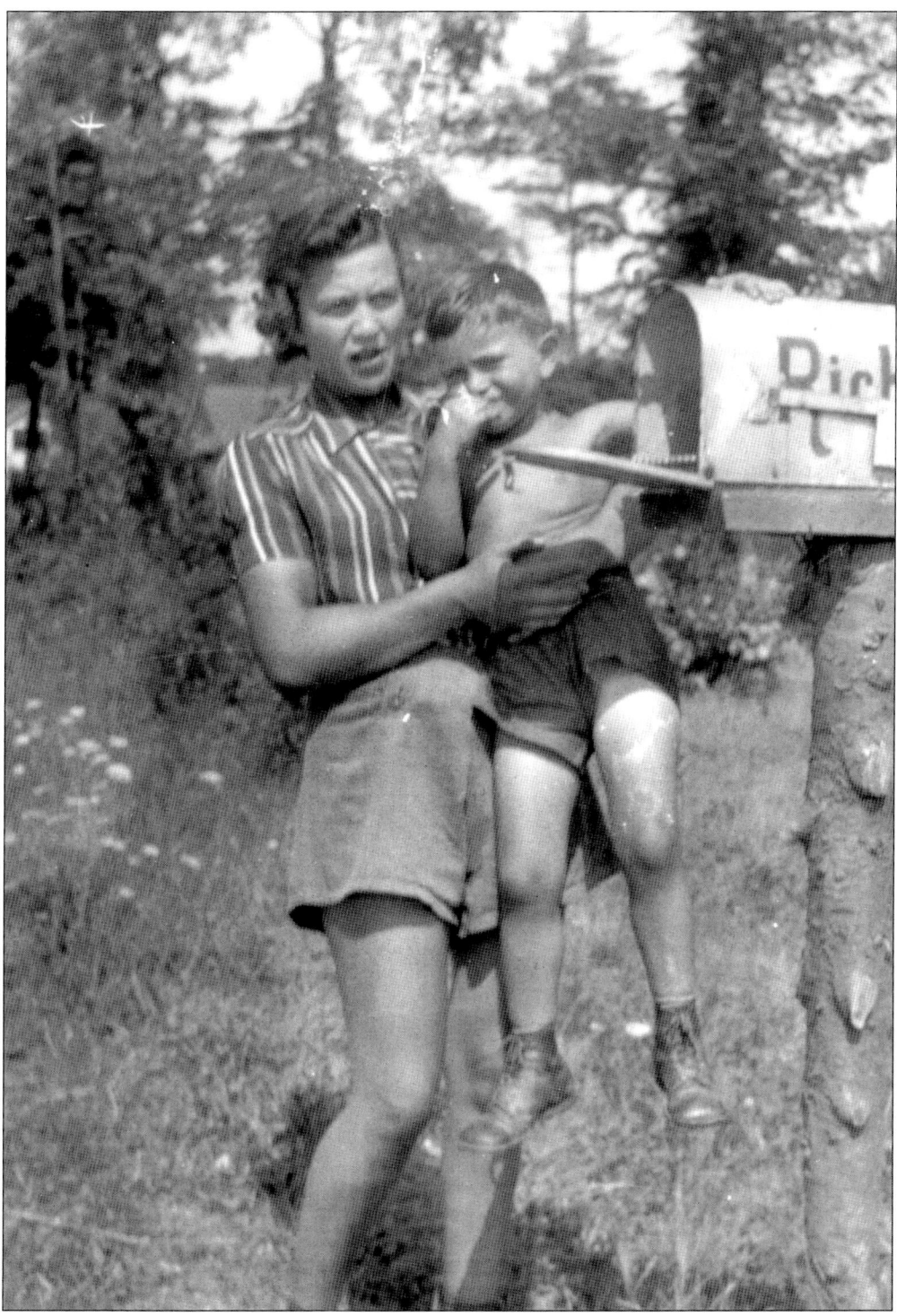

Everyone waited for mail deliveries, which came twice a day in 1941, when this picture was taken. Mailbox snapshots are a very common summertime genre. To many city dwellers, these ordinary, galvanized-iron rural delivery boxes were exotic artifacts that spelled summer.

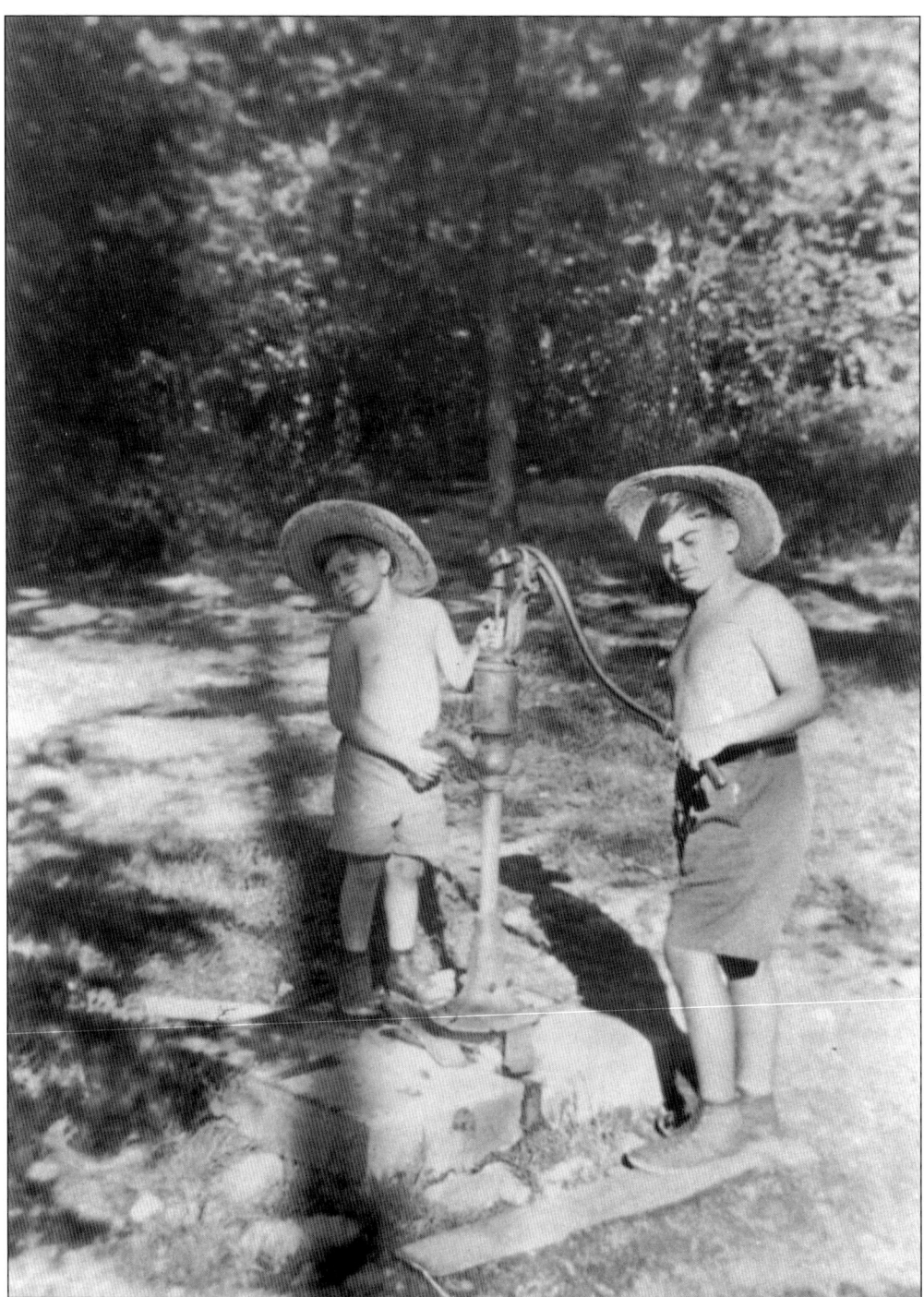
Hand pumps were irresistible to city kids, especially when they were wearing straw hats. In 1943, when this photograph was taken, most bungalow colonies had running water, but many also kept old wells. The water drawn from the wells was cold, delicious, and was often drunk with meals as a replacement for the seltzer of New York City. A favorite competition among children was to see who could pump up the most water in the quickest time.

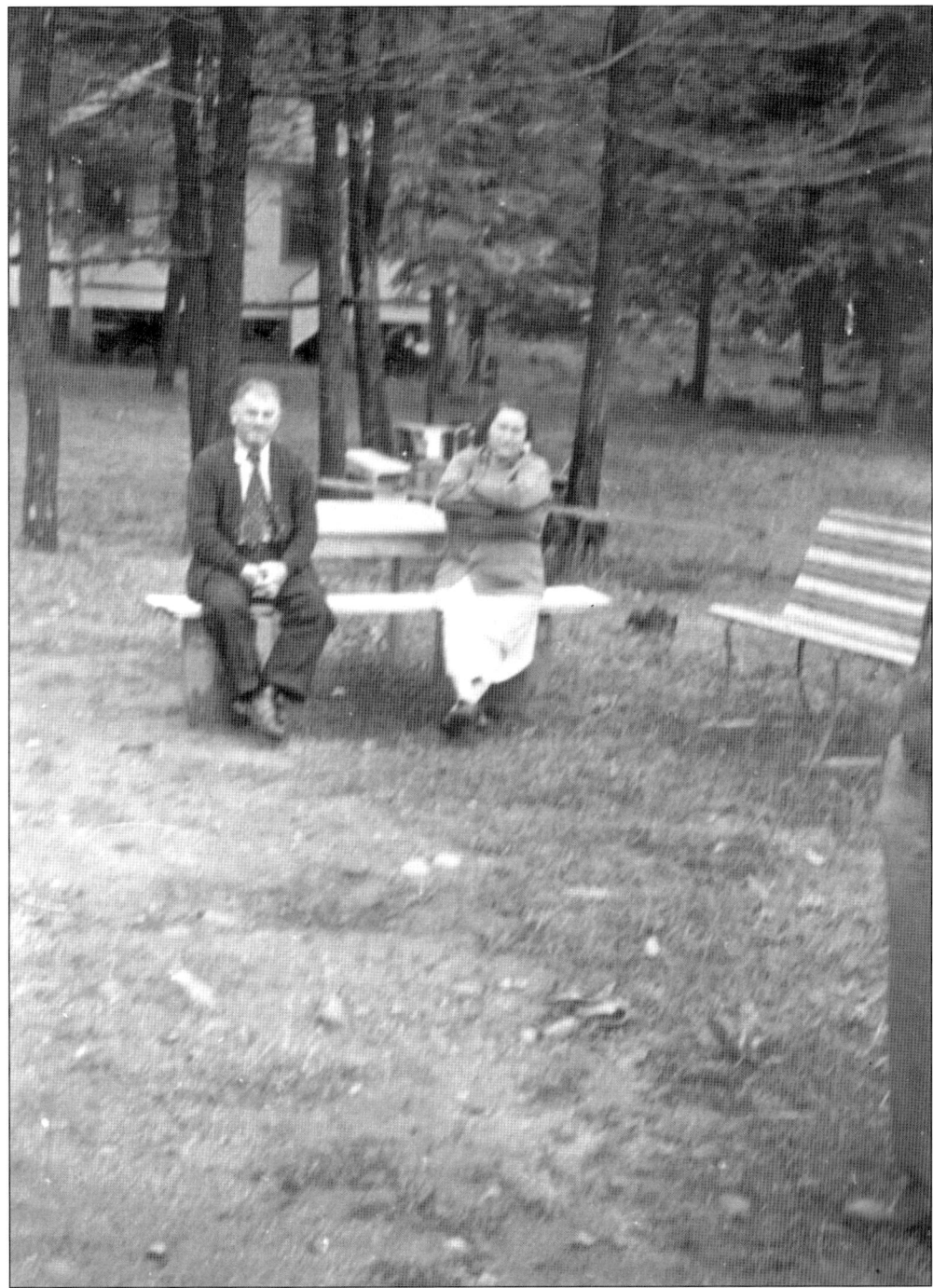

Late August sometimes saw cold snaps—a sharp contrast to the shirtless days of summer. Before the age of power mowers, the lawns at most places were generally rough. Many bungalows were nestled in the trees. These folks sit on a homemade bench typical of the early 1940s.

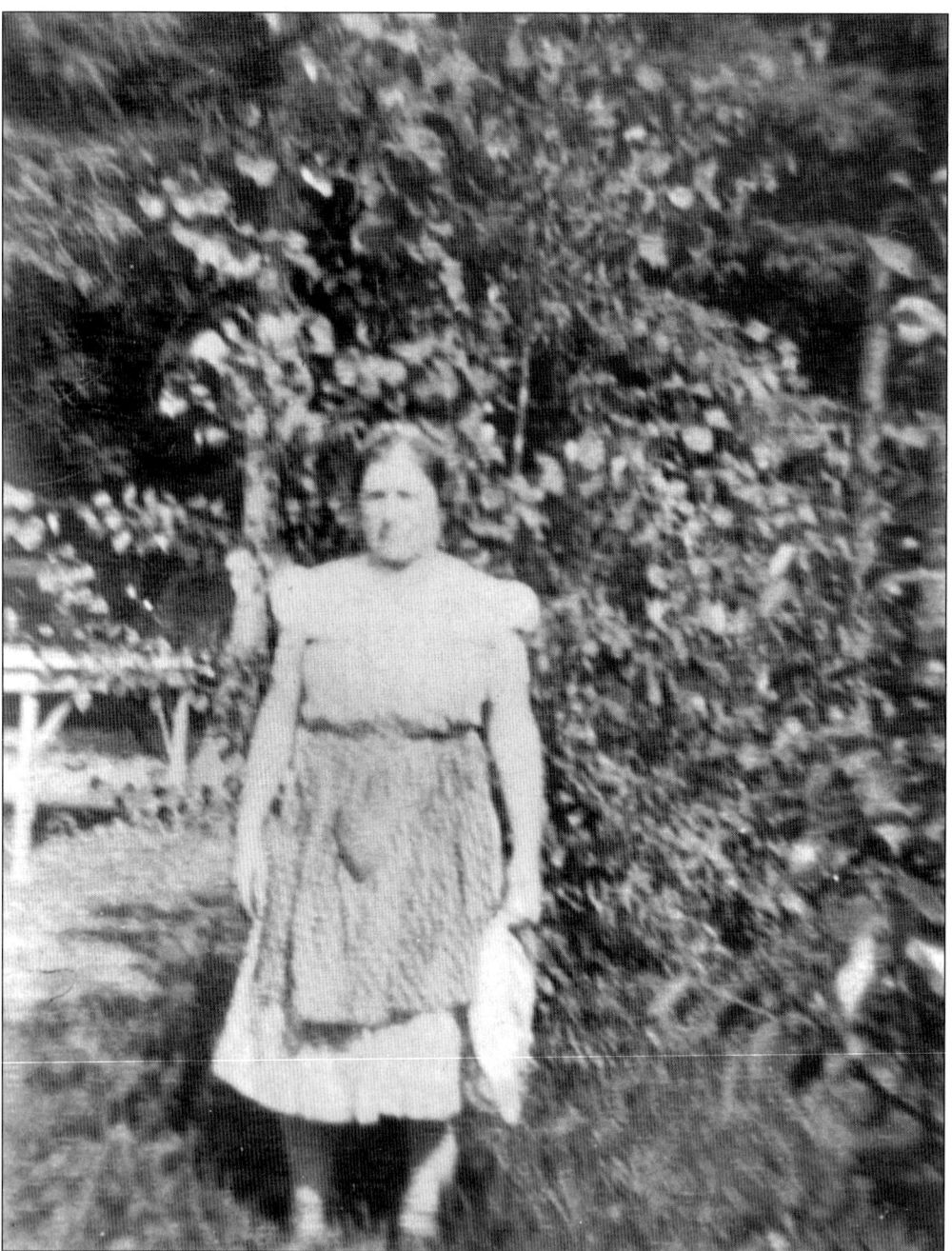

Many bungalow colony owners, like their hotel owner compatriots, were European born. Bayle Richman, who operated a small colony in Woodbourne, was born near Wilna (modern Wilnius) in Lithuania in the 1880s. Her husband was a builder, and she owned a candy store in the Williamsburg neighborhood of Brooklyn until they bought *die plotz,* "their place," in 1936. To her tenants, she was the *farmeka,* "the farmer's wife." She did have a small vegetable garden. Although the quality of this photograph is poor, the image is poignant. In comparing this 1940s picture to the one of Miriam Damico on the next page, you can see what a difference 50 years makes.

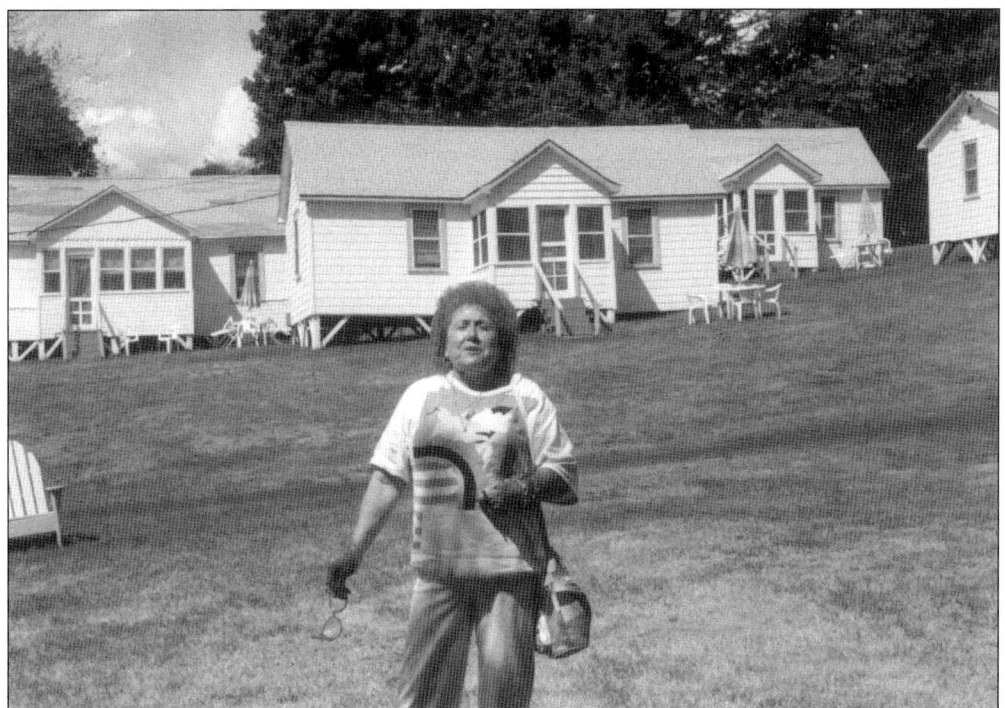

Miriam Damico is the proud owner of the beautifully kept Moonglow Inn in Loch Sheldrake. Her colony offers furnished cottages and duplex apartments. Catering to "snowbirds" (those who winter in Florida but return to the Borscht Belt in the summer), she even provides her guests with bedding, pots, and dishes. Her motel-style units, below, were built about 50 years ago. The corner units, with cross-ventilation, were rented at a premium in the days before air conditioning. The lawn furniture is pressed resin.

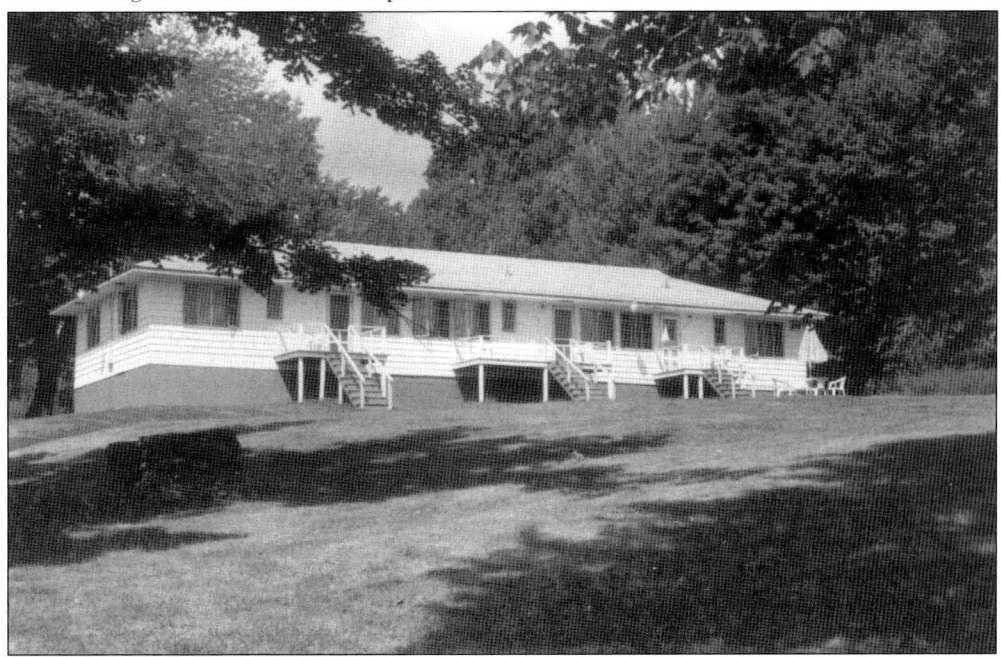

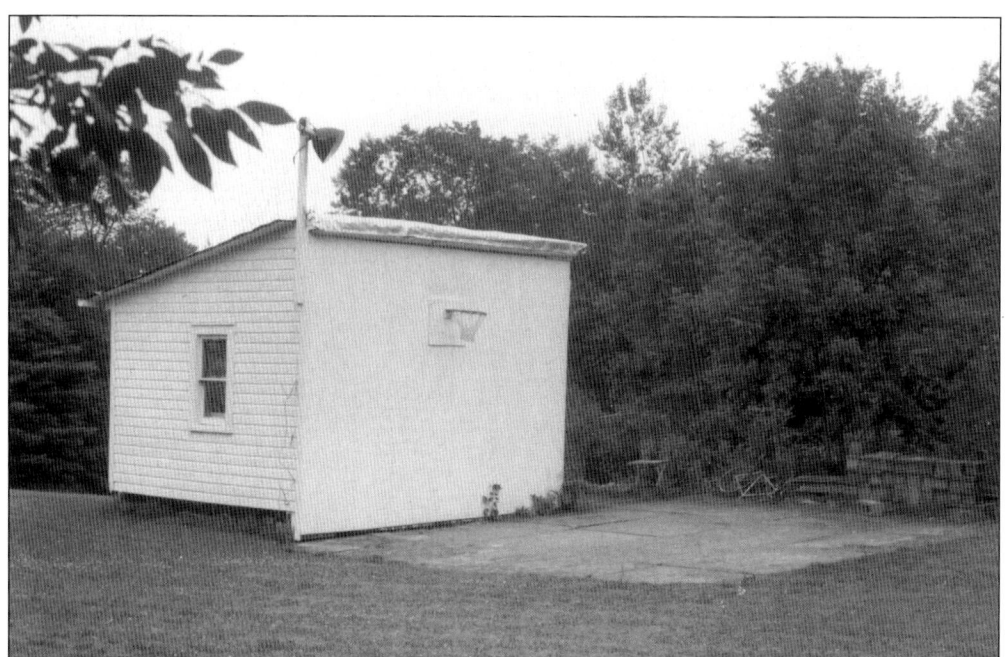

Shown here c. 1950, this bungalow (one wall of which served as a handball court) survives as a remnant of Meyer Furman's large colony. Now used for storage, this strange building on the road to Hasbrouck reflects a time when anything could be rented. The basketball court reflects the interests of the owners in 1993.

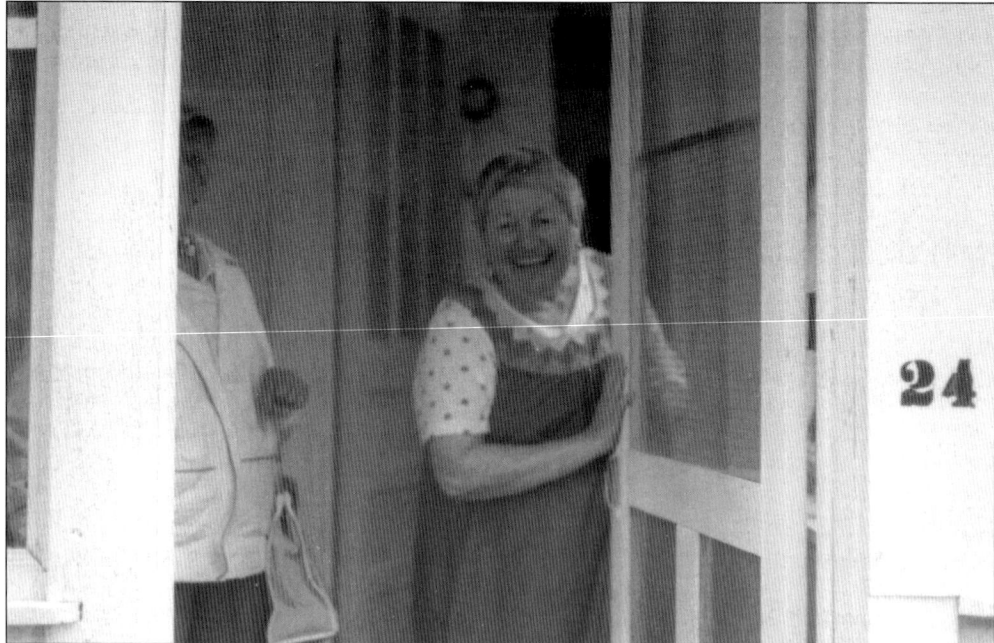

Fran Migden welcomes friends to Bungalow 24 at the Friendship Colony in Greenfield Park in 1993. A longtime resident of Brooklyn, she and her husband, Sid, outlived the colony, which never opened for the 1994 season. They lost their substantial deposit at what had been a premium-quality bungalow colony when a new owner absconded with funds.

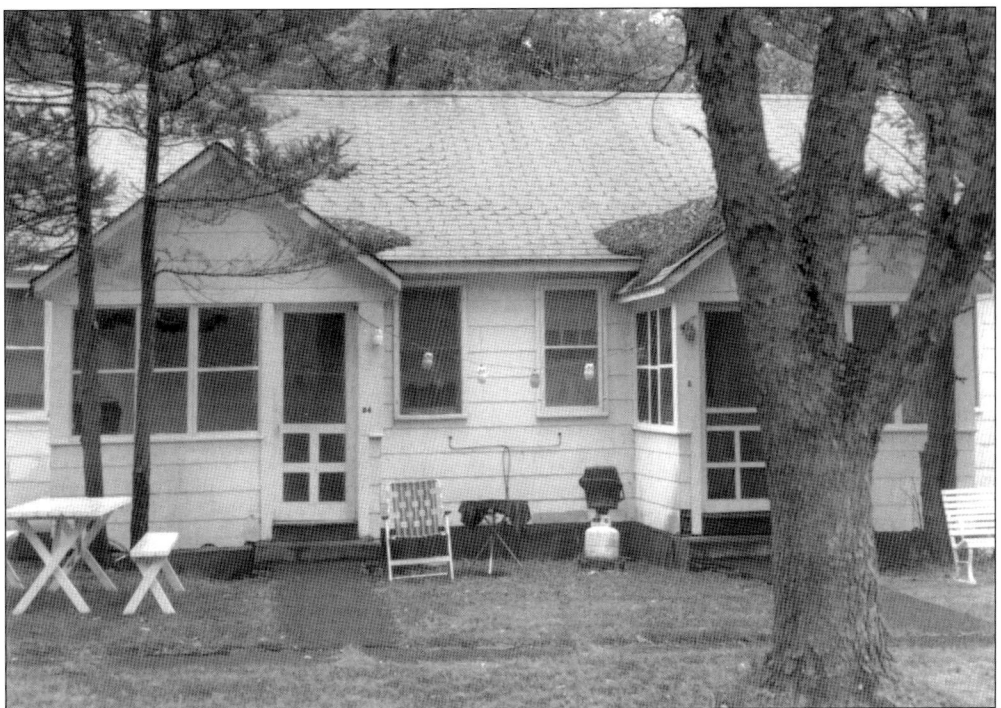

The Friendship Colony, located near Greenfield Park, was owned by the Levinsons, the same family who owned the nearby Tamarack Lodge. The Friendship Colony offered "full hotel privileges," which meant that guests could go to shows and use the Tamarack's athletic facilities and card room. The back sides of the bungalows at the Friendship, like those at most Borscht Belt places, were less appealing than the front sides. Maintenance was often more haphazard. The sheds shown below housed propane tanks.

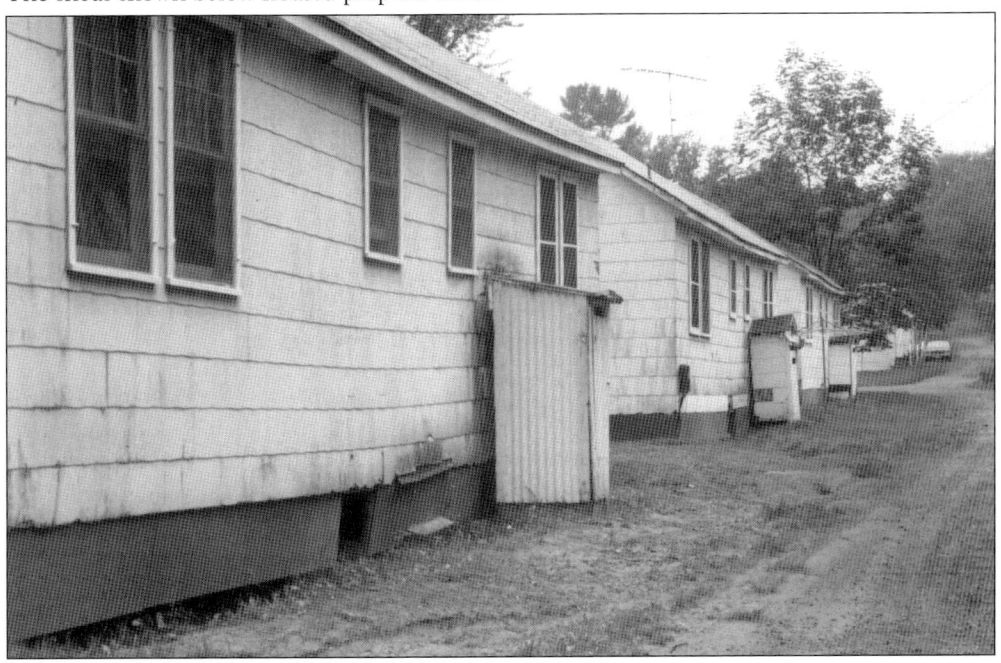

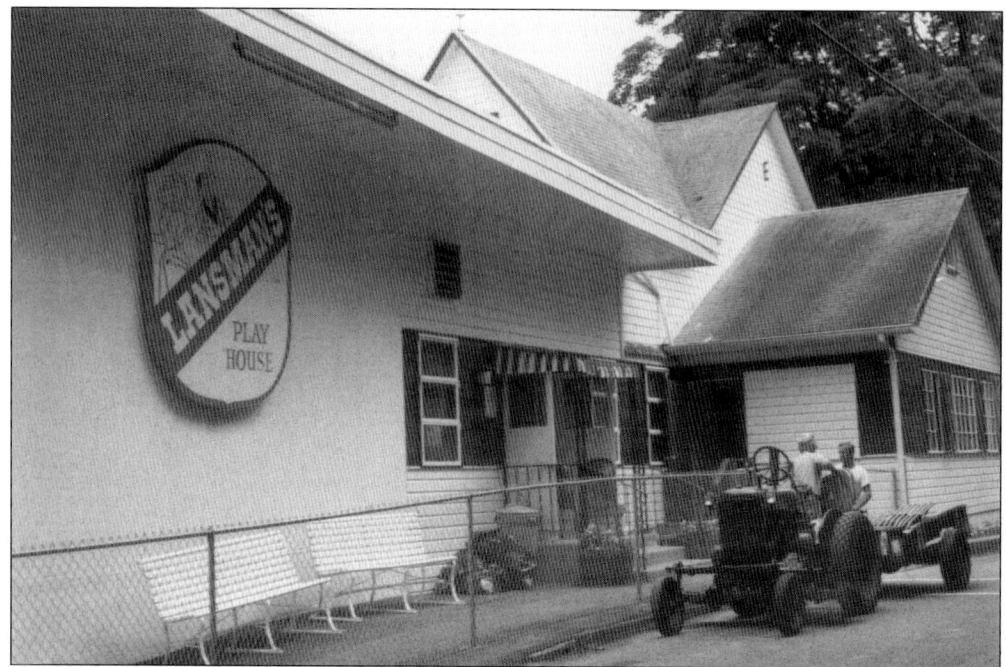

Lansman's Bungalow Colony was one of Sullivan County's largest and finest colonies. It had facilities to match many hotels. In line with changes in the region's resort industry, Lansman's became a co-op. Former rental units were combined and refurbished into summer homes. Today, a professional staff maintains the grounds.

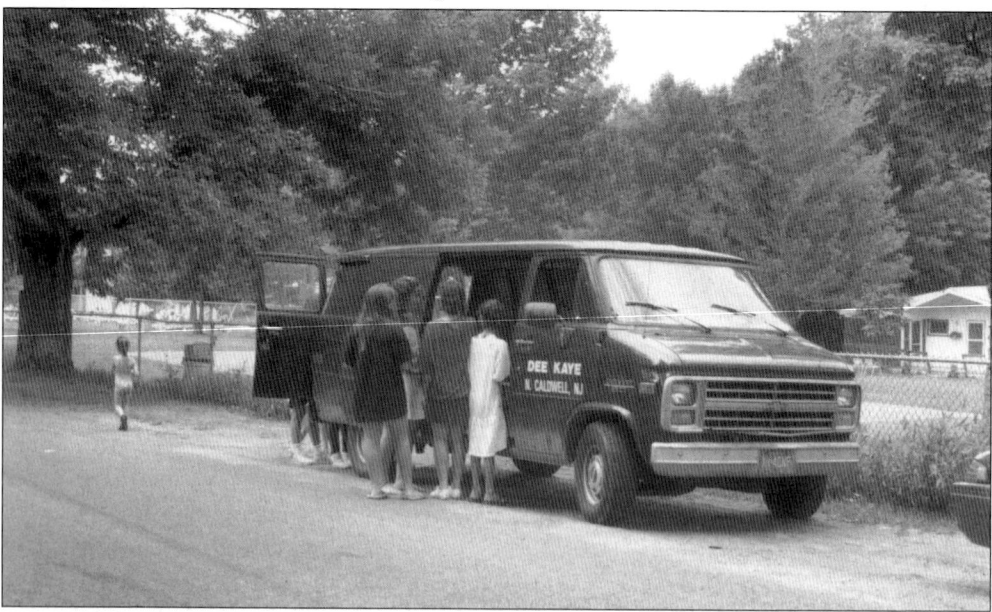

A vendor sells novelty merchandise at Lansman's in 1993. Peddlers of all kinds visited the colonies in their heyday. "Ruby the Knishman" was a legend familiar to thousands. "The Blouseman" was the lover-hero of the 1998 movie about bungalow colony life, *A Walk on the Moon*. Real blouse men, dress men, swimsuit men, or other vendors never looked like actor Viggo Mortensen, a blond Adonis. Most were middle-aged, overweight, and very Semitic.

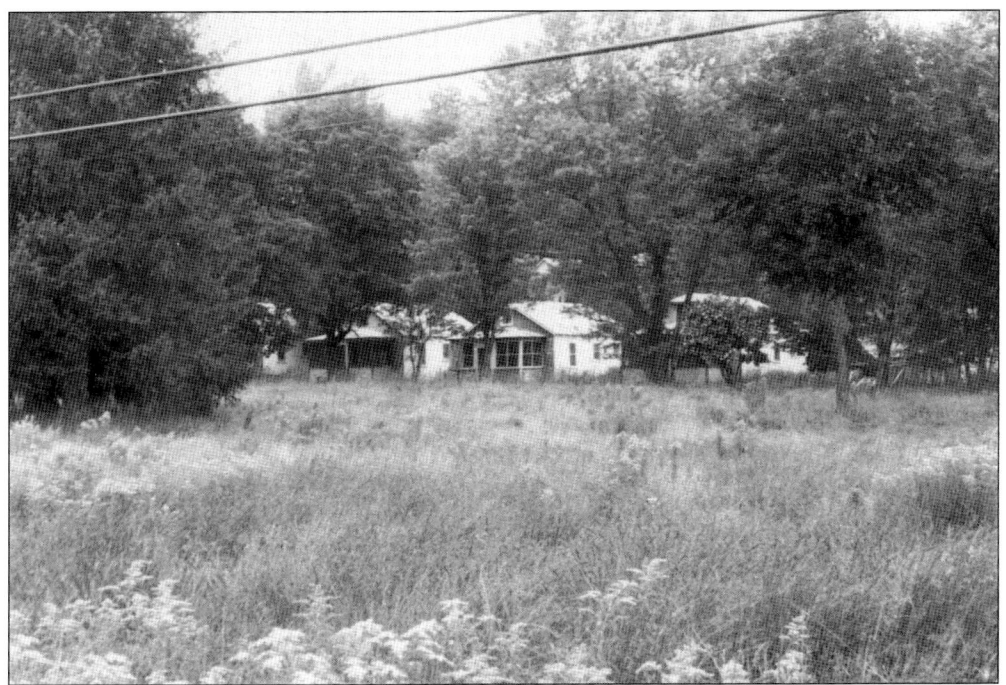

Most bungalow colonies were not as lucky as Lansman's. The Friendship Colony never emerged from its bankruptcy in 1994. Today, colonies survive by renting to a shrinking number of regular guests who winter in Florida. Some colonies rent to recently arrived Russian Jews. The most vibrant segment of the industry caters to the modern Orthodox and the Hasidim, now the bulk of bungalow renters.

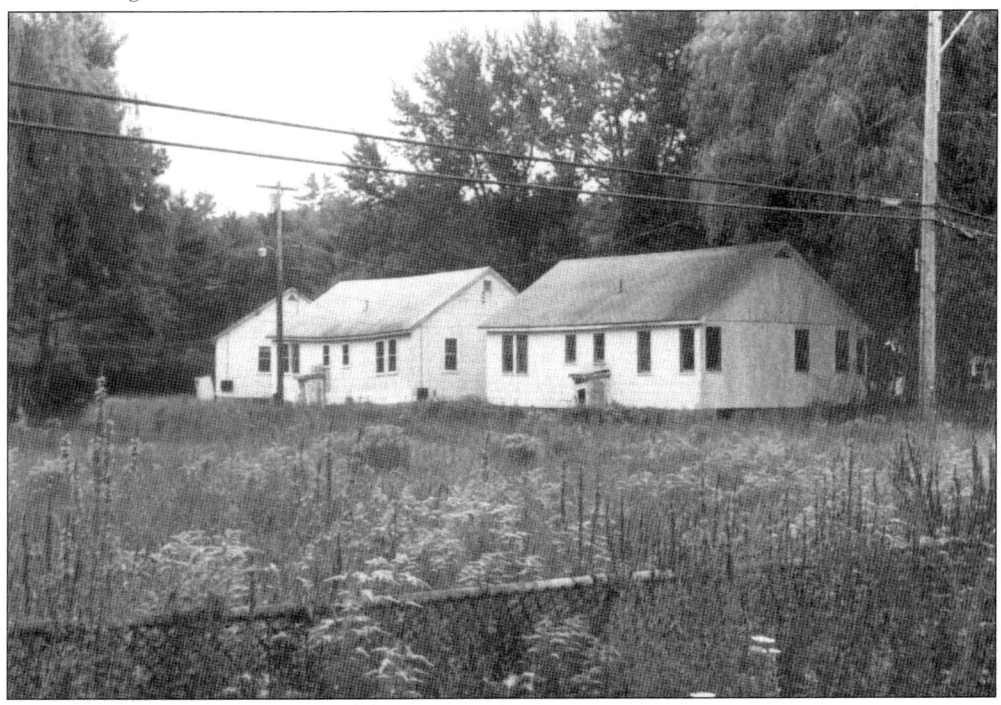

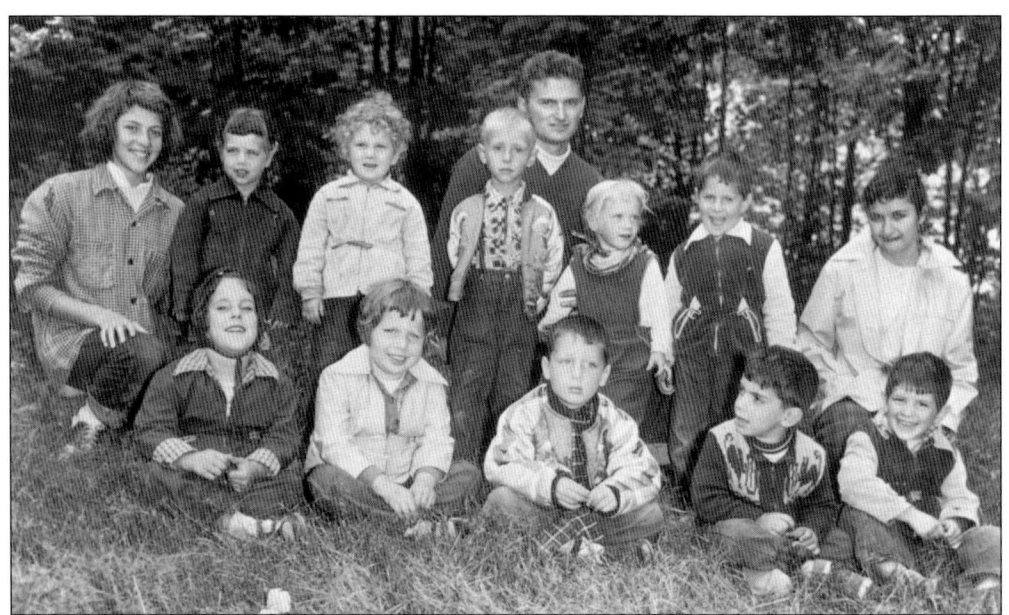

Day camp was a facility copied from hotels. The day camp allowed mothers to have a real vacation, which for many meant lots of time to play mah-jongg and cards. Day camp ran for eight weeks, starting after the Fourth of July, the official start of the summer season. Kids usually attended from 9:00 A.M. to 5:00 P.M. At most places, they walked home for lunch. The cool-weather picture above was taken at Doctor Locker's Bungalow Colony in Mountaindale. The picture below was taken at Kassack's Bungalow Colony in Woodbourne. One camper, Charlotte Feigenbaum, appears in both pictures (standing second from left above; sitting fourth from left below).

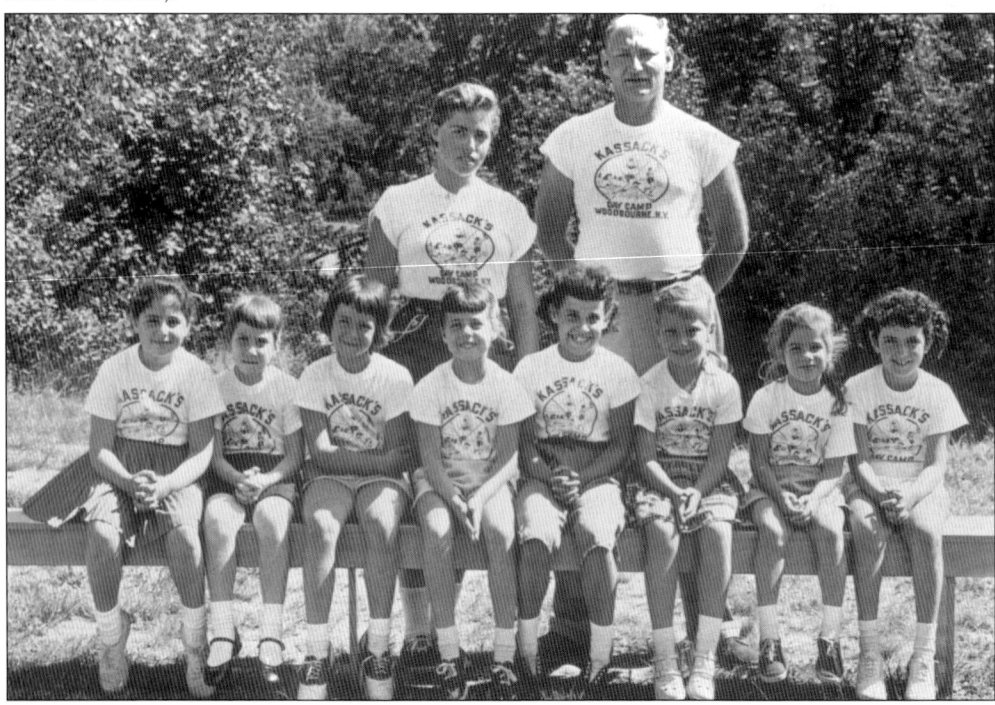

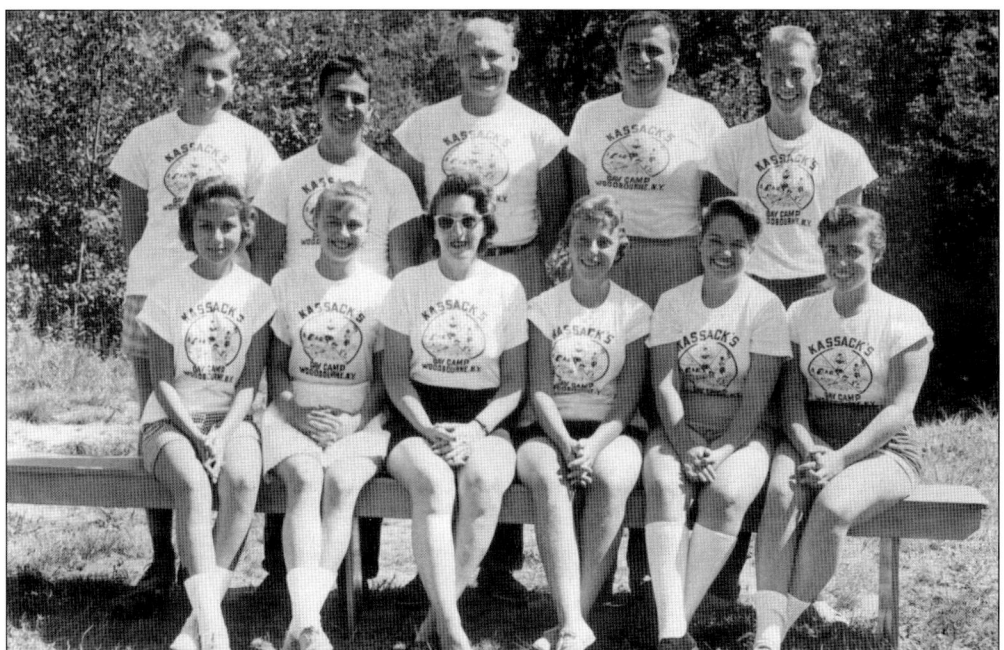

A camp staff was mostly made up of high school students and a few college students. The director (who always posed standing in the middle) and the nursery teacher were the only adults. Many counselors began their careers as campers. Pay was minimal, but many counselors returned for several years. Kassack's Bungalow Colony in Woodbourne had about 75 kids in its camp. Camps needed a minimum of 40 kids to be viable. Some day camps had as many as several hundred campers. Camp teams played softball and punchball games against other bungalow colonies, including Lansman's.

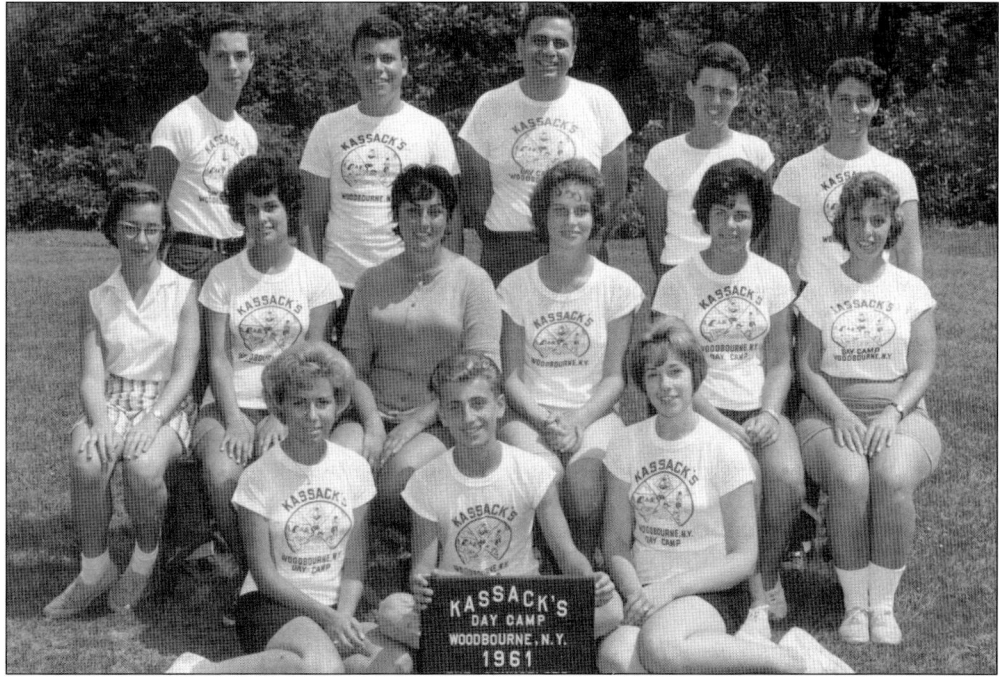

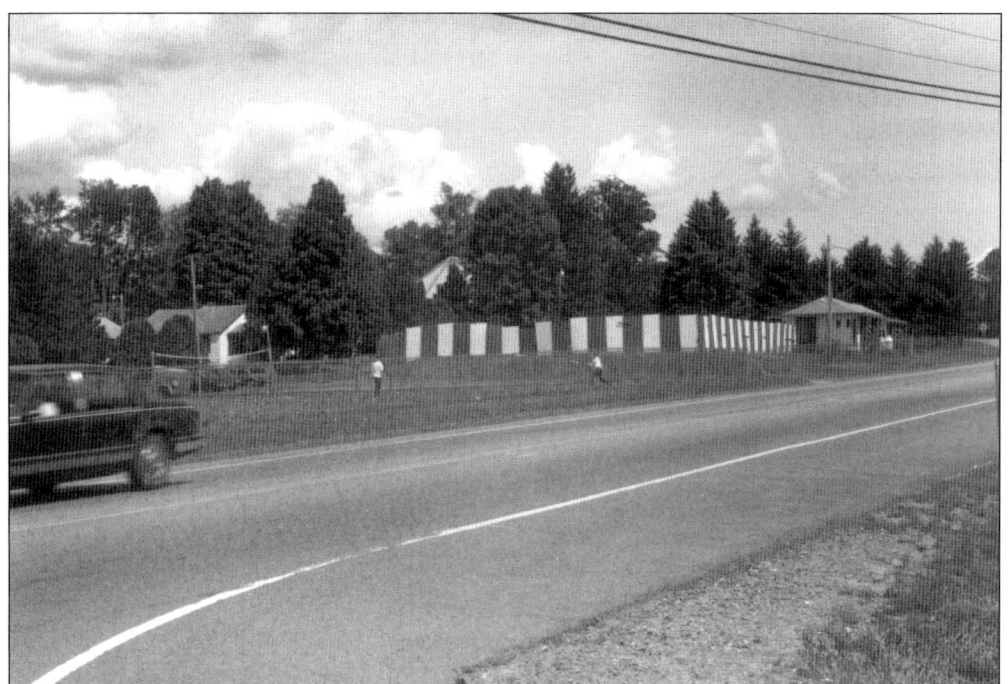

The *mechitza* around this swimming pool delineates this Orthodox colony near Loch Sheldrake, which closed in 1996. Plastic sheets were attached to the chain-link fence surrounding the pool, providing the required modesty for separate-sex swimming. Below, a Hasid looks through the fence surrounding his colony. Toys reveal that there were many children present. The air conditioners are evidence of a new level of comfort expected by bungalow guests. Air conditioning is especially welcomed by the Hasidim, who always wear body-covering clothing.

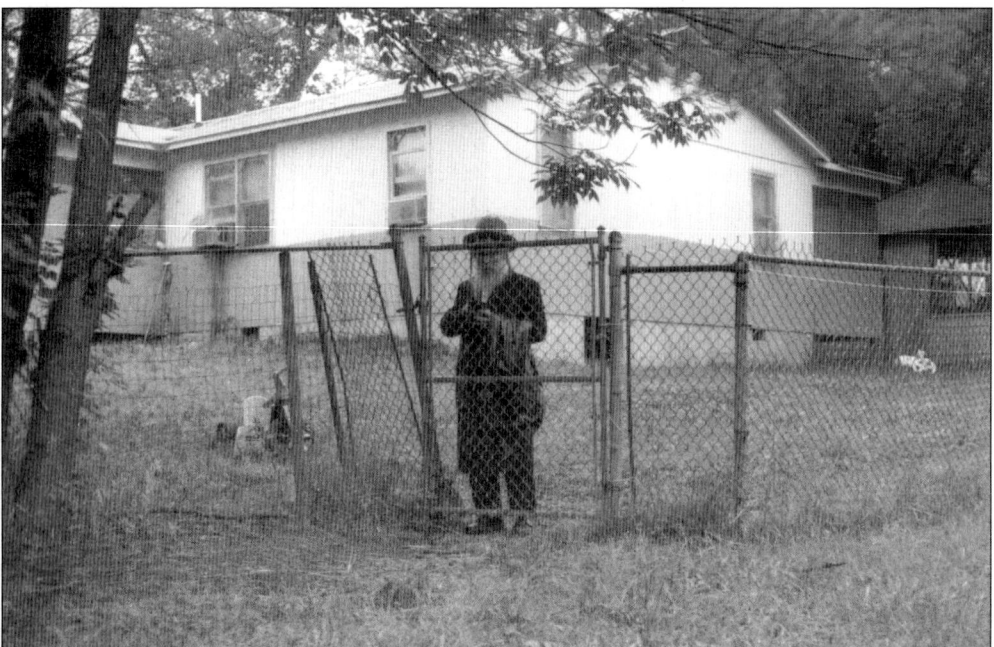

Four

THE HOTEL AGE

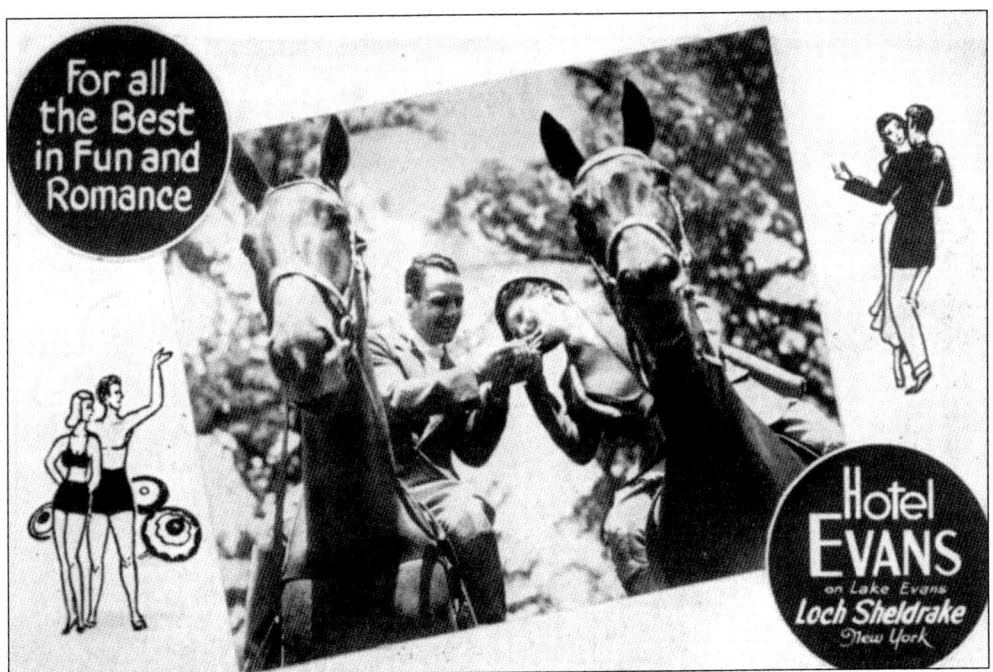

America's Jews were becoming increasingly sophisticated after World War II. Hotel Evans was catering to the new image. This postcard encourages guests to swim, to dance, and (most of all) to go horseback riding. The true gentleman even lights his riding partner's cigarette. The legend on the back of this card promises a "beautiful 5-mile bridle path" and invites guests to "live, laugh, and enjoy the ultimate in vacation happiness."

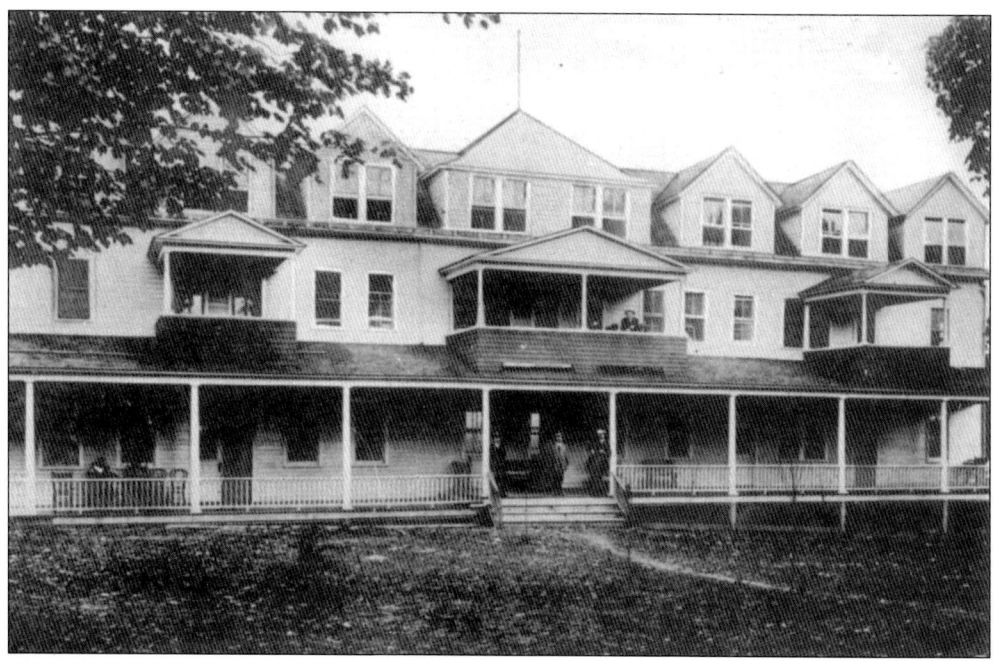

The Morningside House, above, later became the Morningside Hotel. It was located on Morningside Lake between Hurleyville and Loch Sheldrake and is now included in a public park. Like most hotels (including the Lake House), the Morningside was built of stucco-covered wood. It burned to the ground in 1964. The Lake House, below, was a "modern hotel of refinement." A guest in 1947 adds on this card, "Enjoying a good rest. Lots of borscht and sour cream." One wonders if she was staying at the Ritz, the extravagantly named annex.

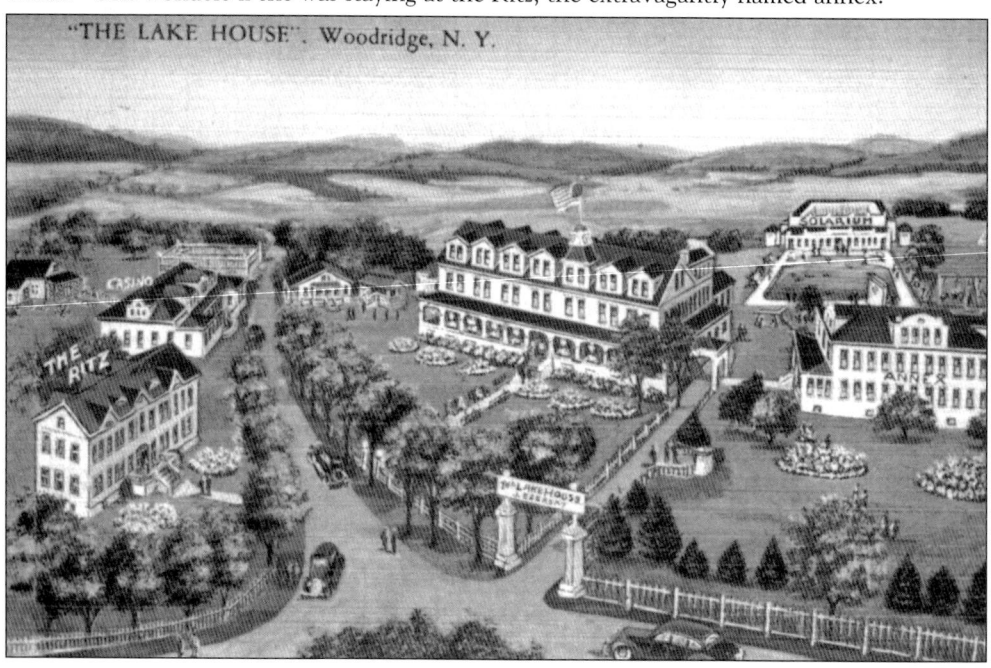

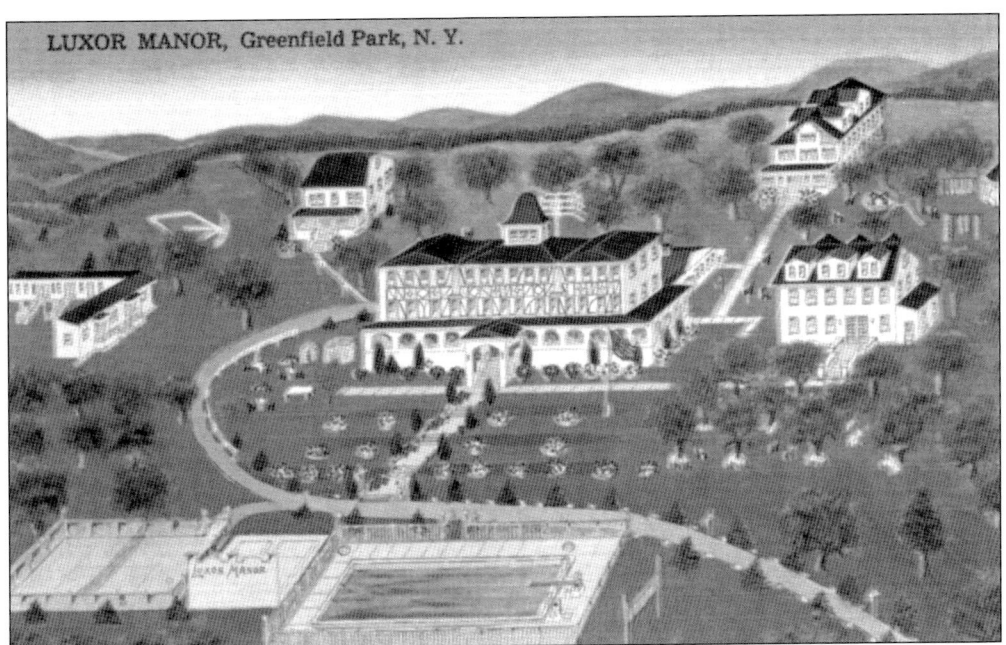

The names Luxor Manor and Hotel Irvington both exude class. After the discovery of King Tutankhamen's tomb in the 1920s, Egyptian motifs and names became all the rage. "Irvington" is an expression of English refinement. Both were kosher, but with different emphases. The obverse of the postcard above reads, "On the mountain top—elevation 1800 feet . . . Kashruth and Sabbath strictly observed." On the postcard below, the Irvington (run by the Charlow family) is described as a "hotel of refinement" and guests are simply reminded of dietary laws.

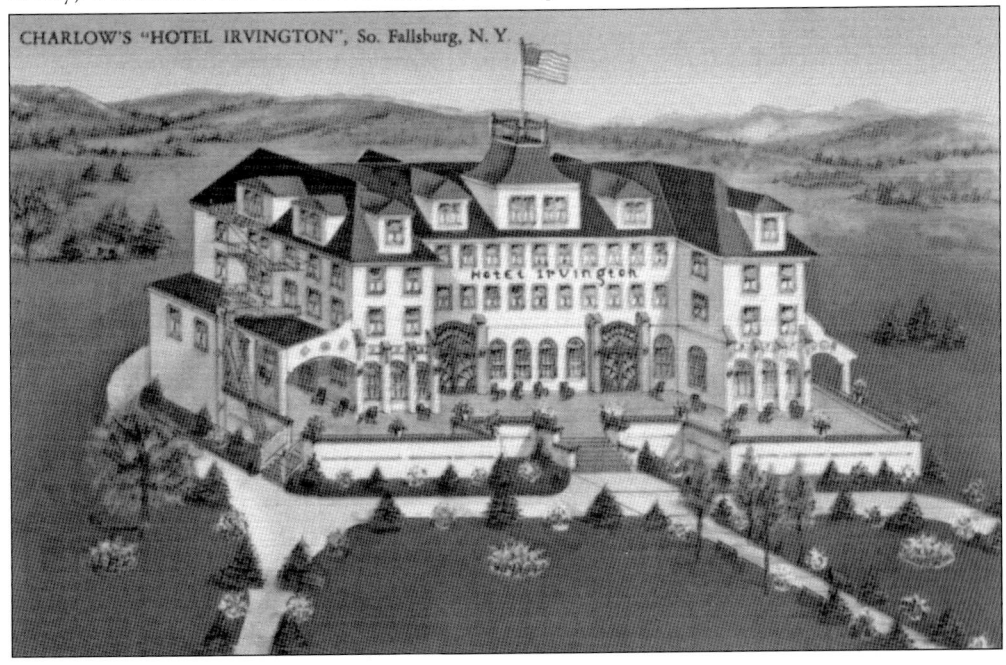

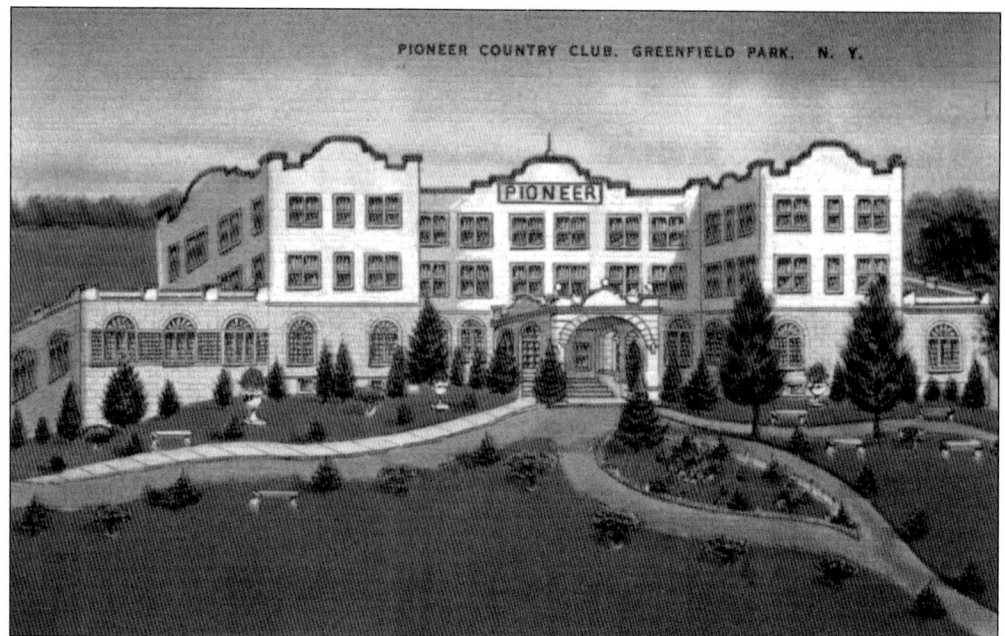

Two of the most popular architectural styles for Sullivan County hotels in the 1920s and 1930s were the vaguely Spanish Colonial style of the Pioneer Country Club and the English Tudor style of the Windsor Hotel. The card above describes the Pioneer as "modern and up-to-date" while advising guests, "Please use Mountaindale Bus and Mountaindale Train." The dietary laws at the Pioneer were "strictly observed." The more liberal Windsor promised "interesting vacation days," noting, "The faultless table settings and service is matched by the superb meals. The cuisine is under the supervision of the ownership-management."

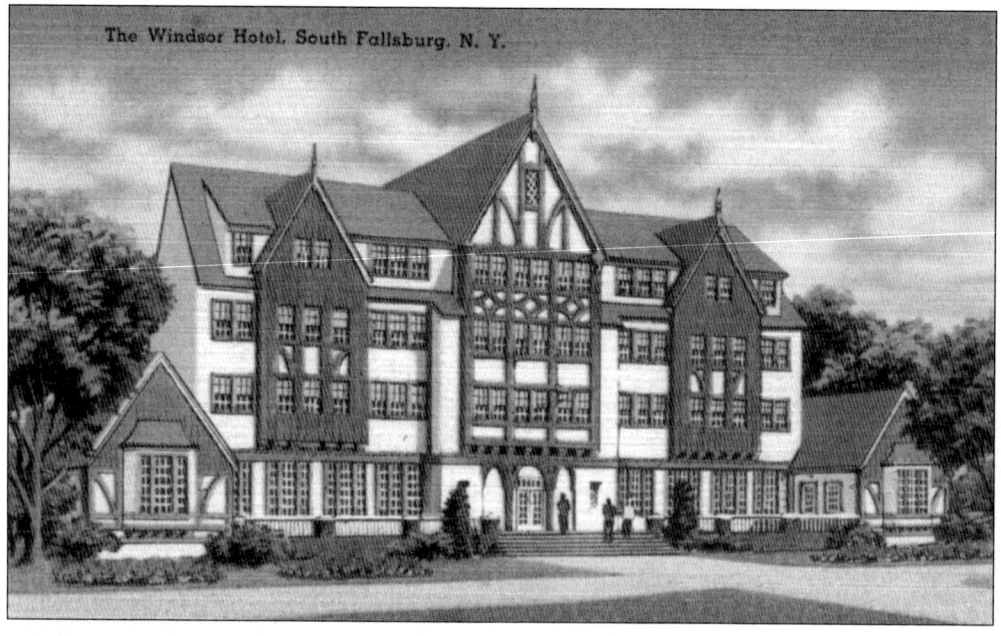

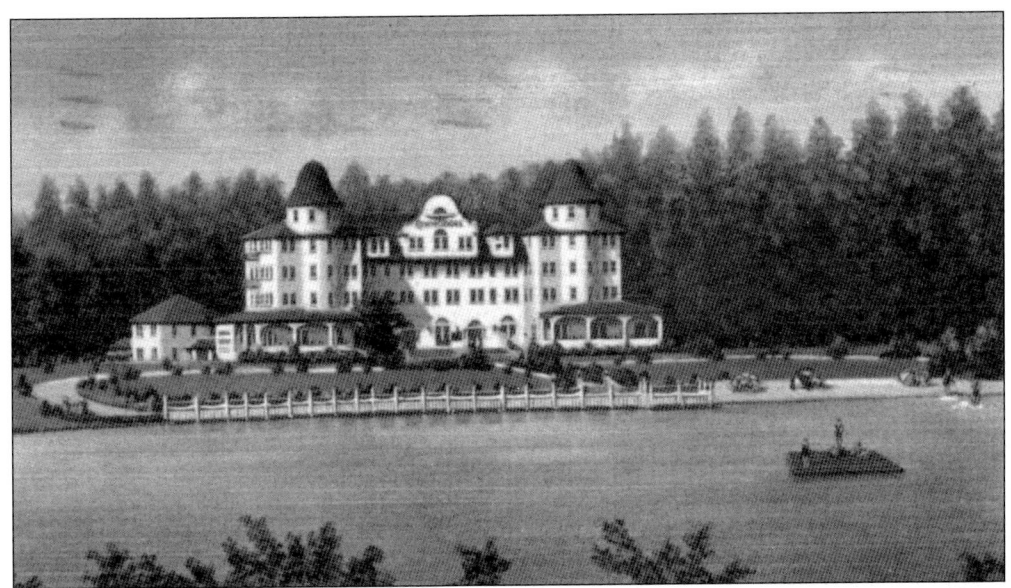

Swan Lake was originally named Stevensville after the operators of the local tannery. About 1895, Dr. Alden S. Swan started buying real estate in the area, and the town was subsequently renamed for him. Many of the town's hotels suffered fires. The Commodore, which billed itself as a "haven for young folks," caught fire in June 1932. Early discovery and prompt work by Swan Lake and Liberty firemen saved the hotel. On the postcard above, guest Julia writes to Naomi in 1958, "They keep you up most of the night. We are having a nice time." The Swan Lake Hotel, which featured a sensational social hall, was not as lucky as the Commodore was. In 1954, during the installation of an elevator, "a fire broke out on the first floor and quickly roared up the open elevator shaft [and] the hotel was soon a smoldering ruin." —Manville Wakfield in *To the Mountains by Train*.

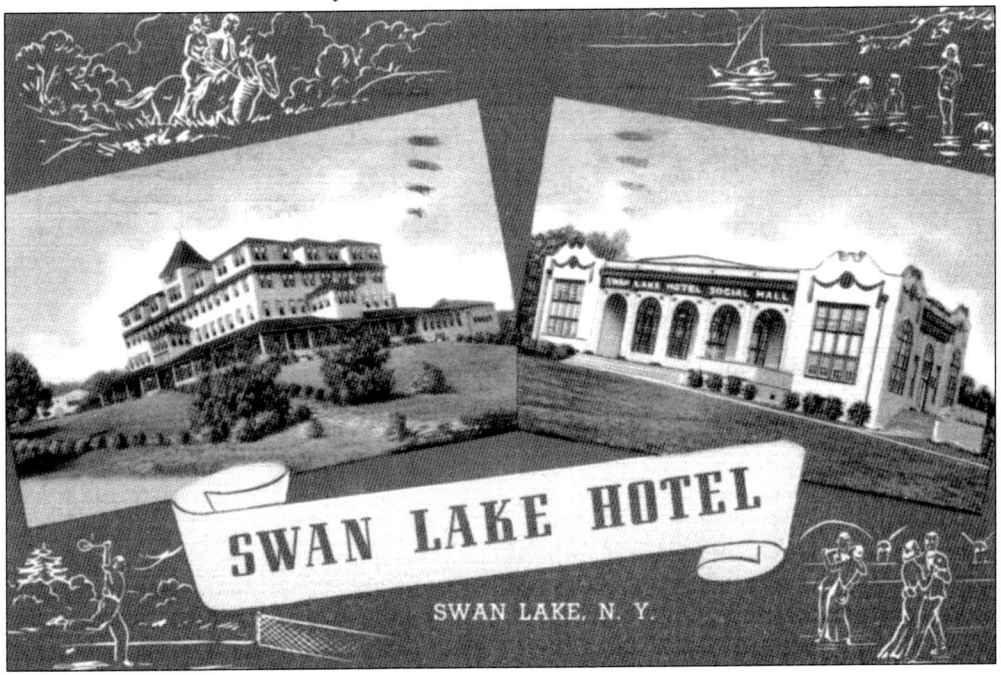

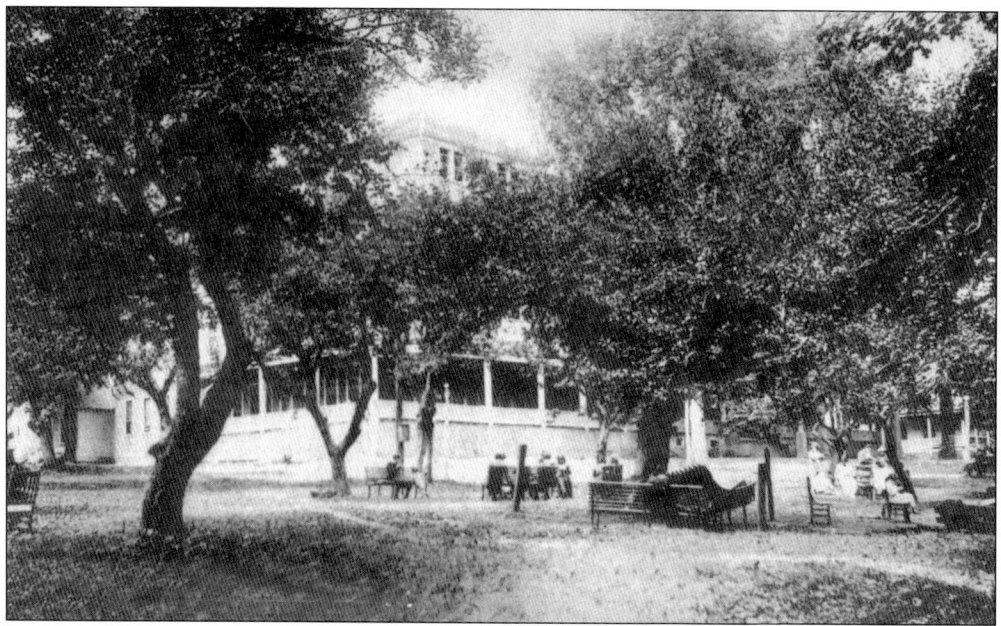

The Hotel Ambassador, along the Neversink River near South Fallsburg, was transformed from a sleepy house into one of the most vibrant hotels in Sullivan County. Its nondescript main building was remodeled into a grand Mission-style structure, and eventually the hotel would have the first real nightclub in the Borscht Belt. Paula, writing to her friend Edna on the postcard below, is a copywriter's dream: "I am having a wonderful time. Tonight we are having a midnight supper. The room I marked is the one I am staying in. I got real dark. We have so many well known stars. We had a basketball game Tuesday night." Here was the hotel owner's ideal—a satisfied customer who loved the food and the entertainment.

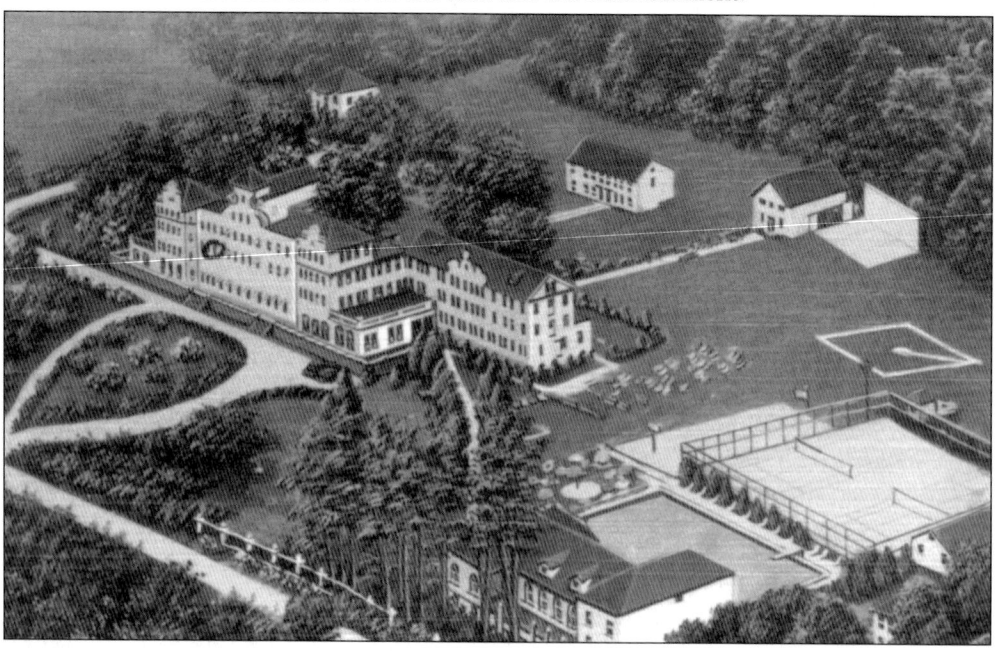

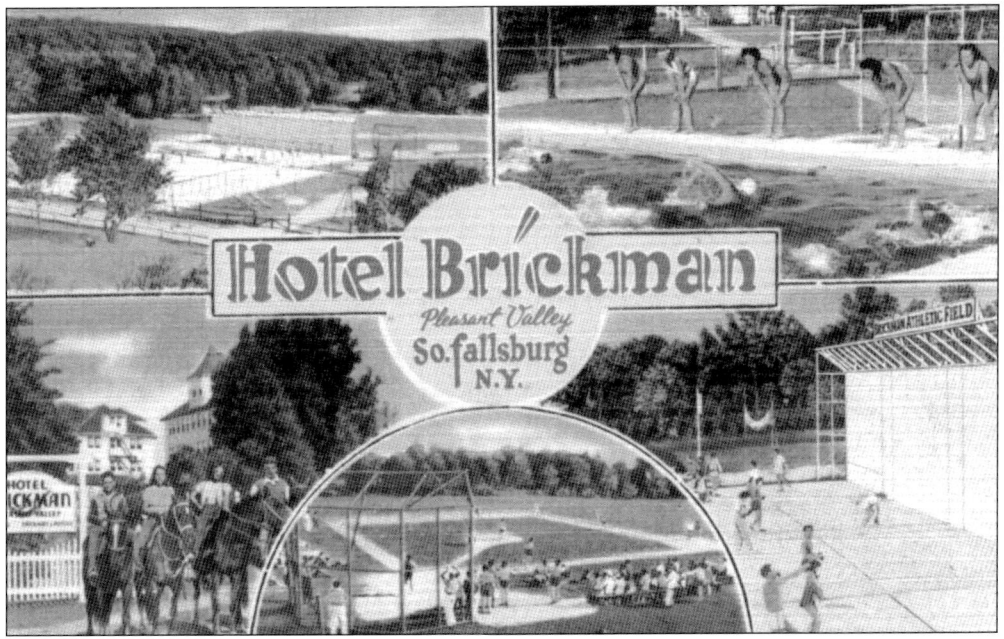

The Hotel Brickman was the Pleasant Valley Farm when it was bought by the children of Pa Brickman. Under the Posner family it was developed into a major resort that featured all of the activities you would expect, including a handball court, swimming pool, tennis courts, baseball diamond, and riding stable. The main house was Mission style. After World War II, the hotel was remodeled to reflect the International style. Trying to attract a suburban crowd, the hotel constructed its Villas-on-the-Green, promoted as "a different concept in resort living . . . Modern Comfort in a charming rustic environment." The Brickman is now part of an ashram, a Buddhist center that counts many Jewish-born followers.

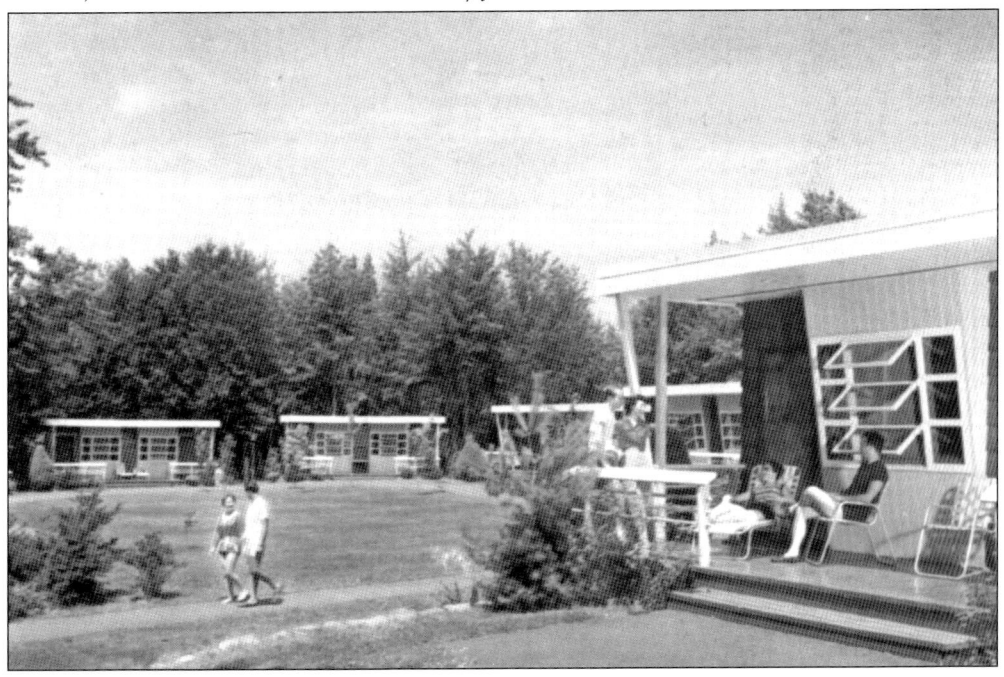

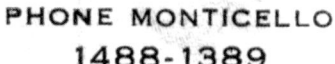

KIAMESHA FAIRMOUNT

PHONE MONTICELLO
1488-1389

PRESTUP & KREISBERG

KIAMESHA LAKE, N. Y.

Business cards were essential for Sullivan County resort owners. Active businesspeople and their families distributed the postcards everywhere they went. It was a cheap form of advertising. The cards reflect the fact that many of the hotels were run by partners—often in rapidly shifting alliances. The more solid the business, the more stable the partnerships tended to be. The card below is especially interesting because it also lists a winter resort. Many resort owners had a second hotel. Lakewood, New Jersey, was a popular site. It was located near New York City, but the temperature was often about 10 degrees warmer than in the metropolis. Other owners, such as the Levinsons of Tamarack Lodge, owned hotels in Miami Beach, Florida.

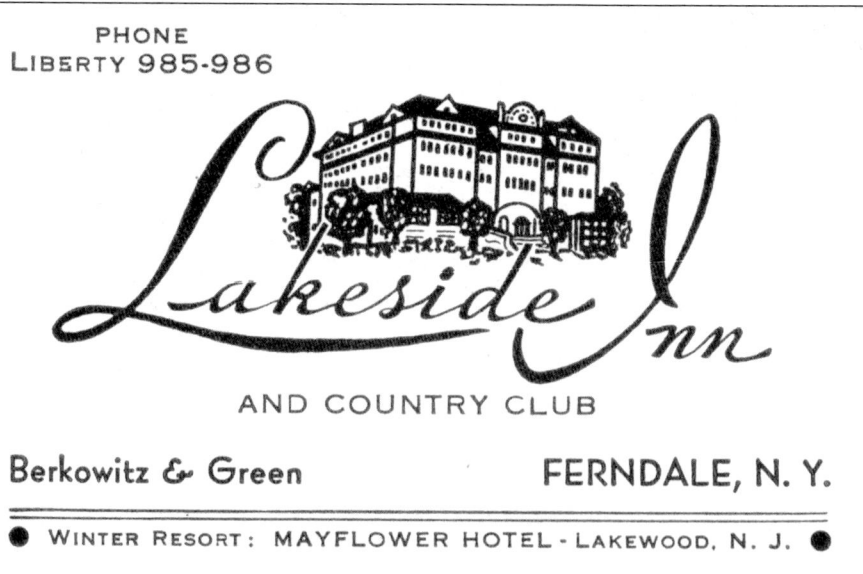

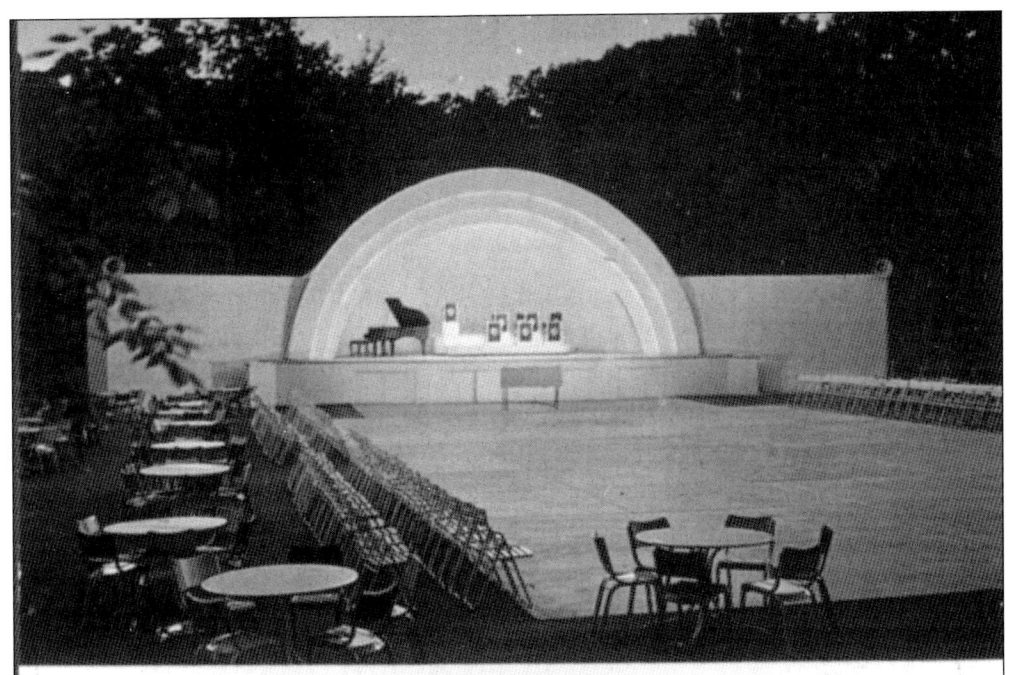

Famous Starlite Theatre at Dusk

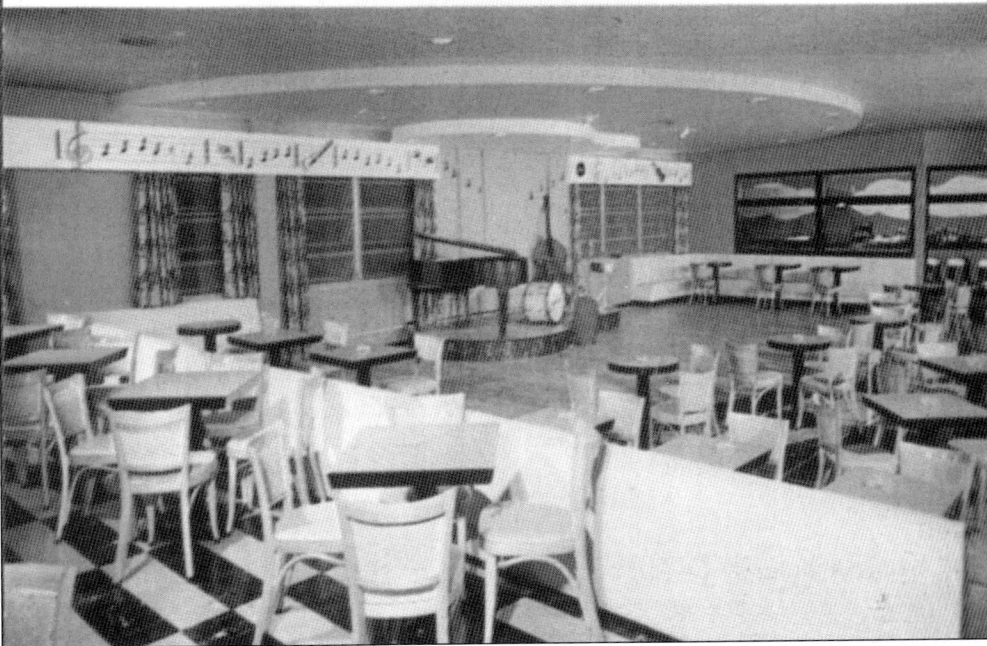

The Sha-wan-ga Lodge, near Wurtsboro, was one of the first large Christian Sullivan County resorts to be purchased by Jews. Sha-wan-ga became a lively place with a racy reputation. People often laughingly called it "Schvenga Lodge," a play on the Yiddish word for "pregnant." It had great facilities. The back of this postcard advertises, "The Starlite Theatre, Melodee Room, and Playhouse make a unique center for every type of show for any kind of weather, for any size crowd." The Starlight Theatre was clearly influenced by the Hollywood Bowl.

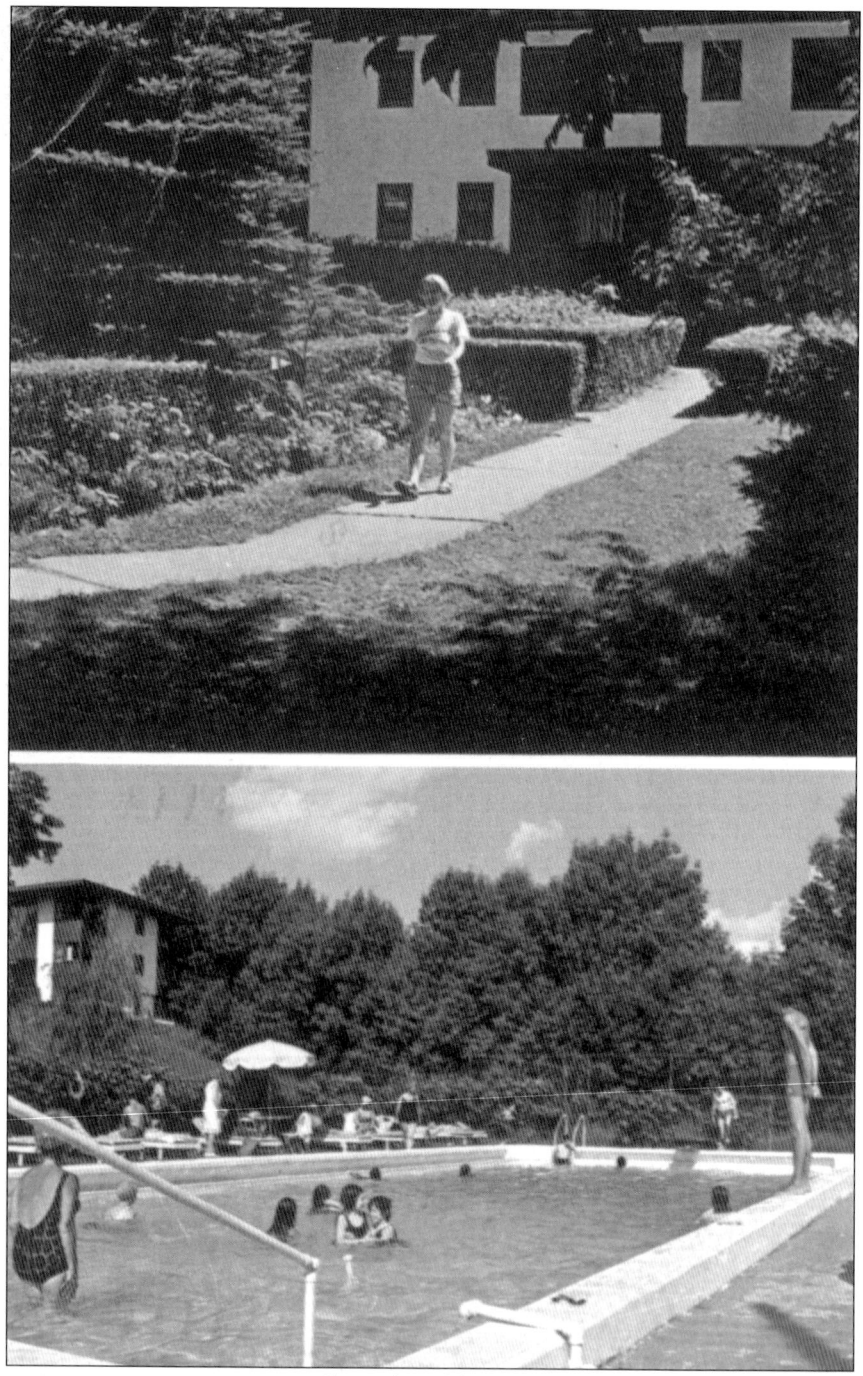

A vegetarian movement among intellectual and health-conscious Jews can be traced to the early 1900s. For many, a vegetarian place was essentially kosher, without making a fuss about the issue. There were several vegetarian hotels in the mountains. Fannie Shaffer's was the best known. Paula writes on this 1978 postcard, "This place is different from conventional hotels. 99% Yiddish. No meat, no fish. Health oriented. Lots of activities. Swimming pool, arts and crafts, sing-a-long, Hebrew-Yiddish, etc."

RATES AND ACCOMMODATIONS

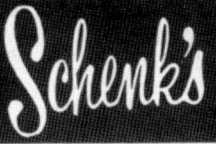 **Schenk's** HOTEL

Direct Wire from N. Y. C. PE 6-9915 Tel. (914) 434-6200

PASSOVER - 1970

MONDAY, APRIL 20th to TUESDAY, APRIL 28th
FIRST SEDER - MONDAY, APRIL 20th
Rates quoted are for EIGHT FULL DAYS per person - two in room

ROOMS WITH BATH OR SHOWER NEARBY
- Colonial $100.00
- Maple or Pines or Virginian 110.00
- Colonial (New Wing) 115.00
- Main Building - (Elevator) 120.00

ROOMS WITH SEMI-PRIVATE BATH OR SHOWER
- Colonial or Ritz or Virginian 120.00
- Texan or Colonial (New Wing) 130.00
- Main Building - (Elevator) 135.00

ROOMS WITH PRIVATE SHOWER
- Spruce or Floridian Terrace 135.00
- Hollywood or Colonial 140.00
- Main Building - (Elevator) 150.00

ROOMS WITH PRIVATE BATH & SHOWER - DE-LUXE
- Californian Terrace 145.00
- Californian 155.00

ROOMS WITH PRIVATE BATH & SHOWER - DE-LUXE - (TELEVISION)
- Colonial or Floridian 160.00
- Californian Terrace 160.00
- Californian - (New Wing or New Yorker) 165.00

CHILDREN'S RATES (in same room with parents)
- Eating in Children's Dining Room $60.00, $65.00, $70.00, $75.00
- Eating in Adult Dining Room $70.00, $75.00, $80.00, $85.00

The third occupant in the room is charged the minimum rate.
Single rooms are available in the Colonial only (bathroom nearby) $125.00
Special low rate for extra days .... $12.00 - $14.00 & $16.00 per day, per person

---

KINDLY PRINT   DETACH HERE AND MAIL

PLEASE MAKE RESERVATIONS FOR

Date _____

Name _____

Address _____ City _____ Tel.: _____

How many in Party? ____ Ladies ____ Gentlemen ____ Couples ____

Children ____ Infants Dining Room ____ Junior Dining Room ____ Main Dining Room ____

Accommodations Desired? 1st Choice ____ Rate ____
                         2nd Choice ____ Rate ____

Arrival Date _____ Departure Date _____

$10.00 Deposit per person required to confirm Reservation
All Reservations are subject to Confirmation

What did it cost to go to a Sullivan County hotel? Most prices were firmly directed toward the middle classes. Traditionally, the most expensive time of the year was the Passover holidays. Even nonkosher hotels, such as the Nevele in Ellenville, became kosher for Passover. This 1970 rate sheet is a testament to the price levels of "the golden age" and the inflation rate we have experienced since.

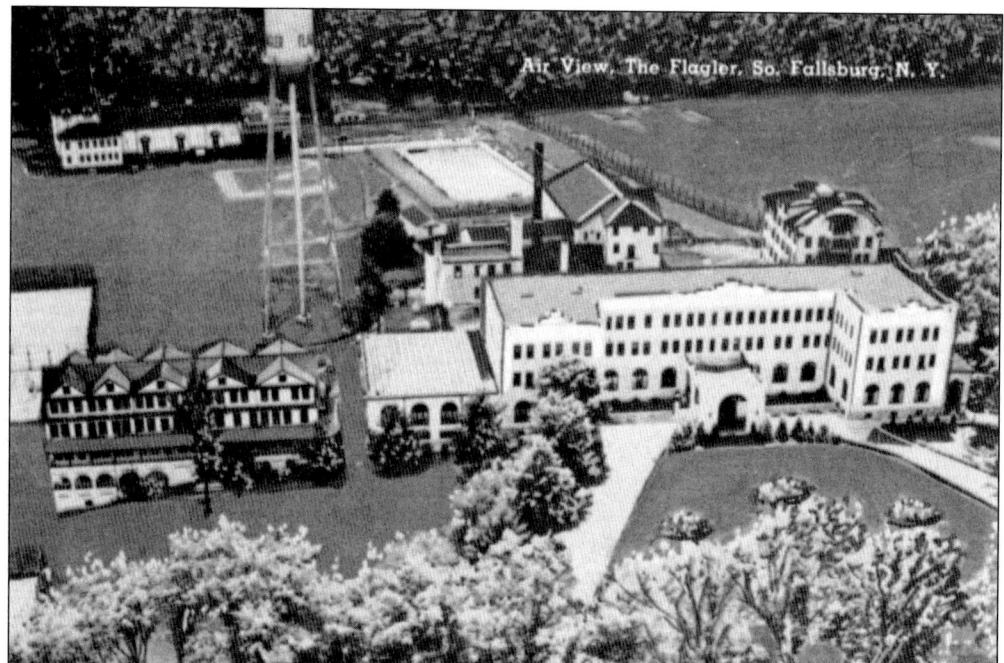

The Flagler was the first great Borscht Belt resort. It started as a modest Christian house, built by Carrie Flagler Angel and named for her father, Nicholas Flagler, a partner in the tannery at nearby Old Falls. Asias Fleisher and Philip Morgenstern purchased the 35-room Flagler House in 1908. The two partners did nothing to dissuade people from thinking that the hotel was really named for (and founded by) Standard Oil partner and Palm Beach pioneer Henry Morrison Flagler. Fleisher and Morgenstern turned their place into a resort that boasted not only running water but also the first in-room telephones in the Catskills. Its 1,500-seat theater was renowned. For several years, future playwright Moss Hart was its social director. The now defunct Flagler was the Borscht Belt's first year-round resort.

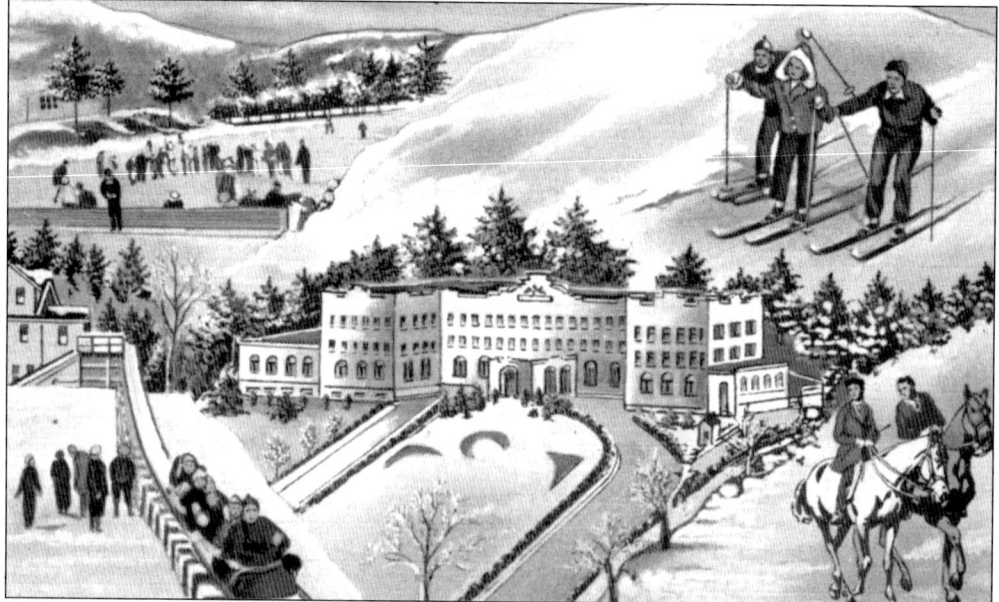

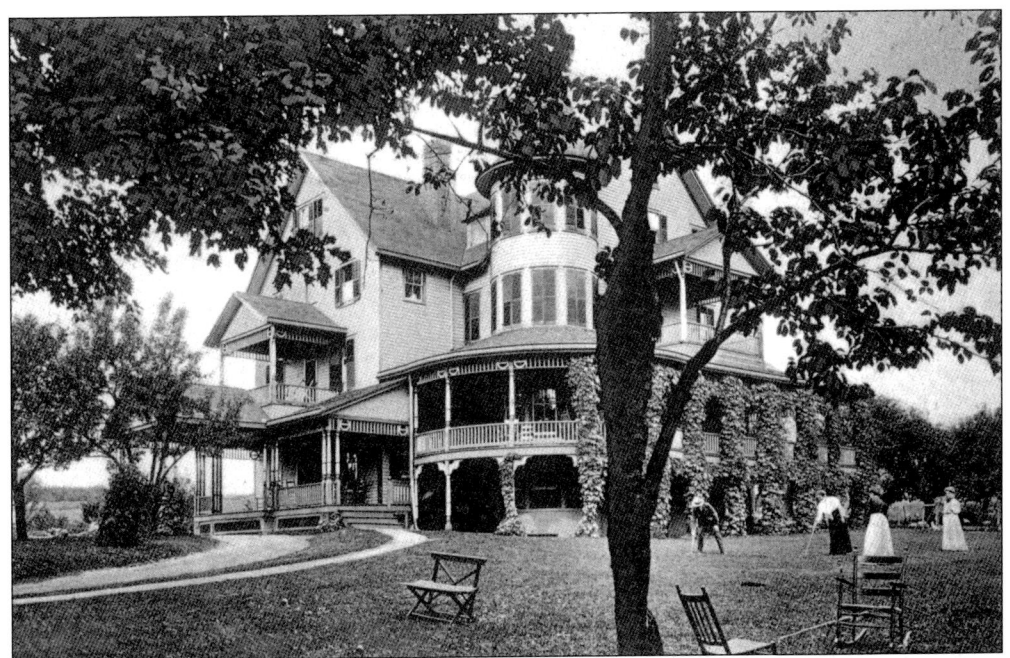

The Nichols (Nicholas) Hotel was purchased by the Grossinger family, who developed it into the most famous hotel in Sullivan County. Soon after they acquired it, they changed the name to Grossinger's and the mailing address to Ferndale in order to separate their resort from the stigma of the name "Liberty," which they felt was tainted by its association with tuberculosis sanatoriums. At the instigation of public relations genius Milton Blackstone, the hotel got its own post office—Grossinger, New York. Author Tania Grossinger remembers getting mail addressed simply "Tania, Grossinger, New York." Offering sports figures and celebrities free vacations, Grossinger's was always in the public eye.

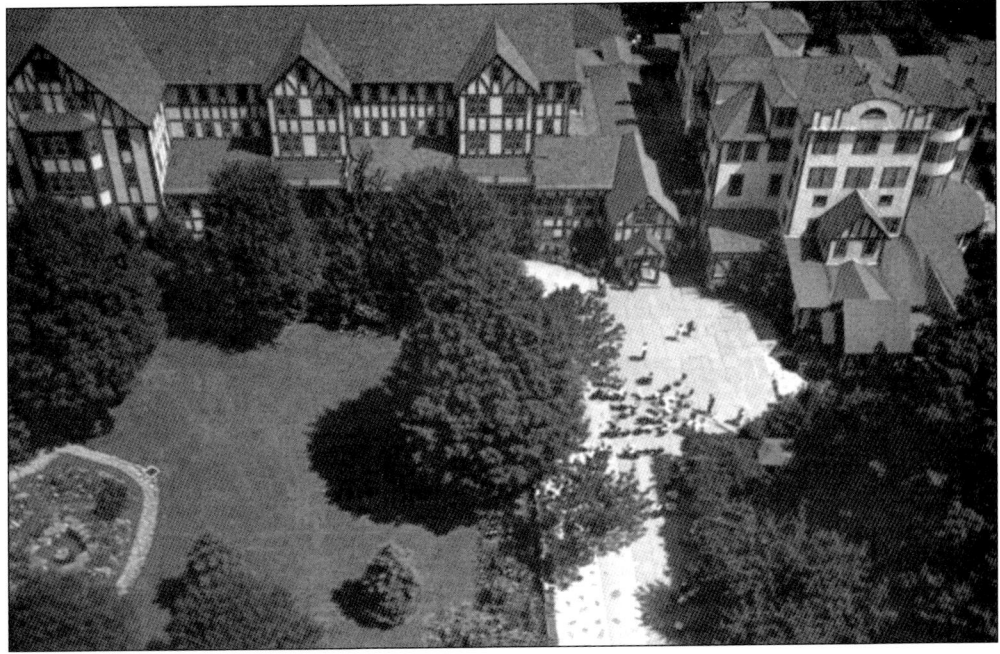

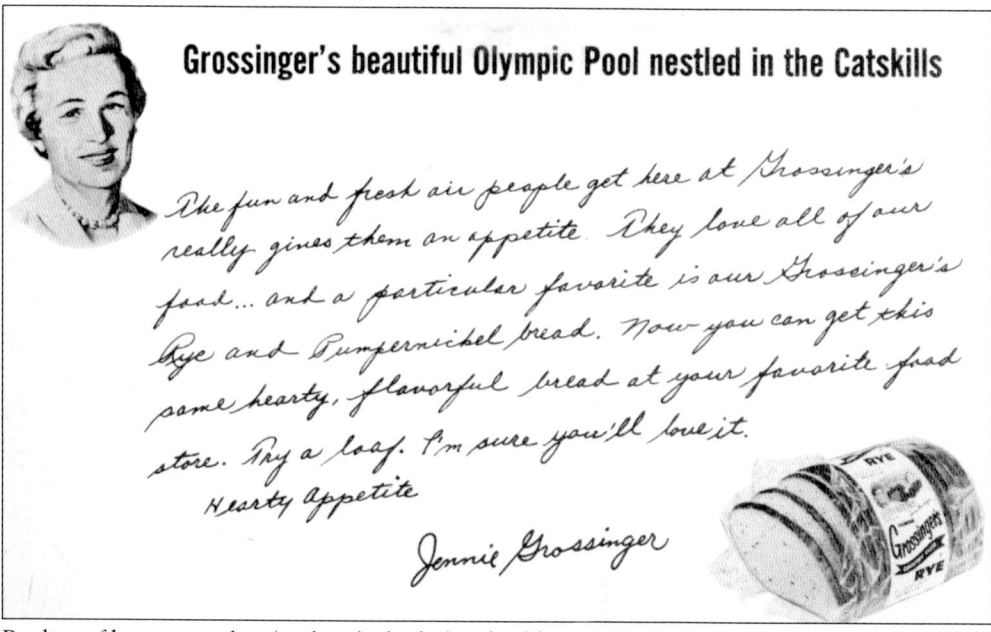

By dint of her personality (and with the help of publicist Milton Blackstone), Jennie Grossinger (1892–1972) turned herself into Sullivan County's only bona fide owner-celebrity. The daughter of the hotel's founders, Selig and Malka Grossinger, Jennie Grossinger married her first cousin, Paul Grossinger. She had a reputation as a gracious hostess to her guests. She claimed that she sent survival kits of gefilte fish and other kosher delicacies to songwriter Irving Berlin when he vacationed at nearby Lew Beach. She was naturally the chief spokesman for Grossinger's Rye, whose advertising slogan was, "You don't have to be Jewish to love Grossinger's Rye."

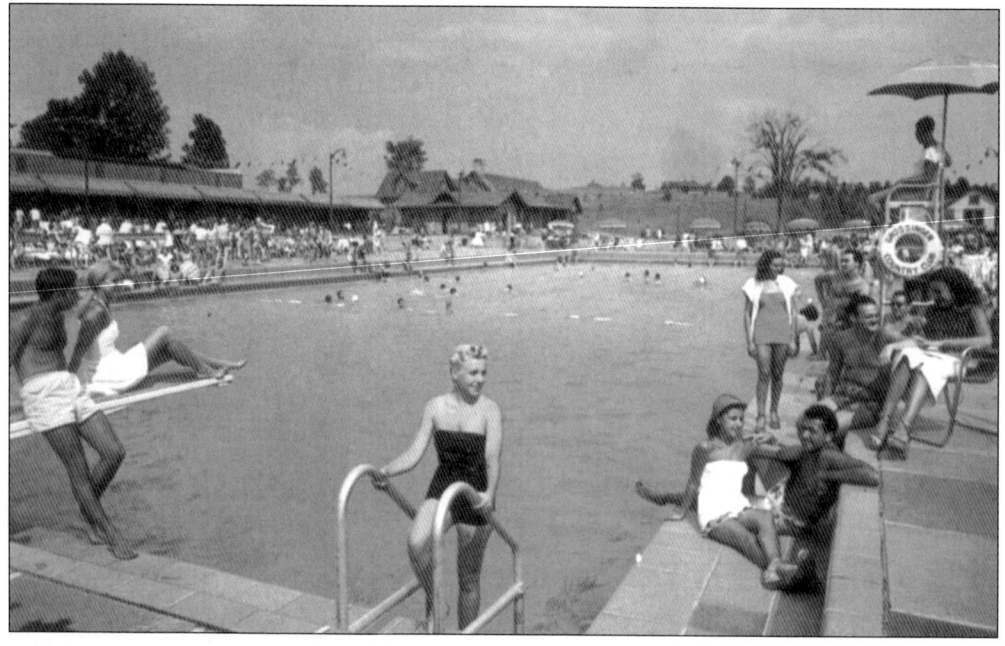

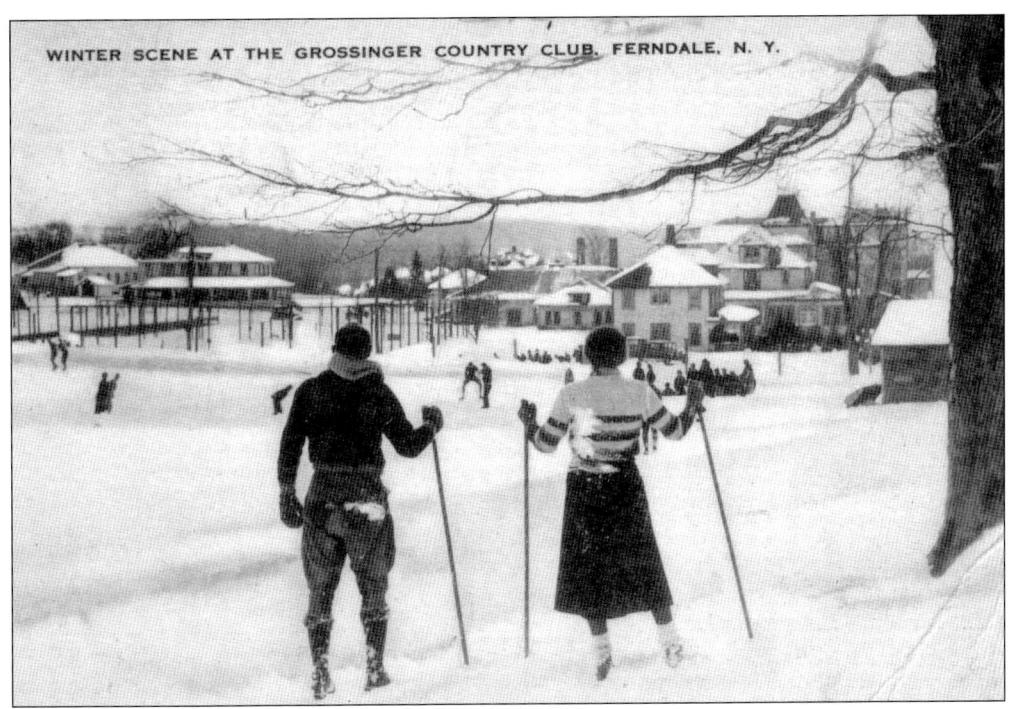

Grossinger's followed the Flagler's lead in becoming a year-round resort. Building superior facilities, it soon surpassed its rival. Ski clothing was rather primitive in 1937, when the postcard of a snow-covered Grossinger Country Club in Ferndale was mailed. Below, in an early-1960s image, guests sunbathing during the winter at Grossinger's look uncomfortably like the tuberculosis patients in Liberty who were given the cold-air cure.

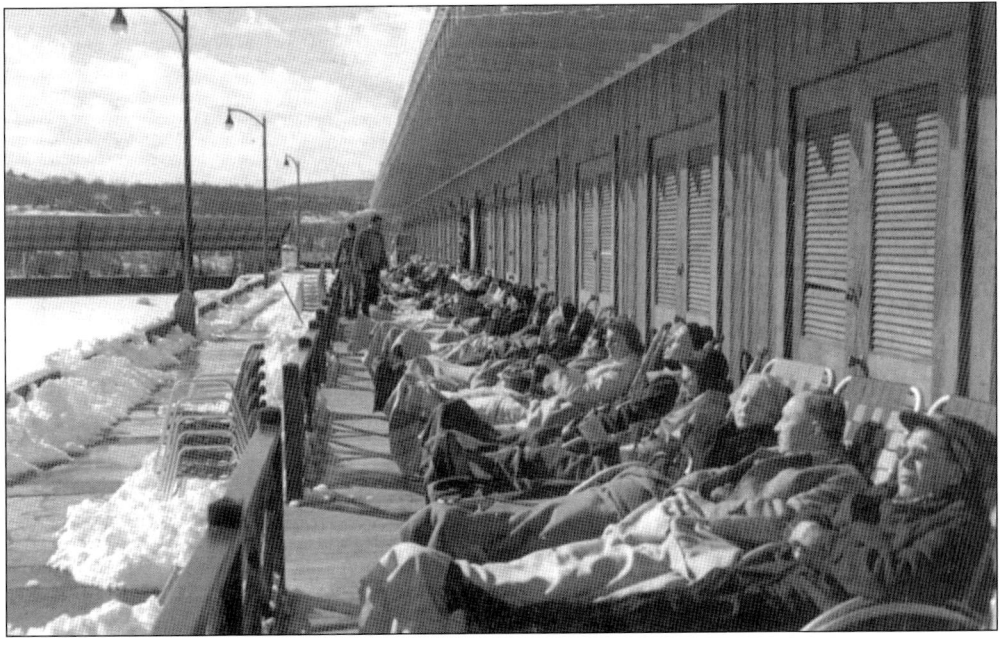

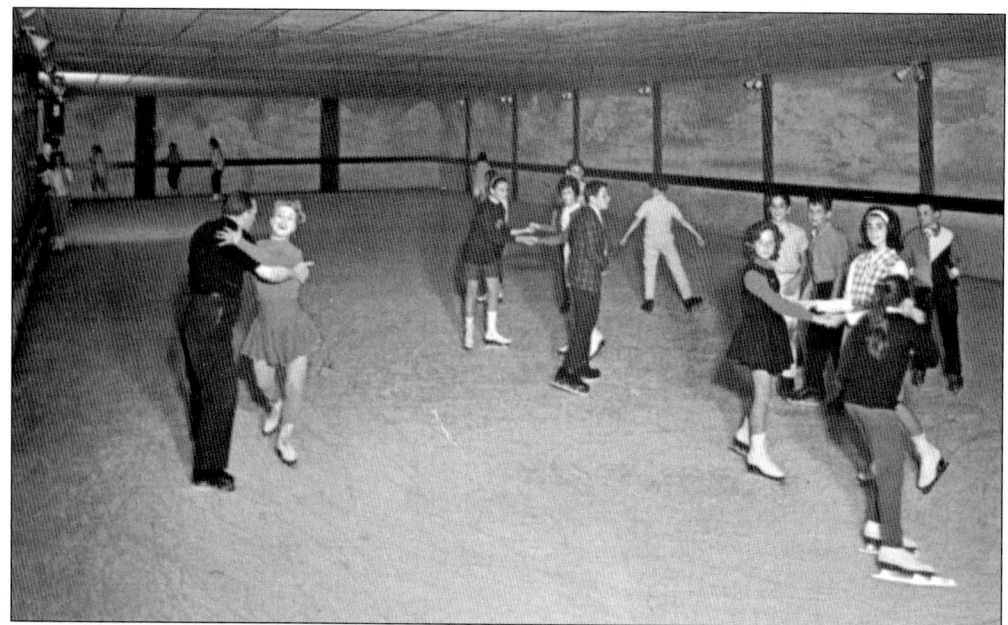

Just as indoor pools allowed guests to have year-round summer, they had year-round winter at the enclosed ice rinks built after World War II. The rink shown here was at the Raleigh Hotel in South Fallsburg. Guests writing to their daughter on this postcard report, "We had a very sumptuous meal and are lounging in the lobby waiting for the entertainment to begin. Tomorrow we expect to play ping pong, go swimming, etc."

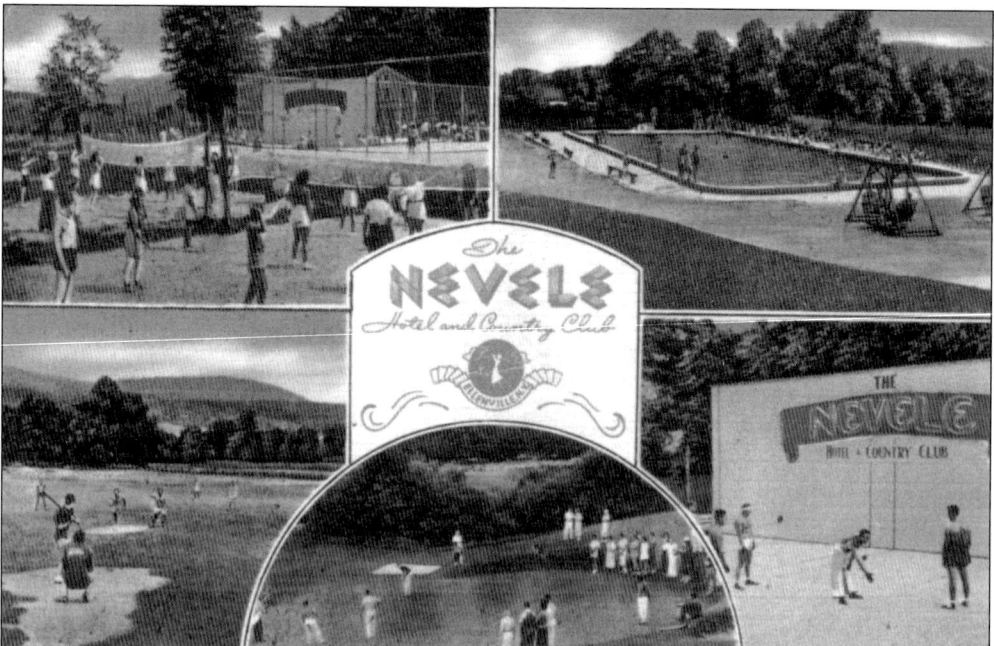

The Nevele Hotel in Ellenville is located in one of the most beautiful spots in the Borscht Belt. The Slutsky family, who owned the Nevele and its neighbor the Fallsview, recently sold them both. Rechristened as the Nevele Grande, the hotel is working very hard to shed its almost exclusively Jewish Borscht Belt image and to emphasize its golf courses.

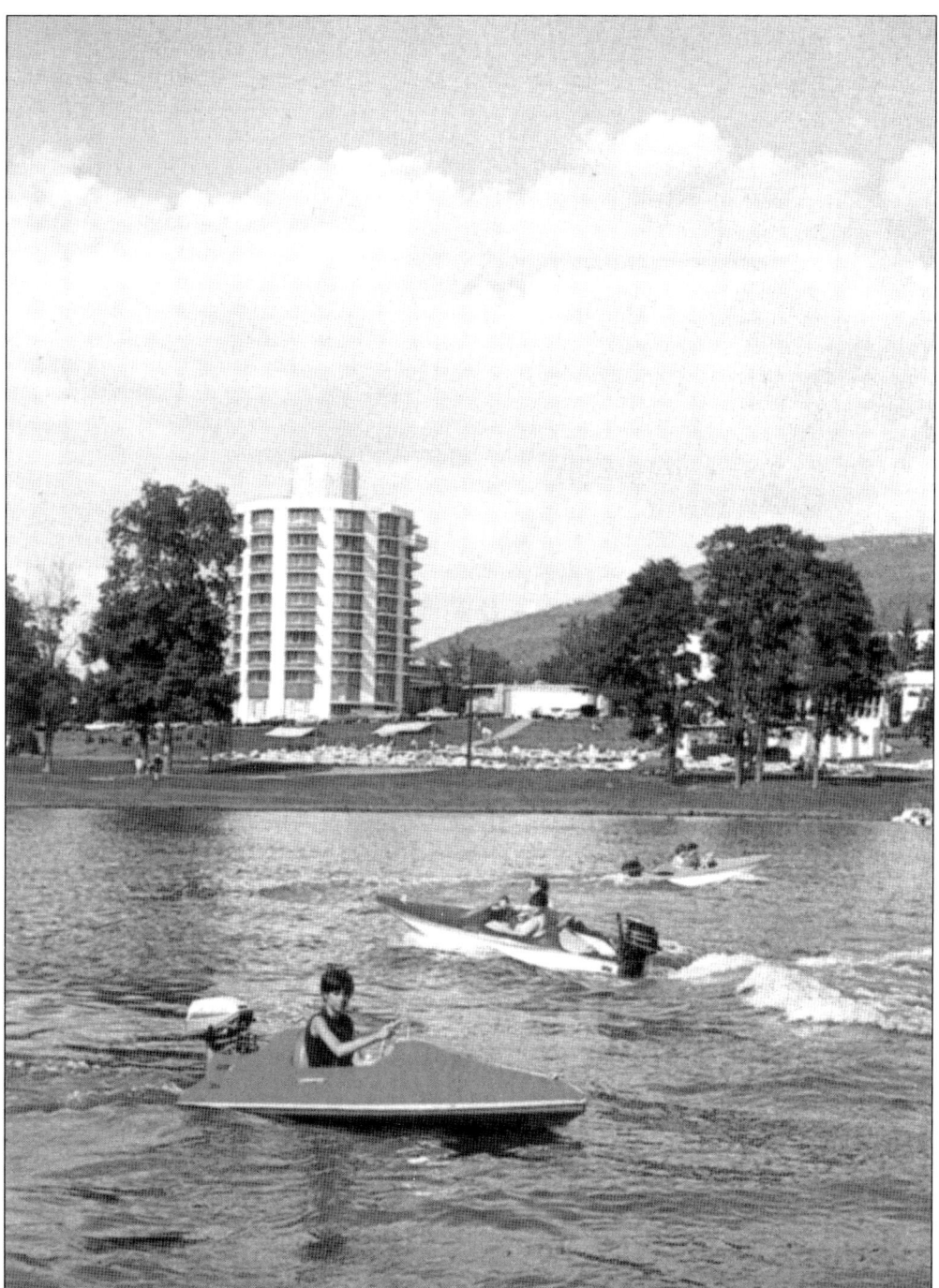

The Nevele's round skyscraper was a sensation when it was completed in the 1960s. At the invitation of congressman and industrialist Joseph Resnick, Pres. Lyndon Johnson came to town in the summer of 1966 to dedicate the new Ellenville Hospital. All of the Borscht Belt was agog, as Johnson was the first sitting president to visit the area. Many were disappointed to hear that the president did not even have a bagel and lox for breakfast—just his favorite dry cereal. Speedboats on the lake demonstrate the resort is up to date and fun.

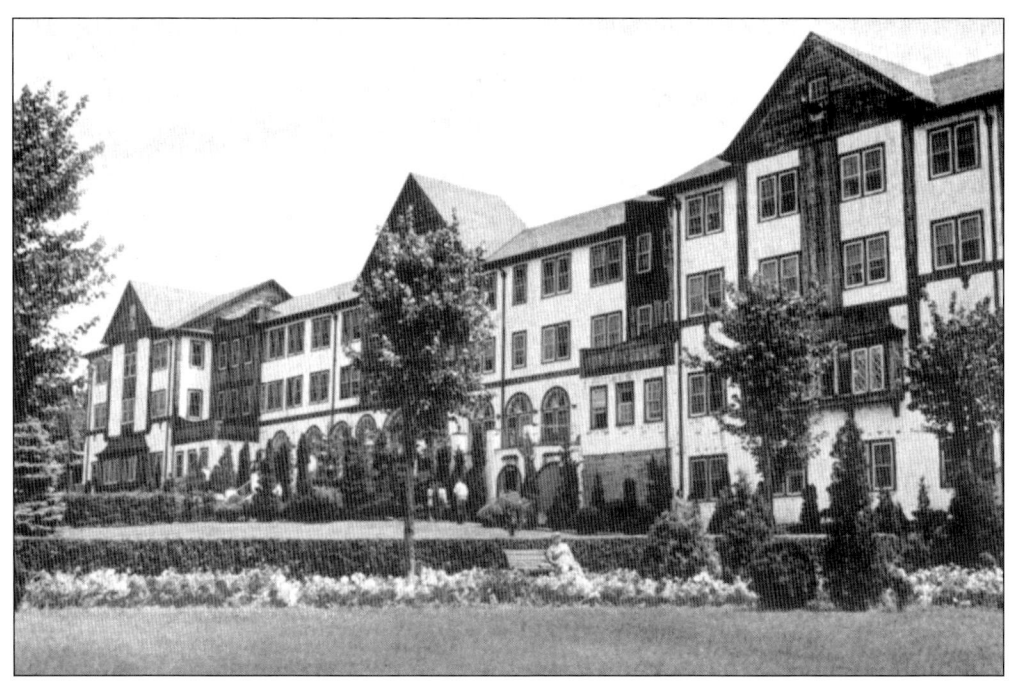

A vision drove Arthur Winarick. He simply wanted to create the largest hotel in the Catskills—and he did. Born in Russia, he immigrated to America with his family as a child. Eventually he made a fortune with Jeris Hair Tonic and other cosmetics and toiletries. Buying an existing hotel (the Kiamesa Ideal) in the 1930s, Winarick rebuilt it as the Concord Plaza. By 1941, the hotel was being promoted as the Concord, with accommodations for 800 guests. In keeping with the times—and in direct competition with Grossinger's—the Concord was built in the Tudor style. Years of competition ensued between the two resorts. Concord sports facilities were always first-class. As shown below in a 1945 view, the very large swimming pool lacked simmers—not an unusual circumstance. Many more guests lounged by hotel pools than went into the water.

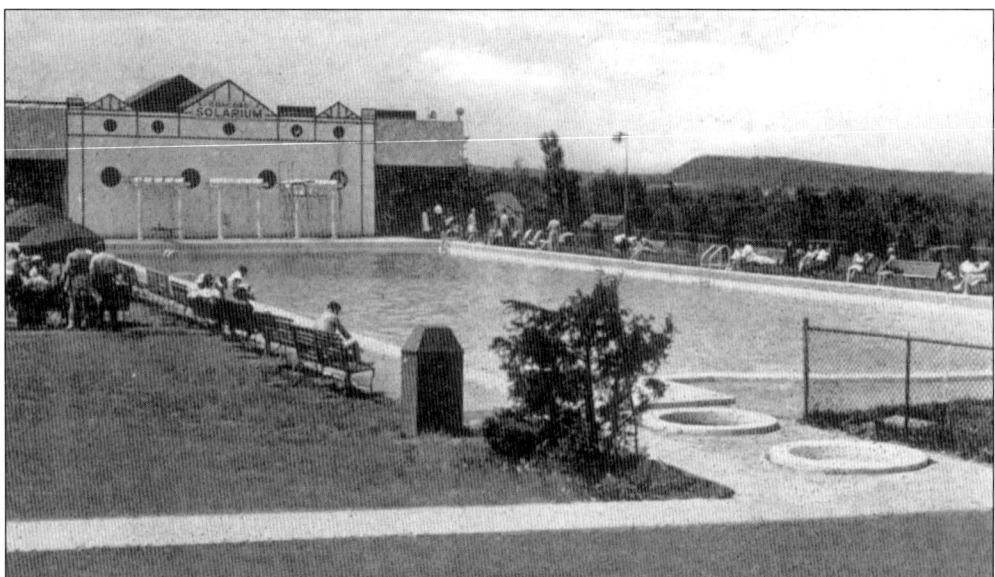

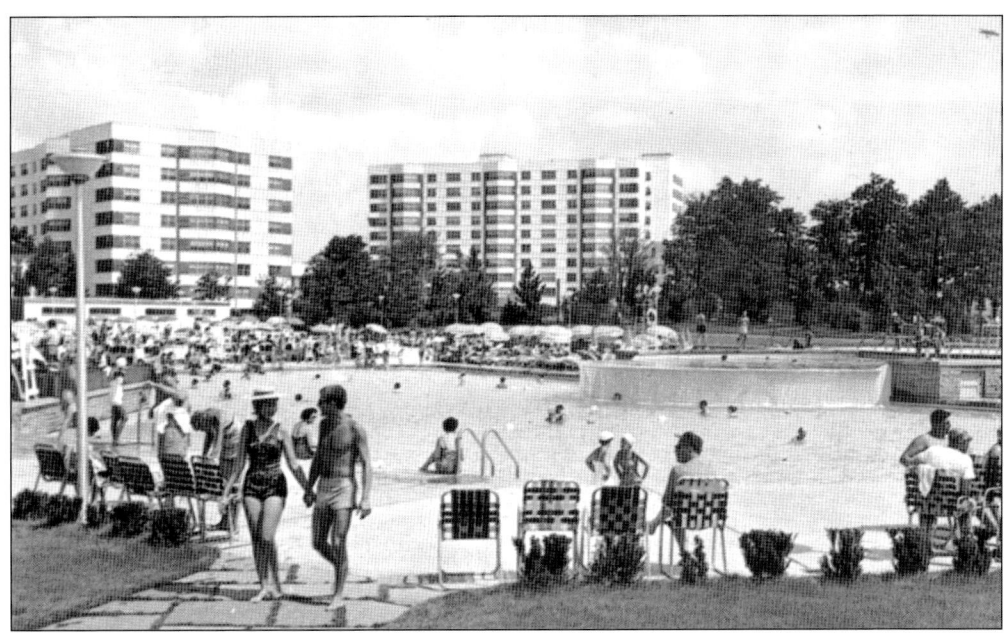

When Arthur Winarick and his general manager, Ray Parker (his son-in-law), hired architect Morris Lapidus (designer of Miami Beach's Fountainblu Hotel), they scored a coup. The white International-style hotel that Lapidus created became the apogee of the Catskill resort industry. The hotel prided itself on the best of everything. Before Atlantic City, the Concord's 3,000-seat Imperial Room presented the most popular entertainers in America. Many performers who starred on *The Ed Sullivan Show* appeared live at the Concord on Saturday nights. In the 1950s and 1960s, the Concord trumpeted the stars in its full-page ads in the Sunday travel section of the *New York Times*. The Concord had Buster Crabbe as its swimming director. The golf course, designed by Robert Trent Jones, overlooked Kiamesha Lake.

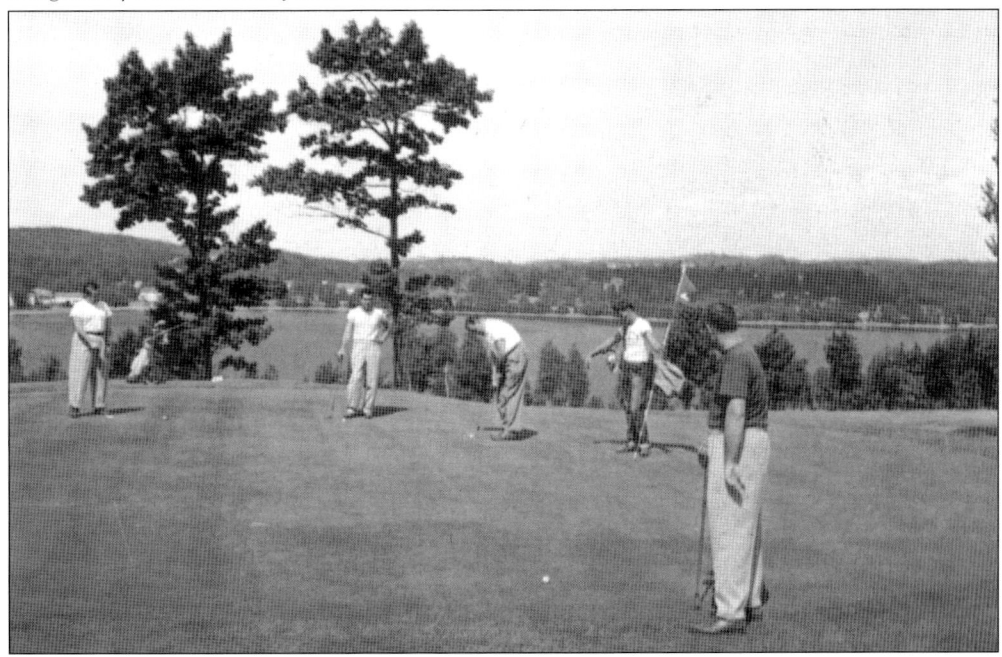

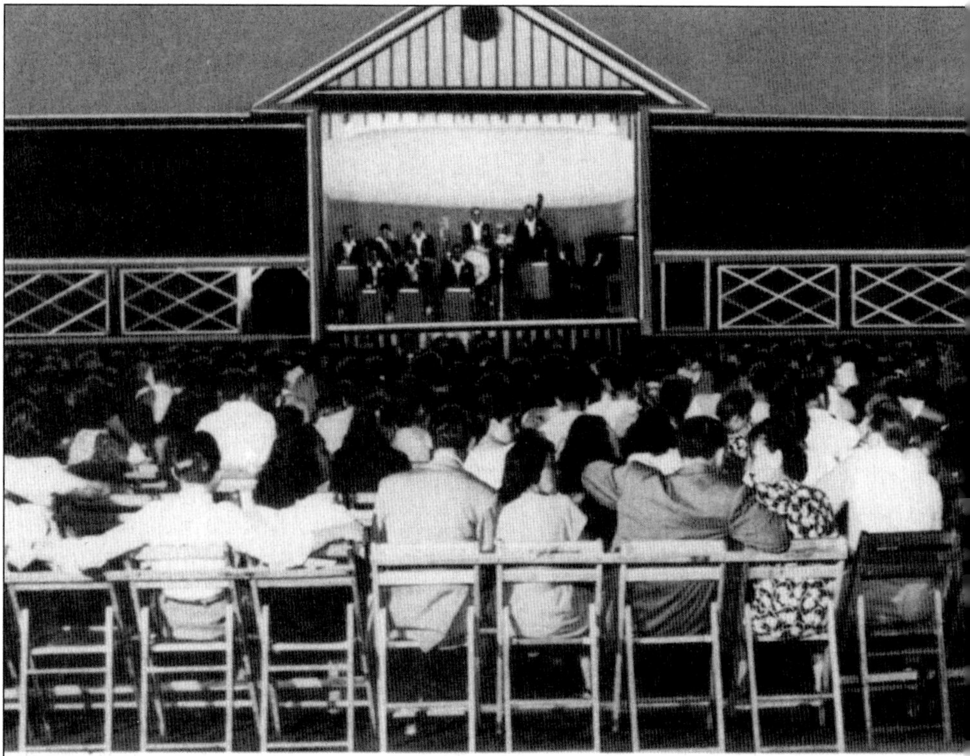

ENTERTAINMENT? Par excellence!

Other areas have their summer theatres. Sullivan County has its summer theatres, too — but they are overwhelmed by a tide of entertainers that saturates every major hotel in the central part of the County with the brilliance and glamour of stardom.

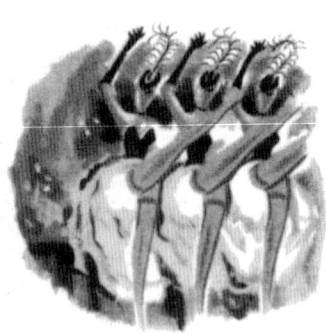

"Summer stock" is, in this neck of the vacationland woods, just one little item in a breath-taking amusement extravaganza that opens as early as May and doesn't close until Labor Day. In scores of hotel nightclubs, playhouses and ballrooms rivalling in splendor the smartest spots in New York, appear famous personalities of stage, screen, radio, television and the world of music. Many of them are back to visit the scene of their "first break." And out on the fringe of dance-halls and small-hotel casinos, headliners of tomorrow are making their debuts. Many hotels cannot do with one orchestra; there are two or more, one usually specializing in Latin American rythms. In many places, too, classes in rhumba and other dances are the thing.

Virtually every popular entertainer between 1930 and 1970 either got a start in the Catskills or played there. These pages from a late-1940s booklet, published by the Sullivan County Board of Supervisors, tell a good deal of the story. Among the other performers who worked the Catskills extensively was Gregory Hines, who started dancing as a young boy in the popular act called Hines, Hines and Dad. To some degree, the tradition still lives. Playing on nostalgia and the

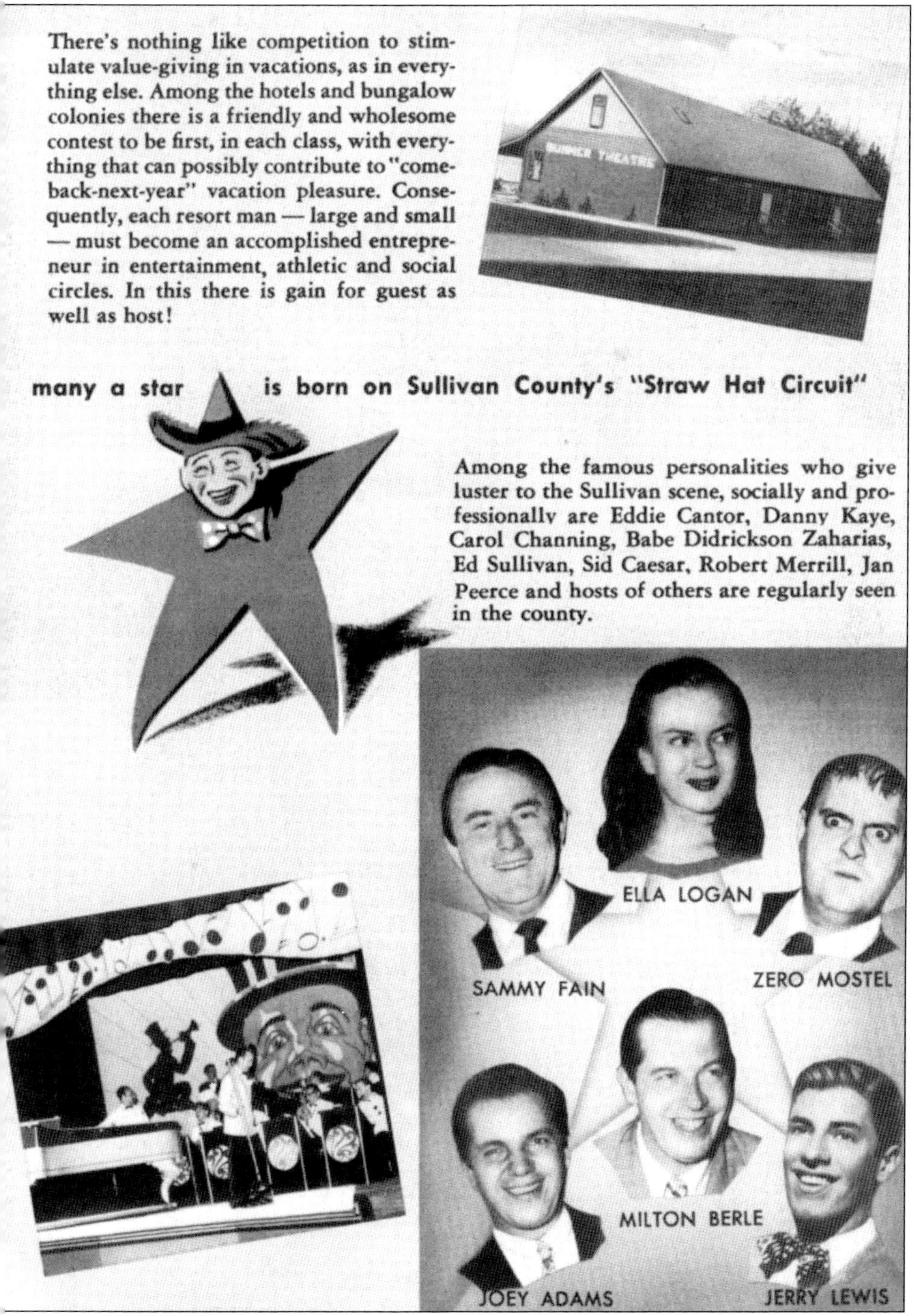

There's nothing like competition to stimulate value-giving in vacations, as in everything else. Among the hotels and bungalow colonies there is a friendly and wholesome contest to be first, in each class, with everything that can possibly contribute to "come-back-next-year" vacation pleasure. Consequently, each resort man — large and small — must become an accomplished entrepreneur in entertainment, athletic and social circles. In this there is gain for guest as well as host!

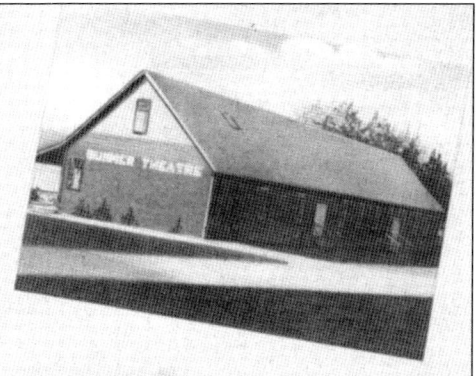

many a star is born on Sullivan County's "Straw Hat Circuit"

Among the famous personalities who give luster to the Sullivan scene, socially and professionally are Eddie Cantor, Danny Kaye, Carol Channing, Babe Didrickson Zaharias, Ed Sullivan, Sid Caesar, Robert Merrill, Jan Peerce and hosts of others are regularly seen in the county.

SAMMY FAIN ELLA LOGAN ZERO MOSTEL

JOEY ADAMS MILTON BERLE JERRY LEWIS

undeniable talent of many Borscht Belt–trained entertainers, comedian Freddie Roman (born Kirshenbaum) brought a comic review (Catskills on Broadway) to New York City. It was a sensation. Roman and his cast subsequently toured the country with the show. Jackie Mason, who honed his craft in Sullivan County, is today a Broadway staple.

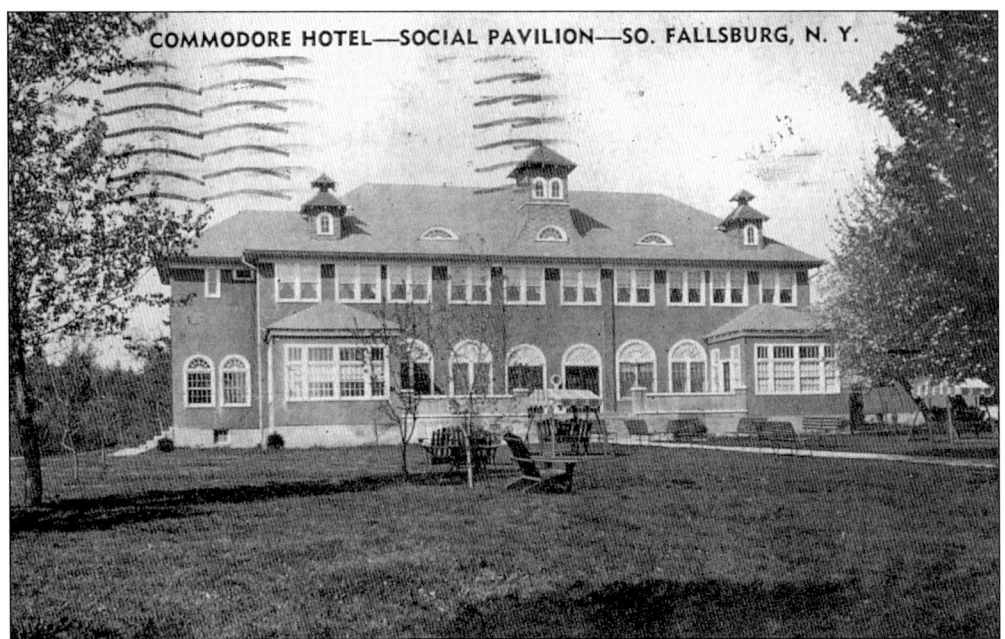

Entertainment was first presented in the barn and then in hotel casinos. Always looking for the newest terminology, the Commodore Hotel of South Fallsburg presented its shows in a "social pavilion" while the Tamarack offered a brand-new "playtorium." On the postcard below, Gertrude writes from the Tamarack in 1942, "Finally decided to vacation here. Place is ideal—lots of activities and I am taking advantage of it all before going back to the old grind." It is interesting to note that there were so many hotels, that several had the same name. There was an unrelated Commodore Hotel on Swan Lake as well as this one in South Fallsburg.

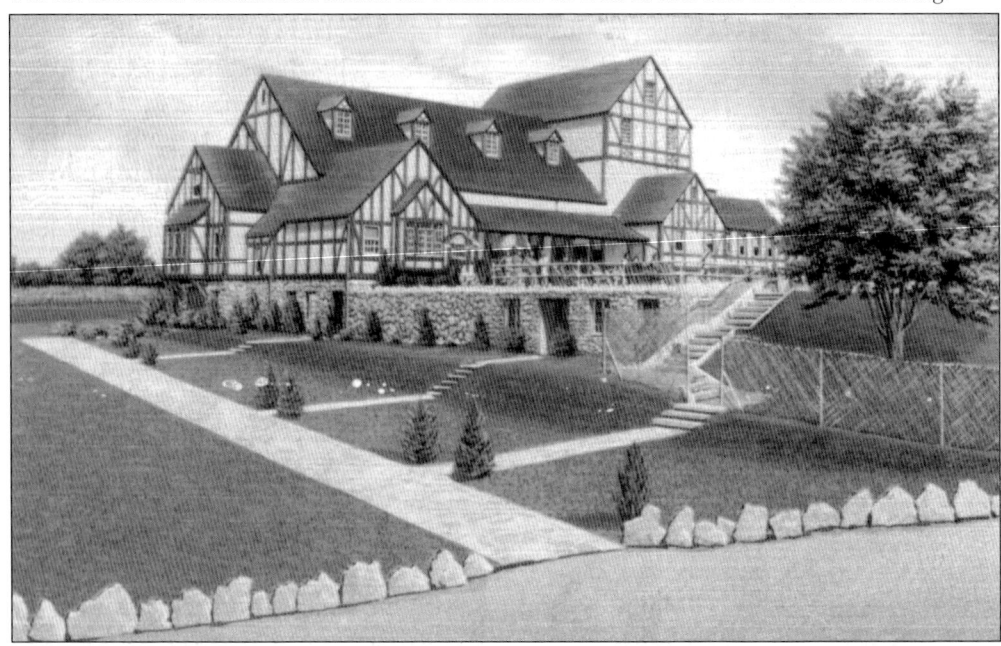

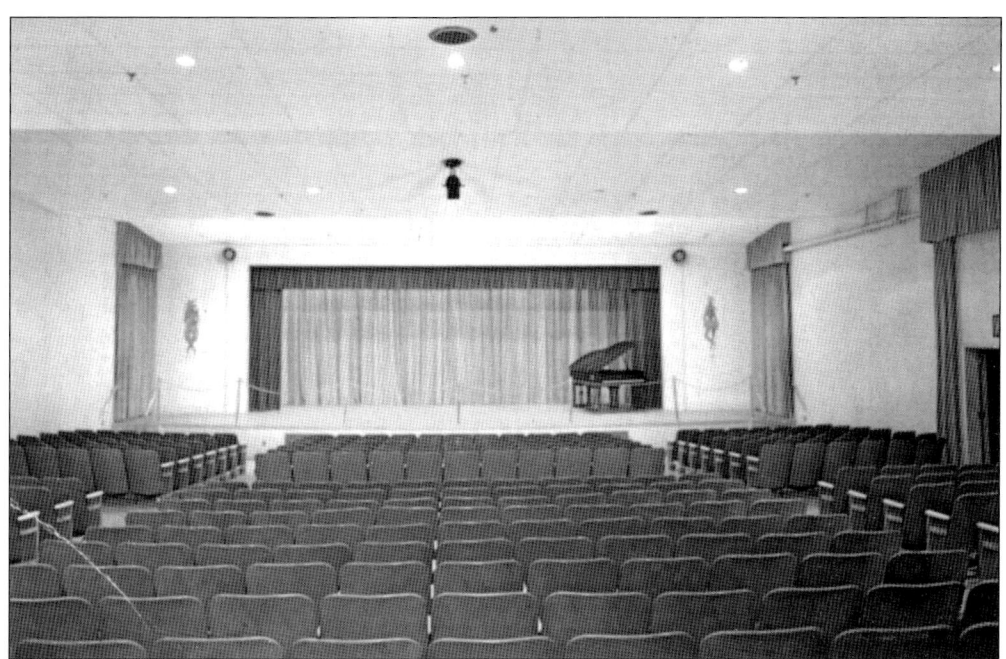

The most elegant entertainment facility was the theater. The finer hotels had them before they were replaced, beginning in the 1950s with the nightclub. The Orthodox Lebowitz Pine View Hotel in Fallsburg offered these attractions: "New Air Conditioned Theatre and Cocktail Lounge. Filtered Swimming Pool. Distinctive Social Staff and Orchestra." Aspiring hotels never had a band—always an orchestra. The Pines in South Fallsburg was very proud of its Persian Room: "The fabulous Nite Club of 1001 nights of top entertainment, featuring stars of B'way, T.V., and Hollywood." Nightclub names were usually grandiose or fantastic. The Aladdin Hotel in Woodbourne featured the Ali Baba Room. The Concord had its Imperial Room.

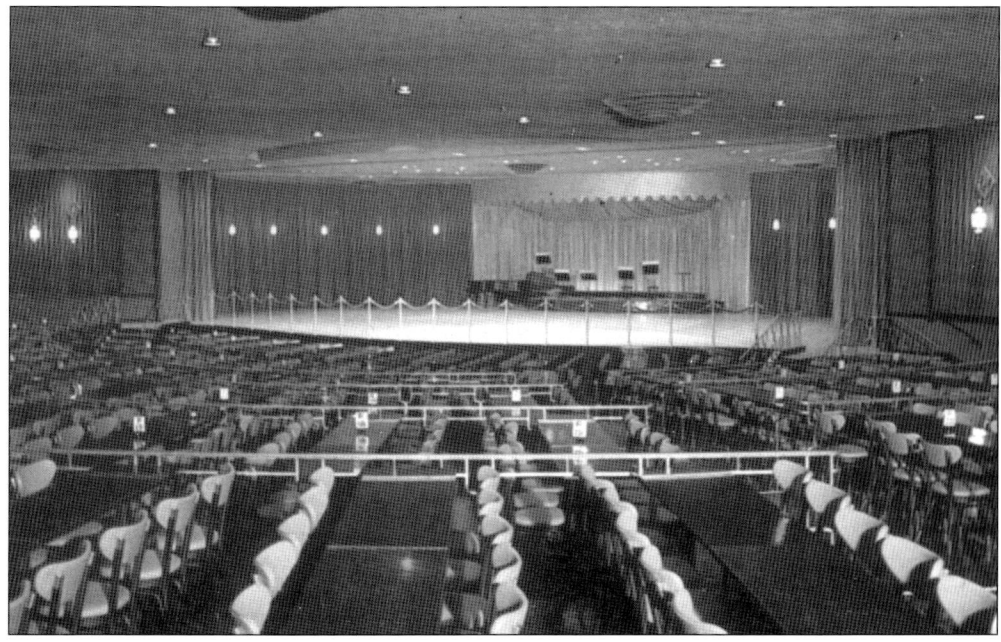

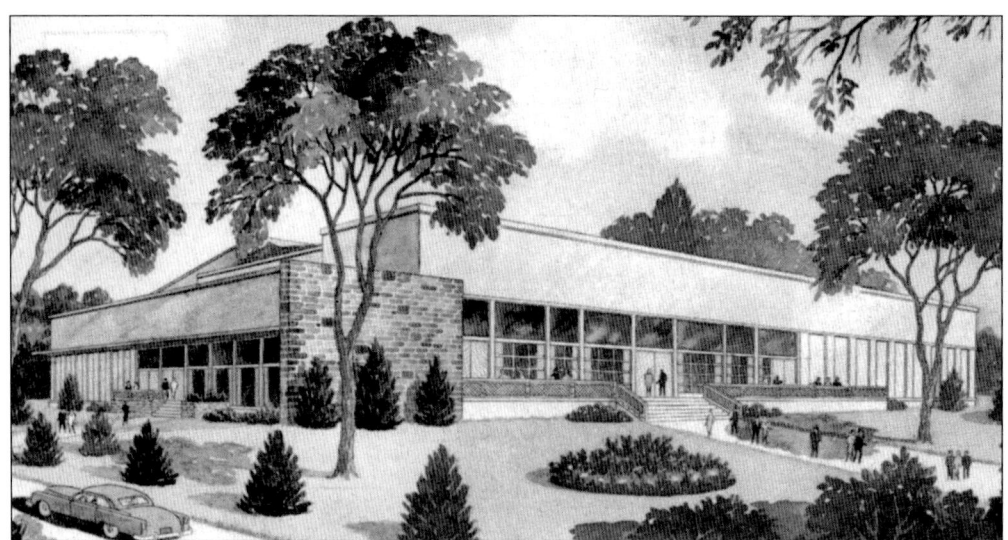

Gartenberg and Schecter's Pioneer Country Club in Greenfield Park already offered a nine-hole golf course, private mile-long lake, and a children's day camp in the early 1960s, when it was planning its new International-style Playtorium, above. Schenk's Paramount Hotel (there still is a Paramount Hotel in Parksville) in South Fallsburg had just completed "the fabulous new Schenk's Playhouse of Stars. Featuring the luxurious new Continental Room, the intimate Rendezvous Room, Coffee Shop and Club 17 for teenagers." Neither hotel survives today. Schenk's Paramount, which featured a soaring abstract sculpture in front of its main entrance, is now a Hasidic boys' camp.

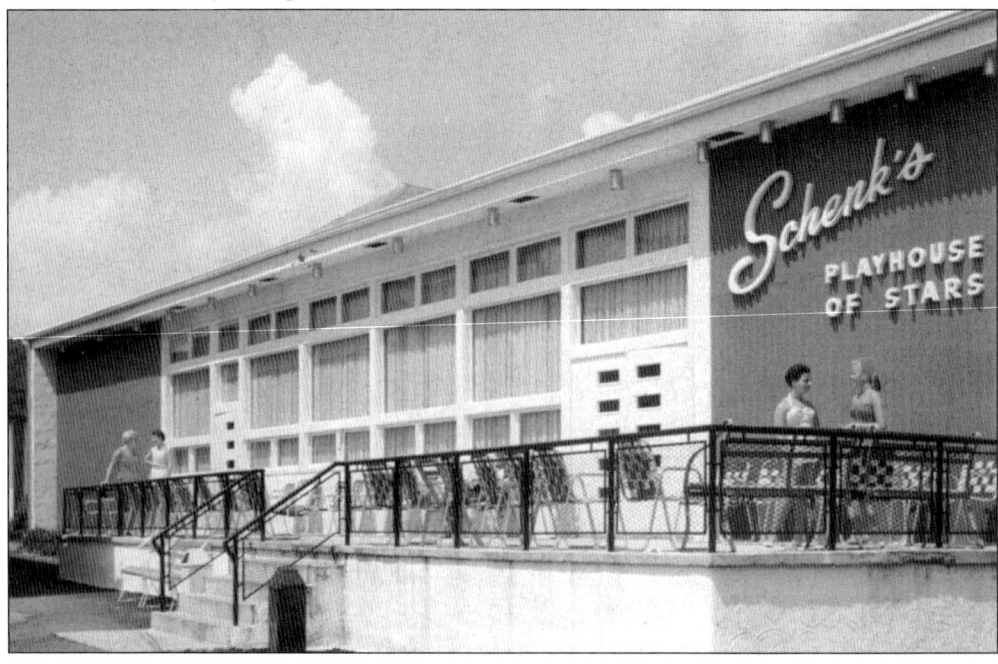

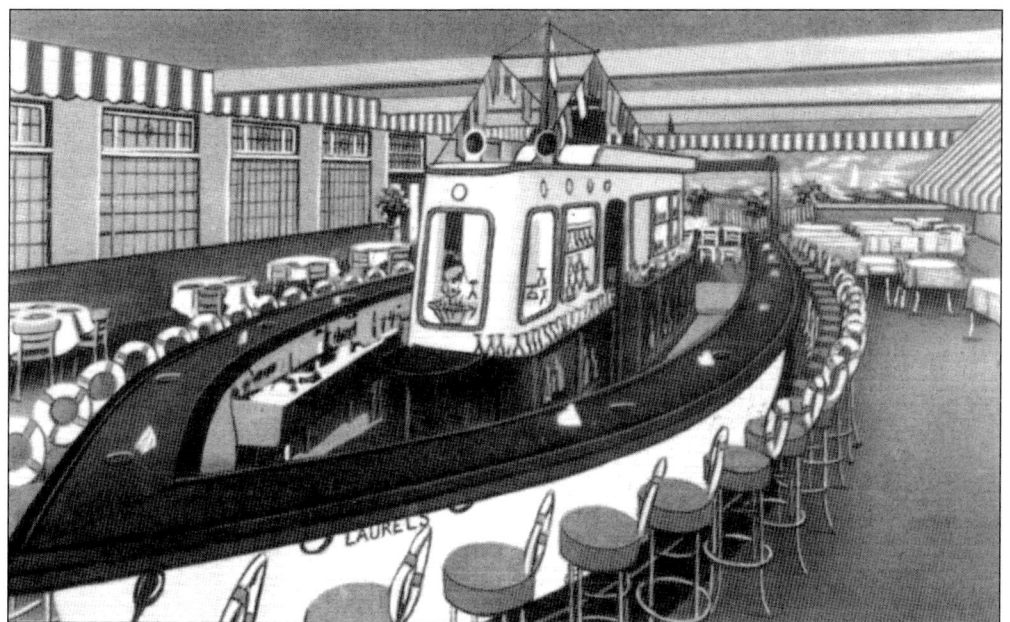

One of the most imaginative Borscht Belt bars was at the Laurels Country Club on Sackett Lake near Monticello, which always tried to attract a younger crowd. The nautical theme was much more common around the swimming pool. Ben Posner of Brickman's in South Fallsburg claimed to have introduced the theme into the Catskills with his new pool in the 1950s.

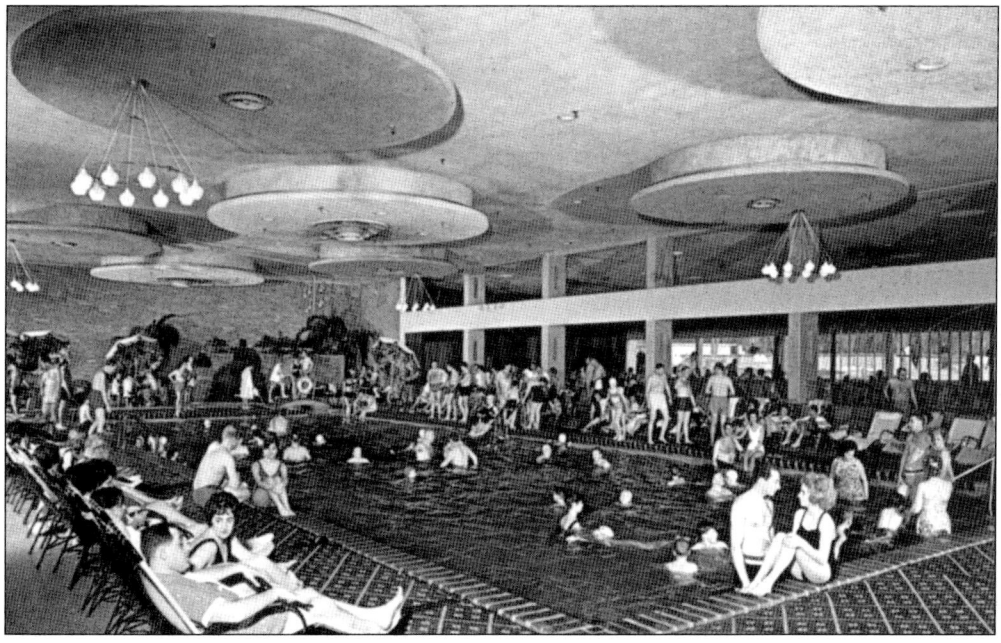

Waiting for the next meal was always an important part of the Catskills experience. When the weather was cold and rainy, you could enjoy the indoor pool, as here at the Nevele in 1965. Even inside, lounging by the pool was more popular than swimming. It was one of the few places where food was not regularly served at Catskill resorts.

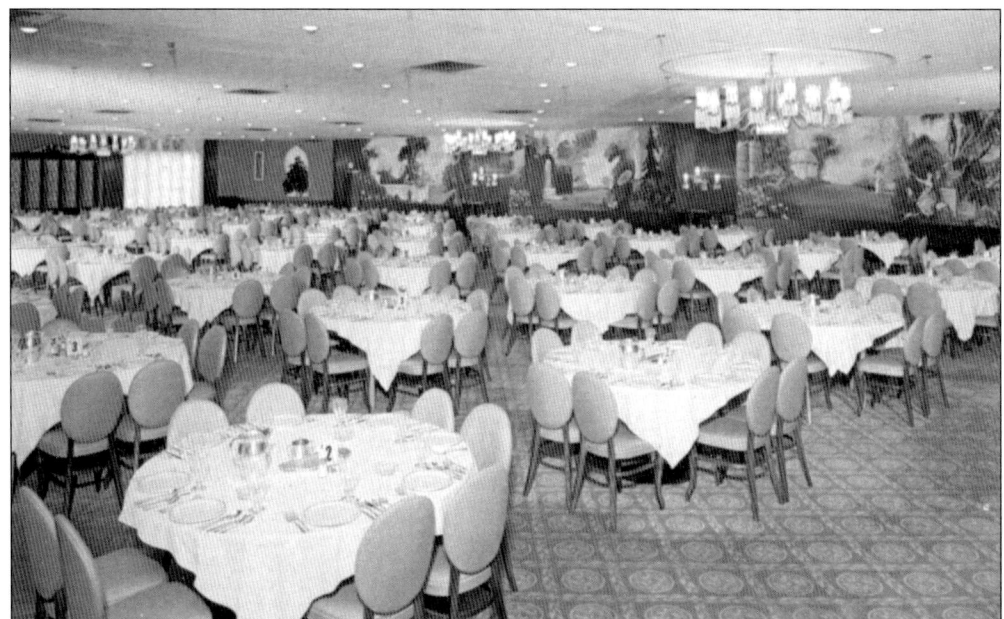

The dining room of Brown's Hotel is described on the reverse of this 1973 postcard as "a bit of California at your doorstep." Mary writes to Dot, "We are having a grand time. We had a live show last nite [she caught the Borscht Belt disease: *night* was always *nite*] and also dancing and the orchestra was very good. The food is great and the place is beautiful, you sure would like it here." Brown's was the "Home of the Brown Derby Nite Club, Fabulous Jerry Louis Theatre Club."

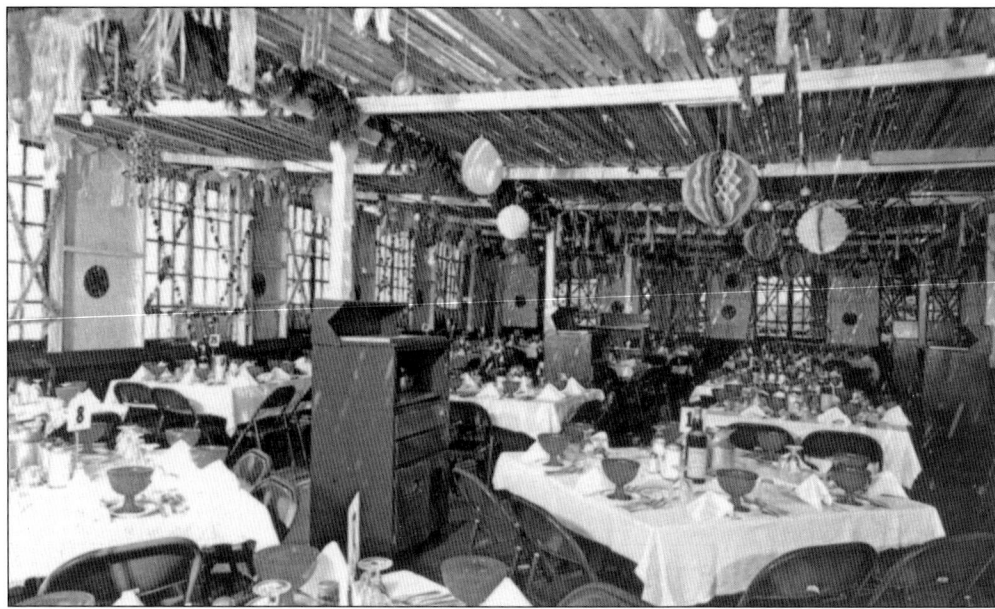

The Pioneer Country Club in Greenfield Park offered "the World's Foremost Succah" according to this card. Most Sullivan County hotels were opened for Rosh Hashanah and even for Yom Kippur, but very few celebrated Succos as did the Pioneer. The back of this card advises, "For A Memory Of A Lifetime Spend the Holidays in An Atmosphere where Sabbath and Kashruth are Strictly Observed."

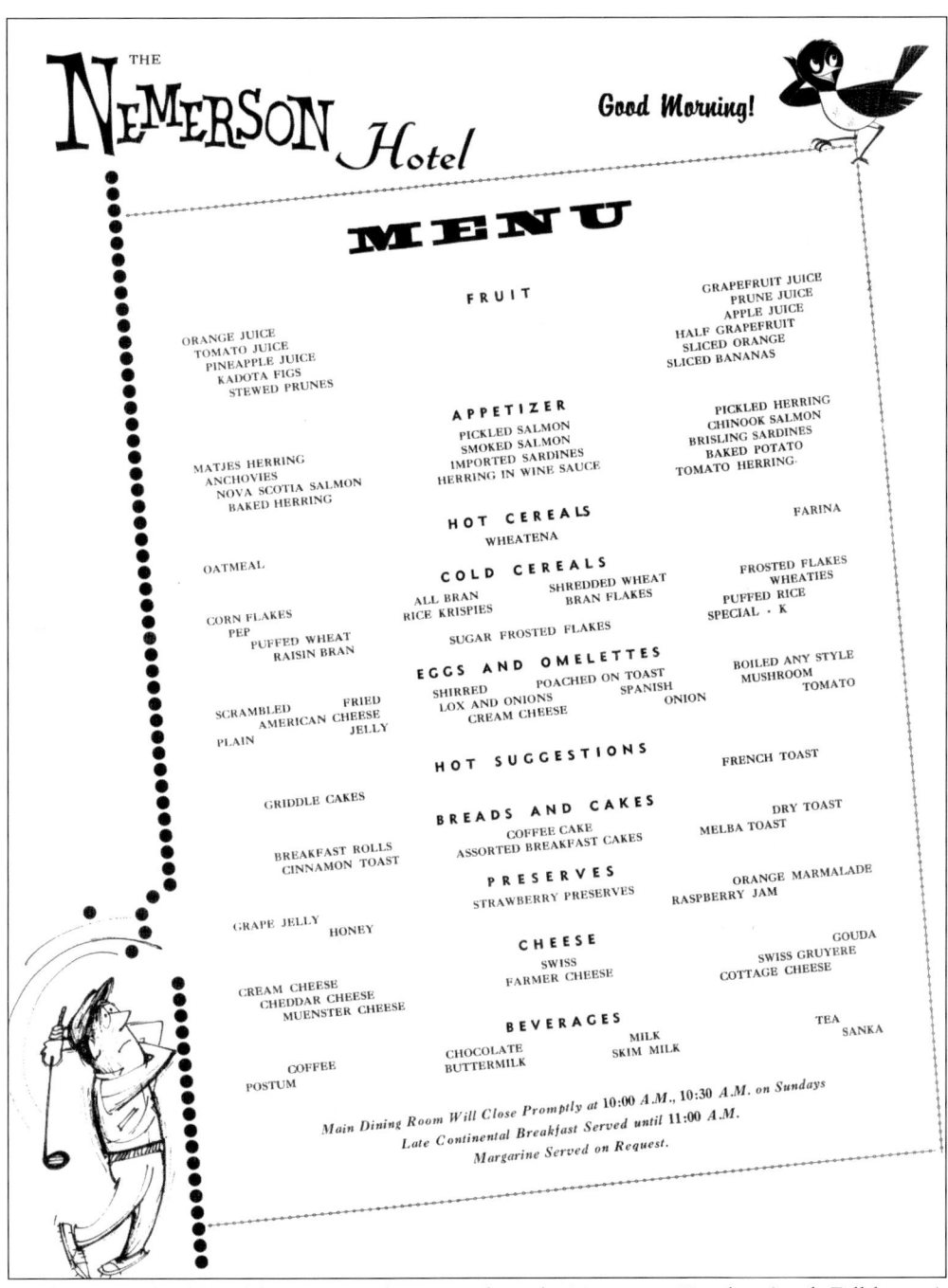

Breakfast was the first of three extraordinary meals at the Nemerson Hotel in South Fallsburg. A guest could order everything on the menu by saying, "Just bring a touch of everything for the table." Writer Sidney Offit—whose novel *He Had It Made* provides great insight into Sullivan County kitchens and dining rooms—was amazed at the popularity of prune juice at Borscht Belt hotels.

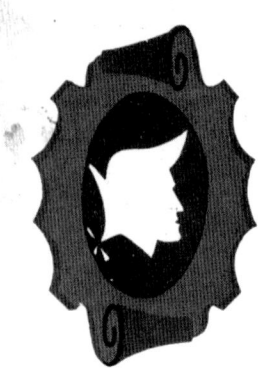

The Concord
KIAMESHA LAKE, N.Y.

Menu

Good Afternoon

Choice of Juice
FLORIDA TANGERINE JUICE COCKTAIL
NATURAL APPLE JUICE

Soup
MANHATTAN FISH CHOWDER
CREAM OF ASPARAGUS
COLD FRUIT

Entree
BROILER ENGLISH KIPPERS, SCRAMBLED EGGS
STEWED FRESH MUSHROOMS, EGG BARLEY
VEGETARIAN LAMB CHOPS, SAUCE SUPREME
SALMON CROQUETTES WITH SPAGHETTI MILANAISE
SPRING SALAD, SOUR CREAM GARNI
FRIED RICE CANTONESE STYLE
SMOKED SALMON WITH CREAM CHEESE SALAD
COMBINATION VEGETABLE LUNCHEON
BAKED SUMMER SQUASH   LYONNAISE POTATOES

Dessert
CHERRY CHEESE CAKE   DANISH BUTTER TWISTS
BUTTER COOKIES

Beverage

The Concord aspired to elegance and rarely served borscht. It did, however, offer "spring salad," which was made of diced vegetables mixed with cottage cheese and sour cream—what is now touted as "sour cream garni." The Borscht Belt standby, lox, was served as "smoked salmon with cream cheese salad." Where was the bagel? Because the Concord was kosher, all of the luncheon dishes were dairy.

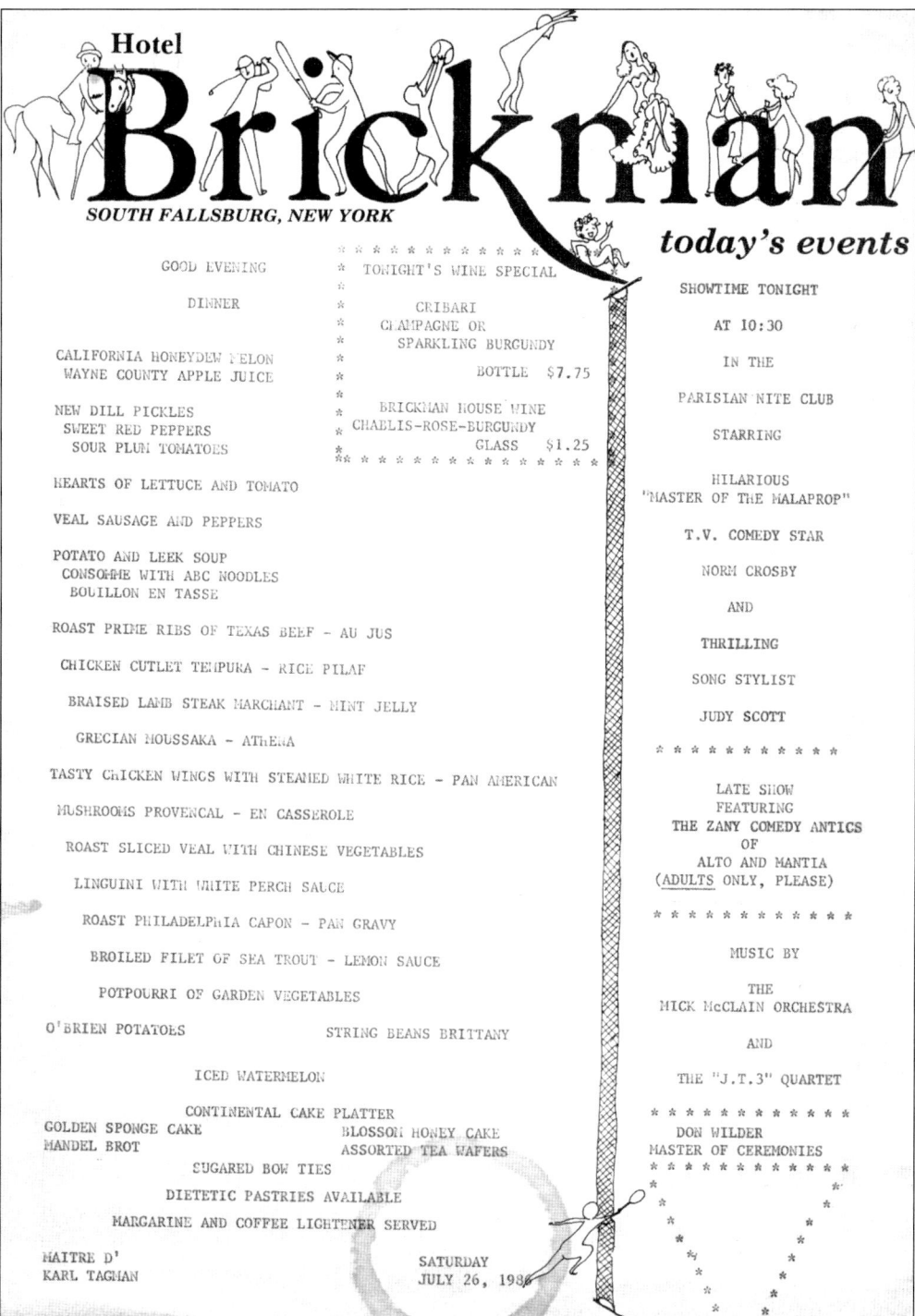

Menus were placed on the tables, and survivors are often stained. The Brickman offered kosher versions of popular international foods. Roast chicken was always on Sullivan County menus. Here it is presented as "Roast Philadelphia Capon—Pan Gravy." Was Philadelphia elegant? Note the coming attractions for two nightclub shows. The late show was for "adults only please."

Hotel Brickman Coffee Shop

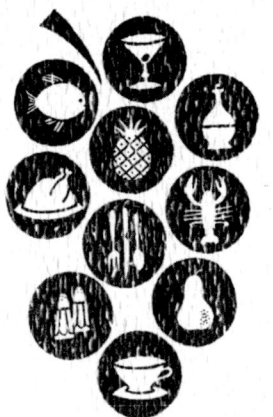

Fountain Suggestions

Dish of your Favorite Ice Cream . . . ~~.75~~ .85
Luscious Ice Cream Soda . . . . ~~.85~~ .95

Very Tempting Sundaes

(With Loads of Whipped Cream) . . ~~1.10~~ 1.15

TOPPINGS — YOUR CHOICE

Pineapple - Fruit - Hot Fudge .25 (extra)

Huge Rich Milk Shake or Malted . . . ~~.85~~ .95
Float (Extra Scoop in Malted) . . . . ~~1.15~~ 1.25
Plain Sodas (All Flavors) Sm. ~~.54~~ & Lg. ~~.50~~ .55
Egg Cream . . . . Sm .45 . . Lg. .60 .40
Ice Cream Cone . . . . . . .45 SPRINKLES .40 .50

Milk - Skim Milk - Buttermilk Sm. ~~.40~~ .45 & Lg. .55
Chocolate Milk . . . . Sm. .45 & Lg. .60
Hot Chocolate with Whipped Cream . . .45
Iced Tea or Iced Coffee ~~.45~~ . . . . .50 .55
Sanka . . . . ~~.40~~ .45
Coffee . . . . ~~.35~~ .40
Tea 35

Weight Watchers Corner

Flavored Yogurt 90
Fruit Salad . . . . ~~.85~~ .75
Cottage Cheese . . . . ~~.65~~ .70
Fruit Salad with Cottage Cheese & Jello ~~1.75~~ 2.00
Pineapple Slices . . . . ~~.65~~ .55
Weight Watchers Malted . . . . ~~.90~~ .80
Jello . . .55 With Whipped Cream . ~~.75~~ .70
Prunes . . . . ~~.65~~ .55
Melon (In Season) .85 with cottage cheese 1.40

Weight Watcher "Losers" Corner

French Toast (3 Slices) 1.20 1.25
Golden Brown Pancakes 1.20 1.25
With Ham or Bacon 1.75 2.10

Should you get hungry between meals or after the show, there was the coffee shop, usually the only place guests were charged extra for food. Hidden behind the fold are "DeLuxe Platters" featuring "Hot Corned Beef Sandwiches" and "Kosher Franks and Beans." Also available were "Heinz Soups—Chicken Rice, Vegetable, Cream of Mushroom." Note the "Weight Watchers Corner." Whipped cream on your Jell-O was optional.

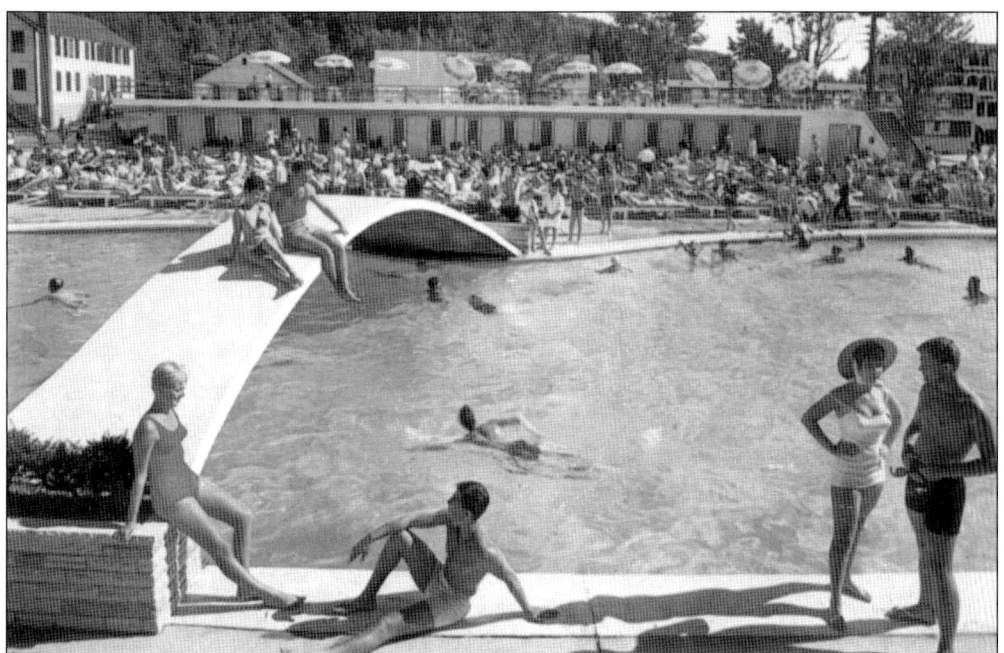

Sullivan County Borscht Belt memories are filled with more than remembrances of meals past. There was the entertainment, the swimming, and the often glamorous surroundings. The outdoor pool at the Pines in South Fallsburg even featured the bridge, shown above in a 1970s view. Below, in a 1940s view, the Hotel Evans in Loch Sheldrake (there was also an Evans Kiamesha) features the more homey sport of Ping-Pong, for many the ultimate Borscht Belt memory. The Evans was a place to "live, laugh, and enjoy the ultimate in vacation happiness." It featured a "complete social and athletic staff" and had a new indoor basketball court. It also offered winter resorts: the Evans Governor Hotel and the Sea Gull Pool and Cabana Club in Miami Beach, Florida.

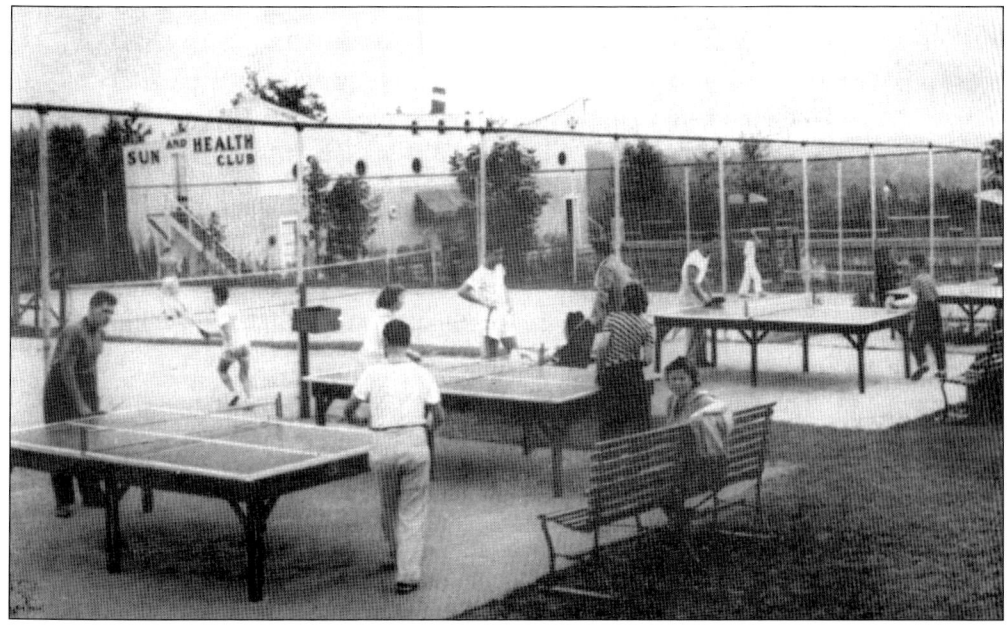

BIBLIOGRAPHY

Adams, Joey, and Henry Tobias. *The Borscht Belt*. New York: The Bobbs-Merrill Company, Inc., 1959.
Blumberg, Esterita. *Remember the Catskills: Tales by a Recovering Hotelkeeper*. Fleishmanns, New York: Purple Mountain Press, 1996.
Boris, Martin. *Woodridge 1946*. New York: Crown Publishers, 1980.
Brown, Phil. *Catskill Culture: A Mountain Rat's Memories of the Great Jewish Resort Area*. Philadelphia: Temple University Press, 1999.
Conway, John. *Retrospect: An Anecdotal History of Sullivan County, New York*. Fleishmanns, New York: Purple Mountain Press, 1996.
Dirty Dancing. Directed by Emilo Ardolino. Vestron Pictures/Great American Films Limited Partnership, 1987. Film.
Evers, Alf. *The Catskills: From Wilderness to Woodstock*. Garden City, New York: Doubleday & Company, Inc., 1972.
Fried, Marc B. *The Huckleberry Pickers: A Raucous History of the Shawangunk Mountains*. Hensonville, NewYork: Black Dome Press Corporation, 1995.
Frommer, Myrna Katz and Harvey Frommer. *It Happened in the Catskills: An Oral History*. New York: Harcourt Brace Jovanovich, 1991.
Gold, David M., ed. *The River and the Mountains: Readings in Sullivan County History*. South Fallsburg, New York: Marielle Press, 1994.
Grossinger, Tania. *Growing Up at Grossinger's*. New York: David McKay, 1975.
Jacobs, Harvey. *Summer on a Mountain of Spice*. New York: Harper and Row, 1975.
Kanfer, Stefan. *A Summer World: The Attempt to Build a Jewish Eden in the Catskills*. New York: Farrar Straus Giroux, 1989.
Lavender, Abraham and Clarence B. Steinberg. *Jewish Farmers of the Catskills: A Century of Survival*. Gainsville: University Press of Florida, 1995.
Ober, Norman. *Bungalow Nine*. New York: Walker and Company, 1962.
Offit, Sidney. *He Had It Made*. New York: Crown Publishers, 1959.
Pollack, Eileen. *Paradise, New York*. Philadelphia: Temple University Press, 1998.
Richman, Irwin. *Borscht Belt Bungalows: Memories of Catskill Summers*. Philadelphia: Temple University Press, 1998.
———. *The Catskills in Vintage Postcards*. Charleston, South Carolina: Arcadia Publishing, 1999.
The Rise and Fall of the Borscht Belt. Directed by Peter Davis. Villon Films. Distributed by Arthur Cantor, 1988. Film.
Sweet Lorraine. Directed by Steve Gomer. Autumn Pictures/Angelica Company, 1987. Film.
Wakefield, Manville B. *To The Mountains by Rail*. Grahamsville, N.Y.: Wakefair Press, 1970.
A Walk on the Moon. Directed by Tony Goldwyn. Village Roadshow Pictures/Groucho Film Partnership, 1998. Film.
Wallenrod, Reuben. *Dusk in the Catskills*. New York: Reconstructionist Press, 1957.